Sacred Fire of Public Education©

The Mass Exodus from Public Schools Will Leave Millions of Children Behind.

What Happens to Them?

Public Schools will remain the primary form of K-12 education for the foreseeable future. Are we to abandon all those left behind in a descending spiral of failure?

Aren't Americans the Great Innovators of the world?
Why have we failed here?

By **David Nemzoff**

Part of the, "*I Think, Therefore I Write*" series.

Author of "*Public Speaking Leadership for Kids, Tweens, and Teens* "© (Follow-up edition to the original "*Public Speaking for Kids, Tweens, and Teens – Confidence for Life!*")

LOOK!

IMPORTANT NOTE

The information in this book is based on the <u>opinions</u> of the author and is intended to communicate concepts designed to start a conversation that sparks major reformation towards a new generation of public education. Every effort was made to ensure accuracy in content, data, references, and attributions where necessary. It is <u>not</u> the intent of this book to disparage anyone or anything. **This book is "opinion-based", and no promises or guarantees are made against errors, omissions, factual inaccuracies, incorrect content, radical ideas, wrong think, or changes in your belief systems or world views.** *Read this book at your own risk.* 😊

Sacred Fire of Public Education©
"The Mass Exodus from Public Schools Will Leave Millions of Children Behind. What Happens to Them?"

Published joyfully by **Gabberz Publishing**, Gabberz®, Inc.
First Edition.

ISBN: 978-0-9882738-3-2

www.Gabberz.com

https://davidnemzoff.substack.com/

www.X.com/davidnemzoff (@DavidNemzoff)

www.facebook.com/david.nemzoff

673 Potomac Station Drive #710

Leesburg, VA 20176

Table of Contents

READ ME *(The Forward)*

I am just a ordinary guy. **Father** first, **Husband, American, Entrepreneur,** and **Dreamer of an Amazing Future**. I have no extraordinary credentials or big degrees. I am not an *"educator"* or involved in any capacity regarding public schools (*which is definitely an advantage in this instance*).

So... who am I to write this book?

What I offer is being a father and embracing a passion for the remarkable United States of America that our children will inherit. Specifically, I offer a vision of the America that **OUR children will build** if only we give them the opportunity and the tools to build it.

My professional career has been built on **dissecting large and complex government, military, and business subjects** and distilling them down into absorbable chunks that mere mortals can understand easily. Until now, most of my work has been restricted to government readers. THIS one is for you and your children.

Given all that, WHY should *YOU* read this book?

Our children deserve the best education possible to ensure their best future possible. The current system is failing and many parents are choosing now to **EXIT the public school system** to protect their children. That is great! But what about all those children left behind in a failing system? This book proposes a new way of doing things that plays to OUR strengths as Americans.

So why this book on education? Why now?

I've written several books, but the first book I published commercially was *"Public Speaking for Kids, Tweens, and Teens – Confidence for Life!"*. I wrote that originally as a **guide for my kids** as I thought about how to ensure they could succeed in the world. I ultimately published that one for all children.

During development of that book is where my thoughts regarding the failing state of public education started to focus on what would later become the foundations for this book. I thought back on MY grade school and high school years and how those teachers and classes influenced who I was, how I looked at the world, and how that impacted my life and the lives of those around me. I eventually realized that ***how*** individual teachers *painted* what they taught had a **profound impact** on my own beliefs and my world view well beyond my school years.

How lasting were those beliefs and world views that my teachers painted?

I ultimately recognized that those heavily ingrained beliefs and world views were **extremely one-sided and contrary to what I finally understood of the world as an adult.** As I made my way through life, I began to challenge everything I had been taught. By extension, that led me to question what fundamentals and beliefs we were planting in our children and how that influenced society today.

Do parents matter anymore?

When I had kids of my own **those thoughts suddenly became very personal and very real.** I read all the stories, reports, studies, and endless news articles about the educational environment just because I wanted to know. For myself. For my kids. For curiosity's sake. I had no thoughts about writing a book then. I was too busy raising my children and building my career.

Ultimately, I began to wonder if we could do better. We are Americans; it is our nature to look for ways to do things better.

This led me to ask, *"Is this the best we can do?"*

All those years of subconscious thought finally slapped me in the face and said, *"Write the damn book, our children are worth at least that."* I promptly responded, *"Why me, stupid brain?"* To which my brain snapped back, *"Why **not** you?"* It was hard to argue against that well-reasoned public education debate.

So… here we are. All I ask when you read this book is to ignore that part of your brain that keeps nagging, **"*It can't be done. The system is too big. They would never allow it.*"** Instead, keep forefront in your mind that…

*"We **CAN** we do better if only we choose to do so!*
*We **MUST** do better for the sake of our children's children!"* [1]

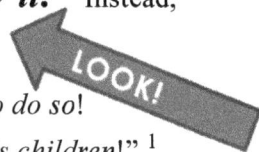

Enjoy!
David Nemzoff

Caution!

You will NOT agree with many parts of this book. You can be pretty confident of that going in. **In fact, you might even hate some of it.** That is okay. Just go with the flow and save your final judgement until you reach the end.

THEN, if you still disagree, **reach out and let's have that discussion**. Offer a solution. Offer a challenge. Or you can even offer to help.

If you **sign up to the mailing list** at www.gabberz.com, you will receive information on upcoming opportunities for discussion and participation. We would love your involvement whether you agree or not.

CHAPTER

1

A PESKY LITTLE PREMISE

LOOK!

Things to consider:

➢ Is this just another *doom-and-gloom depressing book* written to bum me out?

➢ Is this a *"political"* book pushing an agenda?

➢ Why should I read this book?

*"No experiment can be more interesting than that we
are now trying, and which we trust will end in
establishing the fact, that man may be governed by
reason and truth. Our first object should therefore be, to
leave open to him all the avenues to truth."*
— Thomas Jefferson, June 28, 1804[2]

*"The establishment of our new Government seemed to
be the last great experiment, for promoting human
happiness..."*
— George Washington, January 9, 1790[3]

THE GREAT EXPERIMENT

In the very beginning, there was play. We learned the most
basic aspects of survival by playing with our siblings. As with
most animals, we learned to fight, hunt, feed and operate within
societal guidelines through play and parental guidance. We
learned about our history through stories and songs.

Then came civilization.
And eventually... the United States of America.

The U.S. has been referred to as the *"Great Experiment in
Democracy"*.[4] That experiment thankfully continues to this day
due to our tenacity in protecting the **core values
and fundamental underpinnings** of our great
nation. Most of these values are enshrined in
the **Constitution of the United States**. Some
go beyond that into the nature of what it
means to be an American.

From the beginning, we adapted, innovated, and changed
where necessary to continue the experiment. Sometimes, this
blew up in our faces. No matter how many times the Great
Experiment came under attack – **internally or externally** – we
stood up, spoke out, or fought back to ensure our amazing
experiment continued.

America itself is a magnificent innovation that became a
beacon of promise and potential throughout the world. The
American lighthouse of hope also helped guide other nations

away from the rocky shorelines of a tumultuous world and back into safe waters.

> *Unfortunately, the lamp dimmed occasionally.*
> *The lens got dirty and scattered the light.*
> *We even managed to blow a few bulbs.*

Whenever that happened, we were always ready and willing to run out to the hardware store, roll up our sleeves, and **fire up the beacon again with a bright new bulb to light the way**.

Does that mean the "experiment" has succeeded? In some ways, yes. But America will remain an **ongoing process of trial and error** because we are never content with things just the way they are. Our American nature is to keep looking for new, exciting, and ambitious adventures in this grand nation of ours. Except for one critical area that we have ignored.

———— ◆ ————

This book is about a <u>different</u> "Great Experiment." One that has driven who we are, who we will be, and how our children will compete on the international stage as the world changes around us.

Our "**Great Experiment in Education**" ostensibly began in the 13 original colonies when the **Boston Latin School** was founded in 1635.[5] Various forms of education obviously existed prior to that, but this began our formal public education experiment. The Boston Latin School still exists today and is part of a vast network of schools in every community in our nation.

From there, the experiment expanded across the nation and into every community in America. We have had many successes and failures. However, **we now face educational challenges like we have never faced before**. Some of those challenges are detailed in **Chapters 5, 6**, **7**, and **8**.

Before we get there though, I would like to call out the **many wonderful teachers** who serve our children out of a love of education and work hard to give them the best education they can within their power. Do not take anything presented in this book as an attack on any specific school or teacher. **There are numerous examples of greatness in both**.

> *However, there is systemic and endemic flicker in the Sacred Fire of our K-12 Education system.*

A true existential crisis has been burning through our educational system. It cannot be denied that many of our school systems, particularly those in dense urban areas are failing their students and **creating generations of *barely educated, indoctrinated to fail,* and *unprepared to succeed* adults** who struggle to cope with and advance in the real world. Don't worry, I will substantiate this claim over the next few chapters.

Americans are not a people who normally stand idle and let the world overtake us. We act. We innovate. We create. **That's what we do**. What we've always done. Yet…

We refuse to apply all of that creativity to the Great Experiment in *Education* as we have done for the Great Experiment of the *United States of America*.

> → *WHY?*
>
> *THAT is the question we will explore here.*

———— ♦ ————

I intend to present a different Pathway to Fundamental Foundational Reform. One that that has the potential to **Transform** our **K-12 public education system** from a failed "experiment" into a **success model designed from the ground up to actually educate our children and prepare them for a lifetime of achievement**. As Americans, we will once again demonstrate to the world that there is a better way. **The American way**.

A BIT OF A WARNING

I want to assure readers that the *purpose* of the book is NOT simply to shock the reader or to burn down (*metaphorically of course*) an institution that has served us for centuries.

My intention is to **<u>reimagine</u> our K-12 public school system** to focus on the true needs of children and their parents. That presentation will of course entail discussions of the good, the bad, and the ugly (*to borrow a classic movie reference*[6]).

And, yes, some of it WILL get pretty ugly.

This may seem like a NEGATIVE book about public schooling at first. **It is far from that**. The purpose of this book is to provide an encouraging glimpse at how the future of education *could* be if we were to commit ourselves to innovative foundational change.

When Americans set our minds on innovation and creativity, amazing things happen. *This*, **I hope, is** *that*.

There is an abundance of "*downer*" books to choose from. I wanted this to be about **hope and change** (*can I say that?*) to inspire us to blaze a new and exciting trail to a brilliant and glorious future for our children – and for the world.

THIS IS **NOT** A POLITICAL BOOK

I am a **Father** first, a **Husband** second, an **American**, an **Entrepreneur**, and (*this is where the **Warning** comes in to play*) a **Conservative**.

As a young adult **I leaned pretty hard to the** *left*, influenced heavily by my school years and my peers. I was taught to think certain ways about certain people. Indoctrination into believing certain things about our world went beyond the raw teaching of history and civics. i.e., I was taught "*what*" to think.

But I always felt something was a little off.
I ultimately had to learn "how" to think for myself.

As I journeyed my way through life – marriage, children, career – I began to realize that **those world views I had been imbued with in my early years didn't really connect with who I was**. Ultimately, I began to understand that I was a conservative at heart and had been one for many years.

But don't hold that against me,
I really *am* a nice guy, even if we disagree.

So, *why am I telling you all of this*. I want to be absolutely honest with you so that you can accept that this book is derived from my belief in America and is **not presented simply for political agenda**. → Other than to accomplish the stated goal of reforming our public school system to benefit our children.

Do not let my political leanings stop you from enjoying and considering the merits of the ideas in this book (*whatever your political beliefs are*). The solutions presented here are intended to initiate a discussion on how to **secure a future for our children that transcends political lines**.

However, I am a creature of my beliefs and those will most likely creep through in the dark of night to color my words. My intention is **not to blame anyone or to relitigate the past**. It is to reimagine and reform the K-12 public schools to **ensure none of our children are disenfranchised or left behind**.

———— ♦ ————

Controversy is often necessary to build a useful premise and solution for any innovative approach to fundamental foundational change of major institutions.

I ask that you put aside any political disagreement with me and keep focused on our mission.

Read this book with an open mind and an absolute belief that these ideas are intended for the **greater good of our children and** society. Politics are irrelevant when looking to reform that **must necessarily remove those very politics from education**.

THAT PESKY LITTLE PREMISE

This book is about __fundamental foundational change, NOT "fixing" things__. You'll learn why "fixing" is not an option in later chapters. In the past 100+ years, our world has changed in ways that we could never have imagined. Technology, science, medicine, and overall knowledge have all grown beyond what we could have even conceived of just 50 years ago.

Looking at these changes <u>simply as the expansion of access to data</u> (books, literature, articles, news, videos, social media, etc.), **we have created more information and data in the past two years than in the entire previous history of mankind**.

Interestingly, the volume of data and information created and consumed worldwide was approximately **97 zettabytes**[7] of stored information in 2020 (*don't worry, I had to look up what a zettabyte was myself*). Considering the advent of Artificial Intelligence (AI), our universe of data is projected to explode beyond 181 zettabytes in 2025.[8] That is more information than any person could ever even conceive of consuming.

Yet, our K12 educational system has NOT foundationally changed in hundreds of years – except arguably to stray from core academics into politics and social agendas. The questions then become...

Premise for Public Education	
	1. **Can we change** and adapt to the modern era while retaining and enhancing core academics in our public education system?
	2. **Can we reimagine** a different way? A truly revolutionary foundational reformation of our existing public school system?
	3. **Can we come together** as a nation and apply innovation and the American Spirit to one of the most important functions of our society? Are we willing to set aside our differences for our children's futures?

<u>**Those three elements**</u> **are the premise of this book**. My intention is to define a way to tap into our American nature of innovation and harness a free-market ideology to bring our children's education back to the core purpose of educating them.

Please join me in this exploration. All I ask is that you **think critically for yourself** and for an incredible future for ALL of our children.

Enjoy!

CHAPTER

2

WHY READ THIS BOOK?

Things to consider:

➤ Why dissect the cow?

➤ Are schools for "*the Public Good*"?

➤ Do I really have to read the *whole* book?

➤ Do band-aid solutions work?

FEEDING THE SACRED FIRE

You may notice at this point that I have not yet talked about what I mean by **"fundamental foundational reformation" of K-12 Public Schools**. That is by design. Before we jump into this very meaty subject, full of gristle and bone – as well as some tasty fulfilling filets and tenderloins – we need to **dissect the cow** a bit.

Huh?

To fully appreciate the meal I am preparing, we must first dive a bit into where we are and how we got here. All of us, even those who don't have children, understand that the education of future generations is critical to ensuring the continuation and security of this great nation. Based on the issues we face in our country today, we have to ask for the first time in generations…

*In 10, 20, 50 years, **whose children around the world will be leading the way** through the next incredible advances in technology, science, medicine, business, and industry?*

Maybe it's arrogant to say, but I believe it is the **Children of America** who should be leading. *Our* children.

We have a lot to cover to get to the meat of things. However, if you are really impatient and hungry, you *could* jump straight to **Chapter 10** and savor the well-seasoned **Filet of Ideas** that I have cooked up for you on the **Sacred Fire of Education**.

Be warned though, if you do that, **you'll miss out on all the warm savory side dishes** I've prepared that make the meal even more tasty and fulfilling. As with any three-course meal, I recommend you take the time to enjoy each dish (*chapter*) to prepare your tastebuds for the next. There might even be a rich, calorie-laden dessert at the end if you read all your veggies.

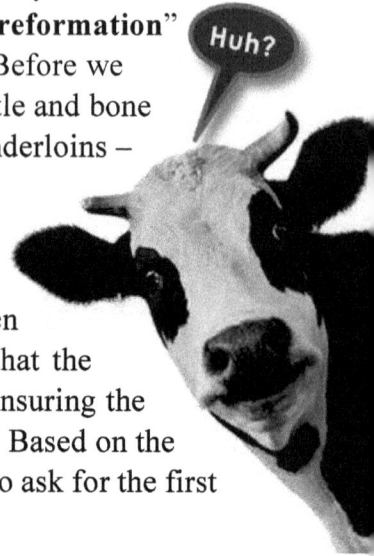

> **You could jump straight to Chapter 10, but you'll miss out on all the yummy stuff.**

APERITIF BEFORE THE MEAL

It's always best to ease into a meal and savor each bite to get the most flavor and enjoyment out of what is dished out. Where better to start than with a *delicious dish of yummy, yummy history*?

Educating our offspring has been the **natural order of survival** since, presumably, our beginnings. Ancient tribes would tell stories to the young ones to teach them about the history of the tribe, sacred or holy beliefs, common dangers, hunting techniques, and great warriors of the past.

As our brains and societies developed, we understood more and more that **the growth of the collective body was fed best by passing on knowledge and experience** to the next generation. This is how we grew stronger and how society evolved into each new and sensational age. We could not have jumped straight into the Industrial Age or technical revolution without solid foundations of earlier knowledge to build upon – passed down from generation to generation.

——————— ◆ ———————

To begin our meal, our educational adventure will start in **Chapter 4** with the **first formalized public school in America, established in 1635**. It is still active and thriving today.

We will also chew on a specially prepared premise of community schooling for the **public good**. It is important to understand *why* we believe in community schooling and what the purpose of it is before we can move forward. Only after we have digested that can we fully appreciate what is fundamentally wrong with today's educational system. Then, we might be able to acknowledge the need for foundational reformation.

If we believe as a nation in the premise of **community education** (public schools) then, as is the American way, **we should be driven to evolve and advance** how we do it to make our educational system the best in the world.

> **We should be driven to be the best in the world at education.**

Sadly, we have not even attempted to genuinely reform or evolve public schools in the past 50+ years. **Chapter 9** cooks up some savory historical small bites salted with a major reform attempt in the 1980s that failed dramatically and was cut from the menu. Finally, you will not want to miss our **spicy dips** into sex education, CRT, indoctrination, and more in **Chapters 6 and 7**.

WATCHING THE SAUSAGE BEING MADE

Everyone knows the old saying, *"if you want to enjoy eating sausage you should never watch it being made."* Well... we need to break that rule and grind up a bit of meat for you.

Education is undeniably an emotional topic for many. We each have different feelings about how well our schools are doing based on our backgrounds, experiences, and contact with the system.

Whatever our feelings though, we cannot deny that there is trouble in the kitchen. And if we *are* failing our children in any way, then **we have a personal and national imperative to pour ourselves into fixing what is wrong**. One of the most important things we can do in modern society is to *ensure that our children do better than us*. Isn't that what all parents want?

Chapter 4 grinds up some of the past, then **Chapter 5** blends in a bit of savory sauce with a taste of what is happening today.

Although the state of our educational system has taken much neglect to get where it is, I promise that the focus of this book is **Not to Look Back** at where we have failed, but to **Look Forward** to how we can achieve an educational system that is successful beyond our imaginations. We must look beyond the way it's always been done.

> **To Truly Reimagine Education, We Must Look Beyond *"The Way It's Always Been Done."***

As I will make clear, this is <u>NOT</u> an attack on teachers as a whole. Although I will lay out the case for a failing public school system, **the purpose is NEVER to negate the power of good teachers.** There are many wonderful, dedicated, loving teachers throughout our educational universe. But many others have been seduced by the system and fail to live up to their students' potential. Some fall to a system that is rigged against them, suffer from the fatigue of bad schools, and *yes… some* of them are just bad and should not be teaching our children.

A successful system needs to **reward** **those great teachers** and **cull out** **those who are just gristle** adding weight to the scales of our system.

IS THAT A BAND-AID IN YOUR SOUP?[9]

Over the last 50 years or so, we have talked exhaustively about the need to "fix" our K-12 public school system. Many grand plans were proposed – we even tried some – but they were always just **band-aid solutions trying to stem the arterial bleeding of fundamental systemic problems**.

We can talk about approaches such as "School Choice," "Charter Schools," and "Money Following the Student," but **none of these fix the foundational and fundamental core problems** with the public school system we have used for centuries. These fixes may help specific children, but are not enough to germinate and propagate a revolutionary change to **help those remaining in the general school population**.

Our primary focus to "fix" the system is almost always to throw more money at the problem, thinking that *"this time"* it will work. We will hire more teachers, reduce class sizes, hire more administrators and counselors, buy computers for all the students, hire consultants, pay for school lunches, pay for more after-school programs, and on and on.

> **THIS time, throwing money at the problem will work! Really!**

None of this has ever fundamentally made a difference.

We've all heard that putting perfume on a pig just gives you a perfumed pig. Add a nice dress, some high heels (*open toe of course*), manicured cloven hooves, a couple of well-placed tattoos, and a curly wig and you still wouldn't want to take it to the Friday Night Dance (*we hope*).

Yet, as a nation, **we keep dancing with that pig** every time we decide that the way to "reform" education is to tack on yet another program or simply feed it more money. The pig will just consume more and more and, in the end, the output only gets worse and worse.

Like everyone else, I love a good barbeque, but we spend roughly **$640 Billion ($12,484 per student)** annually for K-12 Schools.[10] Whereas Private schools average a cost of **$12,350 per student annually.**[11] There seems to be a major disconnect here. Public schools have a mass of scale more than **10 times larger** than Private schools.[12]

In any normal system, this enormous scale of economy coupled with <u>COMPULSORY USAGE</u> *should* manifest itself as huge reductions in cost and higher-quality results. But it doesn't. In fact, **the very opposite happens** in our public school system. Why? See **Chapter 9** to learn a little about why our attempts at reform haven't worked in all these years and why money doesn't fix the problems.

So, what is the solution?

We need to step back and truly reimagine how we do this. We are Americans damn it!

- We know how to reimagine.

- We know how to innovate.

- We know how to be leaders and <u>make</u> change happen.

It is well beyond time that we stepped up to the plate and applied those skills to one of the most important aspects of our society… the education of our children.

Now it is time to take a seat, set your napkin in your lap, and savor the appetizers in the next few chapters while we wait for the main course in **Chapter 10**, **Chapter 11**, and **Chapter 12** to finish cooking.

CHAPTER

3

HOW TO READ THIS BOOK

Things to consider:

➢ Open minds are the only ones that can even imagine the impossible.

➢ You know what they say about assumptions.

➢ We used to KNOW it was impossible to fly.

➢ Will I agree with everything in this book? [**Spoiler Alert**: NO, you won't.]

I KNOW HOW TO READ A BOOK, DUMMY.

Yes, you do. And *thank you* for reading this one. However, this is a broad reaching subject and I promised you I would make it easy to digest as we move from skimming topics to deep dives and back again. I have spent years cooking up this meal, but you are getting it all in one big heaping plate of steaming information. I'm hoping this **primer** will help you enjoy the entire feast.

As you can imagine, **the foundational reformation of a massive nationwide institution** such as our public school system would be a tremendous undertaking with major impacts on the public sector, private sector, financial systems, community services, and state, county, and local legislative and taxation systems. Not to mention the families who would be involved.

In order to keep this book **under 6,000+ pages**, it was necessary to pick and choose the ingredients carefully. The hard part was not finding things to write about – but **choosing what wonderful and enticing flavors would NOT make it into the book**.

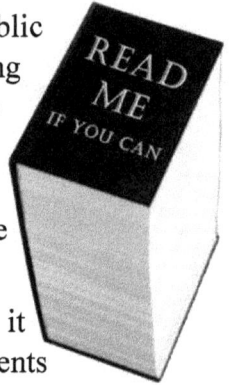

> *The first draft of this book was over*
> *600 pages. Fortunately for you, I've*
> *cut back the calories a bit.*

To make that happen, it was necessary to provide **several assumptions** to limit the scope of discussion here.

ASSUMPTIONS I'VE MADE

There are always two or more sides to an issue. And many flavors to each side dish. **"*The way we've always done it*" momentum will feel like quicksand** and emotions will run high from all directions. We need to remain focused on what is best for our children's futures and debate vigorously with *them* in mind – not politics or agendas.

To **keep from falling down endless rabbit holes** with interminable side jaunts through a warren of countless critical factors that require discussions and decisions, **I have focused on certain high-level concepts.** To maintain that focus (*and keep you from setting this book ablaze in frustration*) **I have made some baseline assumptions.**

LOOK!

For the sake of argument, **please accept that the assumptions in the table below are somewhat settled for the moment.** Imagine that, after extensive debate and some epic arm wrestling to be featured on ESPN™, we came to some basic agreements (*the assumptions*).

These will be the foundations for our discussions throughout this book. **You *may* disagree now with some of these assumptions** (*and maybe even think I'm a bit on the crazy side*), but that is okay. Each assumption could be a book in its own right, so we need to **accept them in theory** in order to move the book forward.

We will never have 100% agreement with everyone on everything. Before we can even begin the discussion though, we need to start with some mutual temporary agreements. So why not start with these foundational guidelines?

ASSUMPTIONS

Assume we have agreed <u>as a nation</u> that...	Why?
We ***MUST implement a major fundamental reformation*** of our educational system, particularly our Public School System.	You will have the natural tendency throughout this book to say, "*we will never agree to change like this.*" To truly enjoy the potential of this book, you need to assume we have come together in large enough numbers to work for the good of our children. We must put the question behind us of "*IF*" we will do something and concentrate on "*WHAT*" we will do when we have that agreement.

Assume we have agreed <u>as a nation</u> that...	Why?
Some form of **"Community Schooling"** *is necessary.*	There are many who do not think that "government schooling" or "taxation for public education" is appropriate. *As a practical matter*, it's pretty safe to assume that well over 50% of voters will agree at this time that publicly funded community education <u>is necessary</u>. Therefore, we must operate for now under the assumption that "community schooling" of some sort, supported financially by the community as a body, will be required. Otherwise, this discussion is moot.
Some form of **taxation is necessary to support education** *for the common good.*	Much debate will ensue about how we pay for community education. If we have agreed that community schooling is necessary for the "common good", then in order for education to be available to all, common taxation appears to be the primary way at this moment. Other possibilities will present themselves in the future (and in this book), but this is what we have now. I discuss funding in detail in **Chapters 13** and **14**.
We want to continue public school **sports**, **music**, *and other group and external* **programs**.	One complaint from parents using private schools, homeschools, and other options is a lack of access to facilities and resources for sports, music, and other extracurricular activities that they pay for through taxes. Most parents, no matter how schooling occurs, prefer to have these programs available so we will make the assumption for now that they must be incorporated into whatever form our reformation effort takes.

    I will make other smaller assumptions along our travels here, but they are not as foundational as the assumptions in the table above. To move us forward, **please accept those other small assumptions and set disagreement aside** for future debate. Once you have read the entire book (*which I am sure you will do*), apply some critical thinking and challenge the assumptions and ideas I've put forth. If you do have challenges or better ideas, I would love to hear them.

I HAVE A FAVOR TO ASK

You would think that buying this book would be enough, but I have more to ask of you.

Our children's futures are _THEIR_ fortunes. LOOK!

The tools, knowledge, and experience we give our children are major determining factors in their path in life, their ability to stand up to adversity, and to take advantage of opportunity. Our legacy is to ensure we do everything we can to **help them succeed and make a better world for themselves and *their* children**.

With that mission in mind, I have a few things I'd like to ask of you as you read beyond this point.

1. **Keep an Open Mind**:
   If your mind is closed to the possibility of change and major reform of our public school system, you will not be open to ideas that stretch the boundaries of what we are doing now. **Chapter 9** will demonstrate that previous efforts we've made towards reform of K-12 have failed. Why? I believe it was because we were NOT open enough to the *possibility* of fundamental foundational reform that didn't rely on existing foundations and power structures.

2. **Apply Critical Thinking**:
   Do not just believe me. Challenge everything I present (*with the caveat of #3 below*). Verify and validate my assertions (*I have **provided numerous references in the end notes**, but there are many more*). If you disagree with my approach, apply some thought to how we could accomplish the intent of the approach in a *new way*. Grab a clean sheet of paper and **think beyond band-aid solutions**. Go to town. Get excited. That's okay, this is too important for fine point pencils. **This demands big bold markers and crayons**.

3. **Assume It CAN Be Done**:
   Just for the sake of argument, just **assume all things here are possible**. Maybe not exactly in the way I've presented,

but *possible*. We just have to **decide to do it** and figure out the steps to get from here to there. Great change only comes when someone says, "*Yes! We can do that.*"

4. **Quit Stressing Over "How"**:
   First, we have to decide **IF** we are willing to do something. Then, figure out **WHAT** that something is. Then, decide to **DO** it. After all that, we can enter the "*Thunderdome*"[13] if necessary (*hopefully not*) and debate through hand-to-hand combat (*hopefully not*) about "how" to accomplish the mission. **"How" doesn't matter if we never decide to do it.**

As you read, you're going to say over and over to yourself, "*Self, this can't be done... that can't be done... people will never go for this crazy stuff.*" Good! Be skeptical. But, always imagine... "**What if?**" *What if it could be done*? Imagine the possibilities are, well... possible.

If you do that, I think you'll truly enjoy the ideas I've laid out for you.

Later in the book, I'll detail just one of many plans for how this *could* happen if we choose to do it. I'll then get into steps you personally can take to spark the discussion. Reformation can never happen if we don't even talk about it.

THE RED MEAT

Yes, believe it or not, we're finally getting to the point of this book. Before we dive into the real red meat, I wanted to leave you with a few light thoughts to stimulate your palate.

If this concept for truly foundational reform of our public schools ultimately makes it to the public square for discussion and debate, emotions will be strung up to high tension with ingrained beliefs on all sides. We have seen in recent years how vocal we can become as a society. This will be no different.

It will be loud.
It will be emotional.
It will be necessary.

Any major societal change brings with it inevitable dispute between **those who embrace change** and **those who will hold onto the existing status quo for safety, security, and "the known"**… as well as for power and money.

Do not fear the conflict. Embrace it. This is natural, although sometimes painful. Just as stubbing your toe is exceptionally painful, it is also a helpful reminder to change paths and turn on the light next time you head off to the bathroom in the middle of the night.

> **The battle between foundational reformation and those who embrace the status quo will be brutal.**
>
> **Neither side will go *"quietly into the night."***
>
> **Nor should they.**

Keeping in mind that this is a heavy, emotionally charged topic, **I try to look at the bright side of things as much as possible here** (*trust me, it wasn't easy*). There is an abundance of negativity, anger, and obstructionism in our society today and I do not wish to add to that. This is a serious subject, but that does not mean we can't have a lively, engaging, and maybe even entertaining discussion.

───────── ♦ ─────────

Finally, I will also be **stretching the boundaries** of what may be possible. There are many ideas in this book that I absolutely love (*otherwise, why write the book?*). There are also some ideas I put forth that **I personally do NOT like at all**.

Why would I do that?

I recognize that there are some things that may be necessary in order to make a fully reformed system work properly. Even if I don't like them, they may be essential to reaching the ultimate goal of true educational reformation. After all, **this is NOT about me**. This is about a brilliant future for generations of children to come.

The **PURPOSE** of this book is to
initiate or trigger a conversation that
<u>there – *CAN* – be another way</u>.

This is not the definitive guide to "*how*" to do it. It will take many people much, much smarter than me to develop the how and to **guide us through the extensive morass of a legacy system that touches nearly everything in our society.** It can be done. But like many good things, it will not be easy. That's what makes it fun.

And finally, finally… before we dive in, here are a couple of inspirational quotes to set the stage.

A famous philosopher once said, *"A mind is like a parachute. It doesn't work if it is not open."*
– Frank Zappa[14]

"An open mind is not an end in itself but a means to the end of finding truth."　　– Peter Kreeft[15]

"They are ill discoverers that think there is no land when they can see nothing but sea." – Francis Bacon[16]

"We used to think it was impossible to fly. Until someone just went and did it." – Me (*and thousands of others*) [17]

4

A HISTORY OF PUBLIC SCHOOLS

Things to consider:

➤ Do we "need" Public Schools?

➤ Is Education a Right?

➤ Do I *Really* have to Learn Some History?

*"OF ALL THE CIVIL RIGHTS FOR WHICH THE WORLD HAS STRUGGLED AND FOUGHT FOR, **the right to learn** is undoubtedly the most fundamental... **we should fight to the last ditch to keep open the right to learn**... We must insist upon this **to give our children the fairness of a start which will equip them with such an array of facts and such an attitude toward truth that they can have a real chance to judge what the world is**, and what its greater minds have thought it might be."*

—W.E.B. Du Bois[18]

---

*"George Washington talked about preservation of the '**Sacred Fire of Liberty**'. As we have witnessed in recent years, the best (and probably ONLY) way to preserve Liberty is to first preserve the '**Sacred Fire of Education**'. Without an honest education, our children will only learn '**what**' to think, not '**how**' to think. Without the skill to seek truth, the fire will fade and man's darker nature will lovingly embrace us all."*

—David Nemzoff

HISTORY OF READING, WRITING, AND ARITHMETIC

There will always be debate about how to best educate our children. Most people mean well, but we have very different ideas about the fundamentals of education.

- Should education be public or private?

- How should it be funded?

- Who controls the curriculum?

- Should we be teaching beyond the core academics?

- If so, what should we teach our children?

- Do children belong to their parents or to the State?

All big questions, but there should at least be **universal agreement** that our children MUST be educated to the best of our abilities. Otherwise, we will surely fail as a society.

LOOK!

CRITICAL SIDEBAR

You may be asking yourself, "*Self, why do I need to learn all of this history and junk? I'm not the one in school.*"

Good question!

Over the next few chapters, we will learn about

- the **history of education**,

- the **current state of our public school system**, and

- the **major problems we face in education today**.

Why? *Before* we can talk about a fundamental foundational reformation of the public school system to maintain the **Sacred Fire of Public Education**, we MUST have a solid grasp of the simple reality that...

We can NOT "FIX" what exists today.

As you read on, you will begin to understand that the foundations of the system are **broken**, **corroded**, **corrupted**, and **shattered** beyond all hope of "*repair*."

In order to accept that **the system must be entirely reimagined and rebuilt from the foundations** – we must first understand what public schools were meant to be and how foundational and systemic the problems we face are.

We must believe in our hearts and minds that _more band-aid solutions simply will not work_. The wound is too deep. The infection is too virulent. **The patient must die and be reborn** with a renewed purpose that is able to **resist corruption and the influences of the moment**.

THAT is why we must "*learn all of this history and junk.*" Otherwise, we will just keep repeating the same mistakes.

If you remember, we agreed earlier to a **baseline assumption** that some form of community education is necessary to a growing and functional society. Let's look first at how this started in America and how we arrived at today.

——————— ◆ ———————

As the old saying goes… *if we do not learn from the past, we are surely doomed to repeat it.* Sometimes though, **the past becomes so ingrained in how we do things that it is nearly impossible for us to change our course**, no matter how flawed that path might be.

This is the case with our educational system. It has served us well in many ways, but we find now that the demands of today's society and **internal/external political and social forces have created some schisms within the system**. These divisions threaten to break the bond between parents and schools as the educational system seeks to **impose more sociopolitical influence on children** external to the parents.

WHERE TO START?

The beginning seems like a good place. Most animals have the same type of built-in instinct to teach their offspring how to hunt (eat), how to hide, how to survive. In earlier days, just as other animals did, we lived as hunter-gatherers. **Our children had a natural way of learning what they had to know to survive primarily by playing and exploring**. This way of life was very skill-intensive but required only a fairly simple knowledge base of the plants and animals on which they survived.

Man in particular understood the need to teach our young what we ourselves had learned over our lives. We don't have detailed records for early man, but we can imagine that rather than the **3R**'s we learn today, they started with the **3E**'s:

1) Don't get *Eaten*;

2) Don't *Eat* things that will kill you; and

3) *Everything* else will kill you.

We are a <u>little</u> more sophisticated these days, but the concept is the same. Elders would teach the younger. That generation would learn, grow, and expand their knowledge. Then, when they were grown, they would teach the new younger, hipper crowd what they had learned (*with some embellishments of course*). **This was necessary for the tribe to grow and prosper.**

Early "education" (*used as a universal term here*) likely consisted primarily of *"on-the-job training"* where hunters took the young males on hunts and taught them how to bring food home rather than becoming food (*remember our 3E's?*). Mothers taught their daughters how to prepare food **without accidentally killing those** who survived the hunt. Elders passed on skills to make shelters, clothing, fire, and weapons... although early records do indicate there were some factions who called for "***spear control***".[19]

—— ♦ ——

As society became more cohesive and complicated, **we needed to convey more information** directly to our children to move beyond being a simple hunter-gatherer animal. With the invention of agriculture in particular, our lives became much more labor intensive (time consuming) and our children had less time for play-to-learn. **They now needed to acquire the skills to function in a society and produce for others** rather than just hunt and gather.

—— ♦ ——

In an incredible leap beyond animal kind, man went beyond survival and **began telling stories and tales** (*and likely a few fanciful fibs*) as a means of teaching the history of the tribe and to explain the unknowns of the world around them (the moon, weather, seasons, death, and why people text while driving).

Suddenly, **education became about much more than just survival**. The community would sit around the central village

One of Man's Greatest Educational Inventions – the Marshmallow!

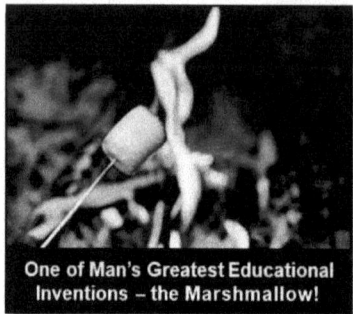

fire pit and tell stories to pass down their knowledge to the next generation, **ensuring that what was learned would not be lost**.

Tales were told of planting seasons, sacred or holy beliefs, common dangers, nearby tribes, and anything else to ensure the survival, growth, and culture of the tribe. When those children grew up having heard these stories over and over, they continued to tell the same stories (*as well as new ones*) to their children.

Survival and non-survival knowledge now persisted beyond the individuals.

It all seems rather obvious and simple, but it's really quite sophisticated if you think about it. Early man went well beyond a simple survival trait to teach history, communication skills, medical skills (*pre-lawyer of course*), pre-planning survival skills, and much more to ensure the continued existence and growth of the tribe. We alone in the animal kingdom were **consciously thinking beyond the <u>now</u>** to future generations.

We understood long ago that a **sense of history and future** separated us from the instinctual animals of the forest whose only thought was of food, procreation, and survival – *not always in that order*. We understood that the passing of knowledge from generation to generation was the pathway to a sort of **collective immortality**.

LOOK!

> When man understood that a sense of <u>history</u> and <u>future</u> created a sort of <u>collective immortality</u>, everything changed – the age of education had begun.

Not only would the collective body grow, but it would grow stronger, smarter, more capable... more survivable.

We ultimately had a sense that our children could have a better life than us. But all of **this was dependent on our willingness and ability to pass on truth, knowledge, and morals** to the next generation.

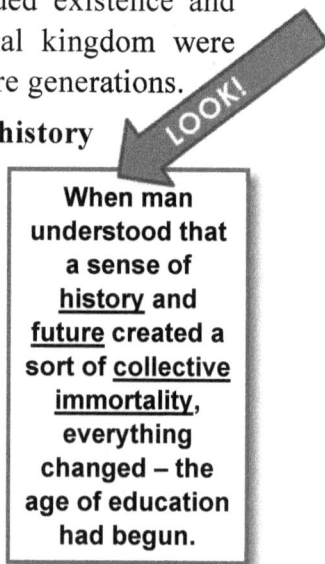

Going from the Village Fire Pit to the University Quad

As humans tend to do, we evolved self and society over time and education naturally evolved with us. Initially, education was entirely survival focused. Most education that followed still retained **some foundation in personal and/or societal survival**. But I'm not quite sure how a college-level course in *"Comic Book Lore and Legend"* helps ensure society's survival. It would seem to have the opposite effect.

The original evolutions of education are lost in the vast reaches of time, but they most likely evolved through several foundational phases:

1. **Survival-based**: Don't get eaten, don't fall off a cliff, don't eat the red berries.

2. **Functional-based**: Planting, making clothes, food preservation, farming, trades, etc.

3. **Community/Cultural-based**: Society, religion, sacred and holy beliefs, history, communication, health and welfare, and more.

4. **Entertainment-based**: Music, theater, lore, tall tales, allegorical stories, sports, fiction, and humor.

5. **Societal/Foundational-based**: Medicine, biology, law, politics, engineering, science, psychology, etc.

6. **Educational/Mental-based**: Philosophy, the Arts, literature, and well... educating the educators.

That is a simplistic list, but we can start to see how as a society we evolved beyond fire pit survival to the vast educational universe we have now. It wasn't easy getting here though.

We went through many eras where education was a primary function of society and considered a right, BUT there were also eras where **education was stifled to separate the classes and keep the lower classes ignorant**. It could be argued that we are currently suffering a limited case of the latter in today's America. But that is one of those **rabbit holes** I promised we would not plunge into.

———————— ◆ ————————

There are many different accounts of where and how formal education (particularly centralized community schooling) started and the truth of it depends on **how we would define what exactly constitutes "formal education"** and how it evolved over the centuries.

We could go back to Mesopotamia around 2010 BC where only the offspring of the rich or royals were educated, or ancient Egypt and their elite corps of scribes, the Buddhists of 1000 BC, or even the government-built schools of the Xia dynasty around 1600 BC. These and many other historical examples serve to demonstrate that formal education in school-like environments has been around for more than 4000 years.[20]

Each evolved out of the needs of the times and were frequently restricted to very specific classes or castes within a societal structure or to those who served the ruling class.

Although some general populations were educated to varying degrees, **formal education was not a "right"** in most civilizations. Education was implemented to **serve the needs of others** – the elites, the Church, or for government needs or military service.

There is rich tapestry of history to dive into across the ages, but that is not the purpose of this book. We need to move forward a few thousand years if we ever want to get to why we are here now.

There is one critical foundational point that we must understand so that we can recognize that modern schools are a product of the history that they grew out of.

*There was NO "**grand plan**" of education*
*developed that provided a **roadmap for***
***formal education in America**.*

If we abandon the concept that schools were "designed" and accept that they evolved haphazardly and piecemeal out of desire, necessity, and the limitations of each era, then we understand that they must necessarily have foundational flaws.

As we saw earlier, "education" began as an instinctual artifact of being a part of the animal kingdom – and a part of the food chain in both directions. *"Eat or be Eaten"* is not just a modern business cliché but was always a natural survival trait. You learned, you adapted, or you died.

> **Modern education evolved haphazardly out of need or necessity in a society – often focused on the needs of the Church or the Ruling Class.**

We eventually moved forward towards more sophisticated tribes (frequently nomadic), then into the agricultural age where we tended to congregate in more permanent settings and start accumulating property. However, there was a **great cost in labor man hours** to make this move and many periods where the lower classes (**especially children**) were exploited for labor to the extent that education was denied for most.

———————— ♦ ————————

When we moved from agricultural feudalism into the industrial age, we sought free-market solutions in capitalist ventures to design better ways for businesses to compete, prosper, and grow. Industry progressed and became more efficient and automated, **driving the decline for the need for child labor.** This offered the luxury of bringing basic community education back into childhood across the socioeconomic spectrum (with some terrible race-based exceptions).

Concurrently, industry began to understand that **a more educated class of laborers provided more competent and upstanding adults** who understood the value of hard labor to prosper.

———————— ♦ ————————

But there was a fundamental problem.

Children learn naturally by playing and exploring as they have done since ancient times. This natural tendency was thoroughly squashed during early agricultural and industrial ages to enforce more productivity from the children in the fields and factories. Play was supplanted by grueling labor focused strictly on the trained task at hand.

When we began to transition back from hard labor to education in a schooling environment, **we treated schooling as we did hard labor** – discouraging play and exploration in favor of a demanding environment of strictly controlled instruction and rote memorization.

> *"As we have no play days, so neither do we allow*
> *any time for play on any day; for he that plays as*
> *a child will play as a man."*
>
> – John Wesley's Rules for Wesleyan Schools[21]

Although children were coming from the brutal and tedious environments of field and factory, they (not unexpectedly) could not adapt well to the school environment. Prevailing thinking at the time was that education – **children's work** – **was most effective through endless repetition and memorization delivered at the end of a ruler, pointer, or back of the hand**.

Eighteenth-century schools had a common theme that **"play" was the enemy of learning** and becoming an adult. It was accepted that education must be grueling work and strictly, even brutally controlled.[22]

─────────── ◆ ───────────

Schools today have become **much less educationally harsh and regimented**, but much of that underlying structure still exists throughout the system. In many ways, today's public school is designed as hard work and not a natural self-chosen activity. This is partially due to the expansive increase in subjects, knowledge, and technical understanding needed to succeed in today's world, especially if moving on to higher education.

On the other side of the equation (*pun intended*), schools have also become extremely weak, soft, and unfocused in many respects. It is an odd dichotomy.

Obviously, play and exploration by itself would never be sufficient to prepare our children for today's world; but **we still rely too heavily on brute strength to force-feed knowledge into young, pliable brains** through an **executive-directed one-size-fits-all educational system** that consumes more and more of their time – arguably for less and less of a positive result.

Additionally, **we have failed at finding that natural balance** between children's work and play/exploration since the current system relies on **teaching to the lowest common denominator. This depresses exceptionalism** by suppressing exploration, play, and choice that would naturally differentiate the diverse types of learners and their capabilities.

EDUCATION ARRIVES IN AMERICA

That was a long way around to get to how history gives us a sense of where we've been, what has been tried, what has failed, and what has succeeded. But that grounding also **helps us understand where we *might* go next**.

After our romp through ancient history, we now need to move forward and explore just a touch of the history of public education in America. Specifically, what has changed (if anything) since we came to this great land?

Remember, we are exploring the past to
prepare us to accept the future.

Upon arriving in America, we evolved relatively quickly into a mix of urban, rural, and agricultural cities, towns, and villages. Education arose piecemeal based on the needs of the time and resources available vs. the value of education to society. **Was education worth the time, expense, and effort?** Early times were rough in America and basic education was not at the top of most people's minds.

But, as humans tend to do, we continued to grow, we procreated (*a lot*), we made life better day-by-day, and we grew a thriving nation that ultimately became a **beacon of hope and freedom to the world** – *often despite ourselves.*

Our story here though is about public schools so let's start where that started in America so we can see how that shaped our current public education environment.

THE BOSTON LATIN SCHOOL

The history of public education in America starts with the long and storied chronicle of the first established public school in the United States – the **Boston Latin School (BLS).**[23]

BLS was established on April 23, 1635 and is still an active and thriving institution today. The school continues to be part of our vast national network of schools nearly 400 years later. The reason for including BLS is not simply that it was the first of its kind, but to examine how it evolved and **how it differs from typical public schools.** Their **387 years of success demonstrates that there can be distinctly different methodologies for managing public education** without placing everyone in the same cookie-cutter environment that we do today.

———— ♦ ————

Most schools of that era (around much of the planet) were **established by the church.** English Puritans believed reading and understanding the Bible was critical to a people's welfare, both here on earth and in the afterlife. They felt that the next generation of leaders must be – for political and religious reasons – **educated in philosophy, classical studies, theology, and government.**

Interestingly, Boston Latin School was *NOT* founded by the Church, but became **the nation's <u>first publicly funded school</u>**.

BLS was established by the voters through the Boston Town Meeting. The school was funded through rents collected for the use of islands in Boston Harbor, **not by taxing the residents**. This is notable in that it made Colonial Massachusetts one of the first places in the world to make education of children an actual public responsibility as we think of it today.

BLS is frequently ranked in the top high schools in the United States by various organizations.[24] Alumni have gone on to graduate from prestigious Ivy League schools and to excel in science, philosophy, business, religion, and other fields. A few notable names **include 5 of the original 56 Declaration of Independence signers** – including John Hancock, Samuel Adams, and Benjamin Franklin (who famously dropped out).

How does BLS maintain such an **intense high-quality education** that is desired by so many parents and students?

All residents of Boston of the right age are eligible to attend which creates a high demand within the city to attend the school. Ultimately, BLS had to implement testing and other qualifications over the years to ensure that students who were accepted to BLS: 1) were capable of meeting the rigors of education there; and 2) *WANTED* **to be there** (*important points to remember for later – there will be a test*).

Look!

---- ◆ ----

Why is this important?

Today we tend to restrict nearly all publicly taxed alternatives to public school, making them **subordinate to the governmental public system.** Unfortunately, the BLS model did not grow as a national model due to the constraints resulting from a funding method that relied on revenue from renting local resources. An interesting concept to keep in mind when we get to **Chapter 13** (funding).

To meet the growing demand for **education nationwide**, the government stepped in with a broader model that ultimately resulted in the K-12 system we primarily use today.

Sticking with Massachusetts, let's look at what else was happening with education. **Most school-aged children received a basic education at home** to learn to read and write. However, Puritan leaders were concerned that parents were not providing sufficient – and appropriate – learning for their children.

In response, the General Court of Massachusetts passed a law in 1642 requiring **heads of households** (or someone hired by them) to teach all of their dependents (children, servants, apprentices, etc.) to read and write English. If they did not teach the dependents as required by law, the household would face a fine <u>or even have their children removed from the home</u>. Even then, the government was inclined to believe our children belonged to them.

Eventually, this approach was deemed insufficient by the General Court and they established **publicly funded district schools**. Ultimately, Massachusetts became the first state to pass a comprehensive **Education Law** in 1789.

> <u>**Public responsibility**</u> and <u>**governmental control**</u>
> **for the education of our children was solidly
> established in America**.
> The rest, as they say, is history.

Advocates for community schooling emphasized the civic benefits of public schools to teach the 3R's and beyond to include history, geography, grammar, and (*in the early days*) **a heavy dose of moral instruction to instill civic virtues** (*Chapter 6 touches on the moral and social teachings in modern schools*).

At this time, they believed society would benefit most through a universal system of education that would necessarily have to **attract sufficient numbers of children from all social classes**, including those from well-educated and affluent families. They had to make universal education attractive to all members of society and **promoted that a more educated population would drive down crime, poverty, and other ills** that are more prevalent in a society with large uneducated populations.

———————— ◆ ————————

The concept of public responsibility was met with significant resistance from citizens who felt it was improper and unfair for them to have to pay for the education of **other people's children**. Proponents successfully countered that the cost to the community would be far less than the larger societal cost stemming from poverty and criminality.

> A more educated society resulting in a culture with less crime and poverty *seems* like a fundamental truth. But that truth is <u>not</u> playing itself out in today's world.
>
> **Why?**
>
> *(See Chapter 6 and Chapter 7.)*

Those who believed public schooling was the answer proposed that **educating children from different religious, ethnic, economic, and social backgrounds** together in one environment would help them learn to get along and understand each other.

> *This was a powerful argument during a time when America was becoming more and more diverse.*

This **shift to universal schooling as a public funding responsibility** was arguably **the *LAST* major reform of our education system to this day** – thus the genesis and premise of this book.

By around 1840, **55% of the 3.6 million school age children attended publicly funded schools.**[25] Today nearly all school age children attend some form of public school, private institution, or homeschooling to get an education.

———————— ◆ ————————

All was not rosy of course. At certain times in our history **particular groups of children were not allowed to participate in education** or were limited to where they could attend based on race, gender, or other reasons of the times. We ultimately overcame those issues and the explosive growth of education in America continues to this day.

This growth has resulted in some advances in teaching methods, tools, and capabilities, but the changes have only been **incremental improvements** or "**deprovements**"[26] within the existing system.

> It may be cliché, but we really do need to understand where we came from to enable us to imagine a different future.

To cover even a small bit of the history of schools over the past couple of centuries would take several books and would drag us way off topic.

However, we should address a few important touchpoints that occurred during more recent history to help set the stage for our discussions later. Although the following events may seem disconnected, **each one of these touchpoints had a factor in shaping our educational system to bring us where we are today.**

The timetable below will help us understand the **evolution of our educational system** and *perhaps* even **why** we have been **unable** to successfully reform it to this point.

HISTORICAL EVENTS AFFECTING PUBLIC EDUCATION

The educational event timeline below provides a rudimentary look at some of the major events in our history that shaped public schooling. This is **not** a definitive list, but will help clarify our historical path to modern public education.

Interestingly, if you look into each of these events, **nearly every one of them served in some way to <u>expand the government's role and scope</u> in operating, managing, funding, and controlling the public school system** (particularly from the Federal government side). Most of these events may seem like great ideas on the surface (*except Jim Crow of course*), but **all <u>served to stifle</u> any possibility of true reformation** in the way we delivery public education. Keep those thoughts in mind as you review these events.

Year	Fundamental Historical Events Affecting Public Education
1837	Massachusetts created the first **State Board of Education**.
1837	**Mann Reforms**.[27] Horace Mann, the Secretary of Education of Massachusetts led the "**common-school**" movement promoting that education should be universal, non-sectarian, free (tax-based), and **should focus on social efficiency, civic virtue, and character, rather than mere "learning."** He also introduced **placing students in grades by age**, then progressing them.
1857	The **National Education Association (NEA)**[28] was founded in 1857 and is the largest professional employee organization (labor union) in the nation today. Their stated mission is to "*partner with communities, parents, coalitions, and students to **build equitable systems**...*" In 2018, the NEA "*overwhelmingly adopted a policy committing NEA to '**actively advocate for social and educational strategies fostering the eradication of institutional racism and white privilege**'.*" The NEA maintains a massive lobbying effort in Federal and State governments to shape all things related to education.
1867	The **Federal Department of Education (ED)**[29] was established in 1867. The scope of their control over public education grew expansively over the following 150+ years. The Department of Education became a Cabinet-level agency in 1980. See later discussion regarding the current and future status of the ED.
1865 – 1968	**Jim Crow Laws**[30] consisted of state and local statutes legalizing racial segregation. Sadly, many schools were segregated during this period, **creating vast disparities in educational opportunities**. Eventually, the nation came together to end this atrocity.
1870	All states in the U.S. had **tax-subsidized elementary schools**.[31] This resulted in the U.S. population maintaining one of the highest literacy rates in the world.
1900	34 States had implemented compulsory schooling laws with 30 of those requiring attendance until age 14 (or higher). Every state in the U.S. by 1930 required students to complete elementary school.[32]

Year	Fundamental Historical Events Affecting Public Education
1929	As **The Great Depression**[33] raged on, tax revenues fell and funding was shifted away from schools to relief projects. The government became hostile to the schools and funding dried up. As we Americans do, we innovate. People and organizations stepped up to create programs to help students and teachers through jobs, "work study" programs, apprenticeships, and more. Of course, once the crisis was over, government stepped back in with lots of cash in hand and a much bigger role in the educational system as a whole.
1940	The **National School Board Association (NSBA)**[34] was founded as a federation of state associations that represent locally elected school board officials. They advocate for equity and excellence in education through school board leadership. **Note**: In the wake of the **NSBA's letter to the Biden administration**[35] in 2021 that characterized parents who protested progressive curricula as potential "***domestic terrorists***", ~17 state school board groups withdrew from NSBA and many downgraded their relationship.
1941	The **Lanham Act of 1940**[36] resulted in significant expansion of Federal support for education during World War II. Provisions of the Act provided assistance to school districts affected by war and industry growth.
1950	Since 1950 the **Impact Aid laws**[37] provided education related assistance to school districts who have concentrations of school children impacted by Federal lands, facilities, bases, or other special challenges. In 1965, this became **Title VII of the Elementary and Secondary Education Act of 1965** (**ESEA**).
1954	**Brown v. Board of Education**,[38] Supreme Court decision (unanimous 9-0) found that legally mandated public school segregation was Unconstitutional. See **The Dunbar Story** below for an interesting sidebar to this.
1958	Primarily due to the Cold War, Congress passed the **National Defense Education Act** (**NDEA**) to ensure we could compete with the Soviet Union in technical and scientific fields. NDEA sought to improve mathematics, science, and foreign language training throughout the public education system.

Year	Fundamental Historical Events Affecting Public Education
1964	The **Civil Rights Act of 1964**[39] effectively ended racial segregation in public schools. It took several years to work through the system to truly end segregation.
1965	The **Elementary and Secondary Education Act (ESEA)**[40] passed by Lyndon B. Johnson is one of the most far-reaching acts of Federal legislation related to education. President Johnson believed that **education was a cure for ignorance and poverty** and **pushed to significantly increase Federal funding** for public schools. Fears of expanded Federal involvement in local schools were somewhat assuaged initially by providing the funding back to states through grants that were then distributed to the local school districts. Many amendments followed. The Constitutional validity of federal involvement is a major topic of discussion to this day.
1966	The **Coleman Report**, "*Equality of Educational Opportunity*", by Professor James Coleman[41] was a massive statistical data analysis effort that concluded additional "*school funding has little effect on student final achievement.*" The report implied that socioeconomic status and other factors had much larger impacts. Additionally, the analysis showed significant benefits to integration.
1983	Reform Efforts triggered by a report titled "**A Nation at Risk**"[42] by the National Commission on Excellence in Education resulted in calls for increased academic rigor, longer school days, and other band-aid solutions that did not result in any real reform. This attempt is discussed in detail in **Chapter 9**.
2002	The **No Child Left Behind Act** (NCLB)[43] provided more Federal aid, but among other things, required states to measure progress and punish schools not meeting goals measured by standardized state exams. Teachers began "teaching to the exam" rather than providing education.
2015	The **Every Student Succeeds Act**[44] replaced the **NCLB** and addresses academic standards, testing, Federal funding, and more. Both the NCLB and ESSA continue to prompt much debate on both sides.

The **massive expansion of scope into all aspects of public schooling by the Federal government** has been ongoing for many years and continues to this day. While many of these powers brought Federal funding to local schooling, **they also carried many caveats, requirements, restrictions, and controls** over schools, reducing their autonomies.

This Federal power also attracted **numerous major lobbying groups** who would come to exert tremendous influence over the schools, their curriculum, teachers, funding, and philosophies. Local communities and parents retained less and less influence over how and what their children were being taught as **control and influence moved farther** *away* **from local interested parties** and became subject to the whims of higher levels of government, politicians, lobbyists, associations, and unions.

THE DUNBAR STORY

I have one last story for you before we leave the exciting world of history. This tale ranges through 150+ years and focuses on an incredible school in Washington, D.C. It's a tale of **remarkable success and epic failure**. But hold judgement until you hear the whole story.

Pastor Corey Brooks, Founder of **Project H.O.O.D.** (*Helping Others Obtain Destiny*),[45] has been working for many years to fight against violence and help the children and youth of the South Side of Chicago live better lives.

While I was writing early parts of this book, he was in the middle of a **100-Day Rooftop Vigil** to build a Community Center to help the youth of his neighborhood. (**Update**: *As of late 2024, his wonderful Community Center is under construction to open in 2025.*) His "*Rooftop Revelations*"[46] each day made for some interesting reading that I highly recommend. I include him here to honor his fight for the safety, education, and futures of youth in an extremely troubled area of Chicago and to introduce the story of **Dunbar High School**.

Pastor Brooks has spoken many times of the importance of a proper education in giving children the tools they need to make better choices and succeed. In his own words, *"America is an **aspirational nation**. We aspire to be somebody. We aspire to create. We aspire to be better. **The American dream at its core is aspirational.**"*[41]

> **When we abandon hopes, dreams, and aspirations, other less admirable choices become more viable and rush in to fill the void.**

His words affirm in my mind that, given the opportunity, we will make tremendous sacrifices for our kids. We will do everything possible to help them aspire to something better.

However, **if the tools, the means, the capability, or the will are not there** to allow us to do that, then youth, particularly in highly difficult environments, can lose hope, shake off dreams, and abandon any viable aspirations that may have existed. **Other choices become more viable, maybe even more attractive to our children.** Which brings us finally to our tragic tale.

———————— ◆ ————————

I first heard about the subject of this story from Pastor Brooks in one of his rooftop vigil talks. The Pastor had relayed one of **Thomas Sowell's**[47] interesting stories about education and it piqued my interest. Mr. Sowell is a renowned economist, social theorist, author (28 books), and senior fellow at Stanford University's Hoover Institution. He is certainly someone worth listening to.

As a result, **I dove headfirst down this rabbit hole** for several days trying to understand what had gone so wrong. I won't go into depth here, but you will begin to understand the importance of this cautionary tale when we get into the current and future-state of education in the next few chapters.

First, a few basic details.

- **Dunbar High School**[48] was founded in Washington, D.C. in 1870.

- It has the distinction of being the **first public high school for black students** in America.

- Throughout the 1800's, the Civil War, and history that impacted our society up through 1954, Dunbar had a magnificent record as an **academically elite school**.

- Dunbar was designated as an **Academic High School in D.C.** (as opposed to other schools in the city that focused on technical or vocational training at the time).

As the first black high school, and carrying the designation as an Academic High School in a major city, they attracted the best and brightest faculty with advanced degrees and doctorates.

Any black student from **any** district in D.C. who desired to go and could find a way to get there could attend Dunbar (*big spoiler alert*). Students (*many encouraged by their parents I'm sure*) chose to come to Dunbar from far and wide within D.C. because **they WANTED to be there, at that school**. *Look!*

This desire to be at that school **minimized the negative impact of disruptive or disinterested students** prevalent at many other schools. They wanted to be there and understood how important an education like this could be to their futures.

The academic standards were challenging, the *esprit de corps* was high, and the **dedication of the faculty and the students was unmatched** at most schools. Any black students in D.C. who aspired to more sought out a place at Dunbar. The triumphs of the school continued to flourish from 1870 to 1954.

Then… everything changed.

In a nation desperate (***and rightly so***) to end segregation, the Jim Crow laws, and anything related to them, **the Supreme Court ruled unanimously (9-0) in Brown v. Board of Education** that legally mandated public-school segregation was unconstitutional. **Excellent ruling! Exactly the right choice!** Nobody would ever doubt that.

Sadly though, the *"unspoken rule of unintended consequences*[49] *resulting from good intentions"* led to the destruction of much that Dunbar High School was.

Important: I do NOT for one second mean to disparage today's Dunbar High School. I'm sure it is a fine school of this generation of city schools. However, in my

> LOOK!
>
> The danger is not always in the *changes we make*, but in the Unintended Consequences we did not foresee.

opinion, the Supreme Court ruling ensured that it could no longer be the same exemplary school of academic excellence that distinguished it pre-1954 as it likely suffers from the same issues that plague many urban schools now.

> *I'm sure I will get many letters from Dunbar faculty, alumni, and students telling me what a wonderful school it is. I will read those and revel in joy over their successes.*

My goal is not to tear down what we have, but to define a reformation for something even grander that would raise Dunbar (and all schools) up beyond what Dunbar was in the early 1900's.

WHAT made Dunbar so incredible pre-1954? If you look back to the previous page, it's pretty simple really... **rigorous academics; desire to be there crushes disruption**; and a **fulfilling sense of aspiration** that something better was possible.

All of this will become intrinsic to our discussions of foundational reformation in **Chapters 10, 11,** and **12**.

———— ♦ ————

Getting back to our tale of woe... In 2015, Thomas Sowell provided an appraisal of Dunbar after the Supreme Court decision. He noted that **political compromise led to ALL schools in D.C. becoming "neighborhood schools."**

This was critical because it meant that **Dunbar could no longer accept students from outside it's neighborhood** and must *"accept only students from the rough ghetto neighborhood in which it was located"*[50] according to Sowell's appraisal.

He noted that since they had to accept all students in the neighborhood, "***unmotivated, unruly, and disruptive students flooded in.***" Many of these new students did not want to be there and had no aspirations to a better education. This quickly led to many of the exceptional teachers Dunbar had collected either moving out or retiring early.

————————— ♦ —————————

This shift in public schooling to remove choice unfortunately also coincided with the **growth of liberalism in the 1960's**. That shift arguably drove some minority communities away from a culture of aspiration to a culture of dependency and victimhood. This combination put the nail in the coffin of Dunbar and it quickly became another troubled inner city school.

Again, I have no desire to disparage any school, especially Dunbar, but **it is necessary to be brutally honest if we are to consider fundamental reform of a massive institution** like our public education system. The time for soft talk has passed.

Once again, you may ask… *why do I tell you this story*? Your time is precious, but I felt this was a great cautionary tale that demonstrated the failings noted above, as well as the **one-size-fits-all** and **lowest-common-denominator** methodologies of a governmental education system that we will talk about later. All of these topics become **important to the tapestry that we'll weave** in finding our way to something new and exciting.

Besides, I have always been a sucker for tales of "**Unintended Consequences**". These particularly plague massive systemic programs such as our educational system. Unfortunately, **those who suffer most from unintended consequences most are NOT the ones making the changes, but those who must abide by them.** Our challenge in foundational reformation will be to recognize potential unintended consequences and eliminate or mitigate them as much as possible.

> **Those who suffer from the "unintended consequences" of changes are not those who made the changes.**

I now return this book back to its intended purpose.

TRANSITION BACK TO TODAY

What an fun romp through history that was. **We laughed, we cried, we even went down a few rabbit holes**. Even so, there was so much we didn't get to cover – but I think we've seen enough of this movie.

To move forward, we need to examine what our public school system really looks like today and **where we're headed tomorrow if we do not change trajectory**. To truly understand that, we walked through the ancient history of education, up through the Middle Ages, and into American history. We saw that education evolved through **three major *eras* of education**.

- **Era 1**: The evolution of education as a survival trait.

- **Era 2**: Education as a way of achieving a sort of immortality for humans.

- **Era 3**: And finally, as a means of improving production, growing knowledge, and competing as the world grew exponentially more complicated.

Era 1 and **Era 2** incorporate many evolutions and reforms in how we perceived and implemented education. However, once we reached **Era 3** (around the 1600's) and implemented publicly funded community education, **all evolution and attempts at major reformation pretty much came to a stop**.

Once the system was up and running, **controlled from the top-down through governmental systems**, the momentum of a juggernaut naturally took over. Our natural propensity to expand power and control of any governmental system (local, state, and Federal) ultimately leads us to accept that "*this is the way we've always done it*" and "*it's too big to change*."

We stepped back as power centers continued to entrench themselves. This resulted in **pushing parents and local interested parties further and further from any control** – or any possibility of implementing any real change that might upset the apple cart.

Abandon the idea that Public Schools were intelligently designed. **They evolved through need.**

Remember → **we must <u>abandon the idea</u> that our public schools were intelligently designed** from the ground up. They were <u>not</u> based on scientific insight or logic. What we have now is a **product of the haphazard history of education**, built up in different fragments, from different eras, and different philosophies – always **driven from the top down** by politicians, bureaucrats, and lobbyists – NOT parents.

That methodology is how we ended up with a system that has **systemic problems that cannot be excised piecemeal.**

To get to an exceptional system **that works for everyone**, we need to build it by design. To borrow from technology development, the educational system must be **<u>Purpose-Built for the success of that system</u>**. It is time for us to apply a different methodology to build a **next-generation educational system**.

To do that, we need to go beyond history and dive into the problems with today's public education system, break down the system's problems, analyze those problems, and develop a product that is **intelligently designed to succeed for *ALL* users.**

Intelligent design should support the <u>Natural Needs</u> of all students: • *education,* • *aspiration,* • *hope.*

Only then can we even imagine a K-12 educational system that will allow **all** children in **all** environments to **aspire to excellence**.

Only then can we educate new generations of children that understand that **education, aspiration, and hope are the natural state for everyone.**

Read on if that concept interests you. But remember…

No more band-aid solutions allowed.

CHAPTER

5

CURRENT STATE OF PUBLIC SCHOOLS

Things to consider:

➢ Are we doing better or worse now than the previous generation?

➢ Are we willing to sacrifice for the next generation?

➢ Who is most impacted by the problems inherent in this system?

➢ What is the real purpose of education?

"Parents give up their rights when they drop their children off at public schools."

—Judge Melinda Harmon[51]

THE STATE OF PUBLIC EDUCATION TODAY

We return now to the present day to explore the results of all that history we excavated through.

- Did we get it right?

- Did we do our best?

- Are **all** of our children receiving the best possible education we can give them?

All evidence we have today suggests that we did NOT get it "right" and it would be hard to argue that even a moderate percentage of children are receiving the best possible education. Which brings us to the core question...

> *Are we ready as a nation to be brutally honest about one of the most important institutions in our country?*

If we are to consider a true foundational reformation of our educational system, then we must be **honest, open, and even brutal** in our assessment – **NOT out of any malevolence**, but out of necessity. The first step in fixing a problem is to fully open our eyes, recognize the *real* problems, and analyze what fundamental change must happen for lasting change.

The development of this book coincided with several major events that unfolded in America and changed how we understood our K-12 educational system (and much of the rest of our world). I had to come back and rewrite much of my original writings and notes due to a **broader awakening** that was happening among parents, educators, politicians, and others during this period.

Interestingly, there was so much going on in the public-school arena that the first draft of this book was over 130,000 words and 600 pages. **Luckily for you**, I am a gentle man who means no harm to you, so I generalized much that was common knowledge to focus on what really matters. There are already numerous books that detail these events so I will just touch on some current events here to set the stage for our discussion.

As the nation continues to be hyper-focused on problems persistent in our educational system, my hope is that this awakening will **drive a movement to push for genuine, foundational, and lasting change** that will usher in a new age in education.

AN AWAKENING

Although much of this focus had been simmering under the surface for a long time, the real **national educational awakening** started oddly enough during the Virginia Gubernatorial election in 2021.

Prior to this boil-over during election season, parents in Loudoun County, VA had started pushing back against Critical Race Theory (CRT)[52] in schools, incidents with sexual assaults, School Board members collecting personal information on parents who complained, and more. **This sparked protests, rallies, and a full-on rumble royale over education versus indoctrination**. The quality of education came into focus as well.

During the middle of all of this, Gubernatorial election season arrived in Virginia and a political newcomer, Glen Youngkin (R), stepped up to run for Governor of Virginia.

He quickly **focused on educational issues and centered on parents** throughout the state.[53] On the other side, his opponent, Terry McAuliffe (D), famously said, "*I don't think parents should be telling schools what they should teach.*"[54] That single sentence galvanized the parents of Virginia and was arguably a major factor in McAuliffe's eventual defeat. The die was cast nationwide.

America's K-12 educational system became the central battleground cause for discussion, debate, rallies, and protests around the nation. Numerous events and issues impacted schools, parents, students, school boards, teachers' unions, and the status quo of education throughout the country.

- **COVID** shutdowns, mask mandates, and vaccine mandates impacted children throughout the nation.

- New at-home public schooling for K-12 students during COVID **exposed the actual public-school curriculum and teachings to parents**.

- The so called "**war on parents**" became a common phrase to encompass numerous issues.

- Detailed **pornographic teachings and sexuality** in schools were exposed (*sorry for the pun*).

- One-sided **politicization** of education grew more visible to parents.

- The integration and indoctrination of **CRT** theories and other race-based teachings in K-12 and college education were revealed.

- **Action Civics** involved teachers sending middle and high school students on field trips to live protests and teaching them how to protest at social activist rallies.

- Many **School Boards were exposed as ideological-driven organizations** who did not believe parents should have a say in their children's educations.

- **Teachers began quitting** or **retiring** in larger numbers than ever before.

- **A Mass Exodus of students EXITING the public school system began** (the point of this book).

We may all have different feelings and beliefs about these topics, but there is no denying that they had a profound impact on education, awareness, and political activities during this time.

It is safe to say that this was an interesting period, and it **exposed much of the <u>underlying and secretive world of education</u>** that we, as parents, had allowed to flourish through our **silent consent**. *Why?* Maybe it's as simple as the fact that we were complacent with the status quo. **It was the easy path** and we'd always done it that way.

> **Parents' distance from the monolithic government school system insulated them and made them feel that the silence in the void was just an echo of their own isolation.**

This is the way **monolithic systems** grow and consume all in their path. The system becomes so big and entrenched that the individuals subjected to the system begin to feel that they are but a small powerless cog in a very large machine. **As parents moved farther and farther away from the core of power, they became more isolated from the system**… they began to feel that they were alone at the edge of the machine. That their detached voice could not and would not be heard.

The silence of millions in the educational void became an echo of their own isolation.

Because of this presumed isolation and an increasing acceptance of the failings of the public education system, more and more **parents began to abandon the system** altogether. We have seen this play out as millions who have moved out of the community pool of public-school education to alternatives like private schools, homeschools, co-ops, and other options. Often at great personal expense and inconvenience.

Of particular note is homeschooling which had dramatic growth throughout this period of time. (Note that <u>at-home schooling</u> of public-school children due to COVID closures are **<u>not</u>** included in the numbers below.)

- Homeschool households grew to 5.4% of the U.S. school population in early 2020.[55]

- By October 2020, households grew to 11.1%.

- Peaking at 19.5% in May of 2021.

During this confluence of events, COVID was of course one of the major drivers (but not the only one) in parents' new focus on the problems with our school system. McKinsey & Company examined **the effects of COVID on public school students** during this period and found **significant social and developmental delays, as well as double-digit drops in reading and math comprehension scores**.[56] Mental health issues such as depression, anxiety, and suicidal tendencies grew as students were forced to isolate themselves from their peers and leave the social environments they were accustomed to.

It should be noted that there is **marked difference** between public school children forced to learn from home in untried environments due to COVID and actual homeschooling by parents. The public schools failed miserably by every metric during this troubled time.

The impacts of COVID, the other factors noted above, and all the issues we are about to discuss combined into a loud chorus that amplified the lone parental voices ringing out across the country. **Those who felt they were tiny cogs with no voice suddenly realized that there were many other voices in the void to join theirs**. Maybe enough even to trigger change.

> **Do we have the fortitude to do the hard things for our children? I believe we do, but parents must band together under a single flag to fight for our kids.**

MASS EXODUS – EXITING THE PUBLIC SCHOOLS

In recent years, there has been a **massive sea change in education** as parents (and children) fed up with public schools sought other pathways to get the education they want for their children. Numerous public, private, and personal paths to the best education have been expanding and **drawing more and more children out** of the public school system.

That is GREAT for those children who can exit the government system for something that works better for them. **The problem is that public schools will remain in place** for the vast majority of K-12 children.

> **LOOK!** → *Do we just abandon those millions of children left behind in a failing public school system?*

If we could replace the entire public K-12 school system with the alternatives mentioned above, that would be amazing. It would then become just a matter of choice.

But that is *not* going to happen. Ever.

Alternative schools will always be around, but we all know that our **publicly funded public schools are not going away**. *Remember*, this was **one of our major premises** in **Chapter 3**. I will make the case for **why this MUST be true** in later chapters. But reality remains that **public schools remain the easiest pathway for most parents**.

So, if millions of children are going to remain behind in the public K-12 schools, **what is the answer** to ensure they get the best education possible and maybe even out-perform the alternatives?

- Are we just going to keep applying band-aid solutions to the ailing monolith?

- When the band-aids ultimately fail, will we then be willing to do the hard things?

- If so, then why not do the hard things now?

The information in the next couple of chapters will help prepare you to **fully grasp the import and impact of the changes I propose** later in this book. But before we go there, we need to understand what education is.

THE PURPOSE OF EDUCATION

DO WE NEED PUBLIC EDUCATION?

We have seen in our dance through history that Americans have a strong belief that there should be some sort of public education supported by the community. We also made that one of our assumptions in **Chapter 3**. If we accept that, then the question on public education becomes:

- what form does it take?

- how is it structured?

- who controls it?

- how is it funded?

All great questions that we will take on in **Chapters 10, 11, and 13**.

The challenge then is… what type of public system would work to provide **all** children with a great education – **regardless of location, socio-economic status, or educational needs**.

———————— ♦ ————————

At this point we must be truthful with ourselves and accept that **there will always be inequities** based on those who have the economic means to pay for expensive alternatives such as exclusive private schools and those who don't. Just as some families will have expensive cars and large homes, others will never be able to afford those things. **That is the nature of our world and we cannot and should not interfere with anyone's liberty** to use *their* resources as they choose to accomplish what they believe is best for *their* child.

> We cannot tear down others to make everyone equal. We must work to raise everyone to a higher standard. Opportunity is there for all who understand how to seek it.

Our goal then is to **make sure our shiny new and improved public educational system will provide an education that rivals the best educational opportunities on the market** (*sorry, you have to wait until* **Chapter 10** *to see what I've cooked up for you*). Every child must be provided the tools, resources, knowledge, culture, and outlook they need to succeed, prosper, and flourish in the world. Only then will education be as equal as it can be in a free society like America's.

Is that then the purpose of education? Let's find out.

WHAT IS THE REAL PURPOSE OF PUBLIC EDUCATION?

"Education is not the learning of many facts, but the training of the mind to think."

—Albert Einstein[57]

LOOK!

Americans will never agree on a single purpose for education. That's okay. That's America. We have different beliefs and goals in life and those personal values drive how we see the purpose of education. None of those purposes have to be mutually exclusive, but **we do need a baseline understanding of the** <u>primary goals</u> **that define the existence of public education**. Without those, <u>how do we define what the next generation of education should look like</u>?

If we define **goals** rather than **specifics** of *what* to teach, then we can allow the system to **innovate and evolve** to better meet those goals. So, for now, allow me to offer a starting point for these goals based on my studies and my beliefs. You may not agree, but let's start with the goals I designed because, well... *I wrote this book.* ☺

> **Education must be defined by** <u>Goals</u> **rather than specifics to allow** *Innovation* **and** *Evolution* **of education to thrive.**

By the time we get through **Chapter 9** we should have a solid understanding of what we want out of our education system. We need that understanding to **determine if this proposition for fundamental reformation has any validity**.

———— ◆ ————

I have pondered much over the years as we raised our children about what education *should* be. I even changed my mind on numerous occasions as the times changed, as the world transformed around us, and as I myself changed.

Do you remember our discussion in early history about the **purpose of schools changing based on the needs of the era and the community**? Education during the agricultural age differed vastly from education needs during the industrial age or the information age. Therefore, I believe that no matter what we decide the actual "purpose" of education is, **it must be fluid and able to adapt** to ensure our children are prepared for *their* lives and *their* futures beyond home and school – no matter how the world changes around them.

LOOK!

A *major Caution* here; → any "**fluid**" purpose for a large system such as this runs the risk of **massive corruption** steering the system away from its original intentions over time. Corruption cannot be allowed.

One last thing before we jump into all of this. To keep things simple, we need to define one complex element we'll be dealing with into a single phrase. From here on out, when I use the term "**Core Academics**", it is intended to encompass all traditional education basics such as the 3R's+. This would include Reading, Writing, Arithmetic, History, Civics, Sciences, and other **traditional academics**.

———————— ♦ ————————

So, what about our educational "GOALS"? As the old cliché goes, *"the one thing we can all agree on is that we will never all agree on everything."* That's the nature of being free minds with free will. This is one of the reasons **we struggle so much with our current one-size-fits-all government educational system**.

We govern our current system in **broad strokes intended to fit all students in all environments** based on national needs, desires, and sociopolitical leanings. Our nationwide efforts for equality and equity have **the unintended consequence of dumbing down the system** to the **lowest common denominator**.

However, we can use some broad strokes for now to **come to soft agreement** on the high-level goals of education. This soft agreement provides us with a mental milepost to bump against when we finally arrive at designing our incredibly bold foundational transformation in **Chapter 10**.

Much of the information in the table below may seem common sense... but is **being demonstrably violated on a massive scale in today's educational system**. Keep these goals and the fluidity we discussed earlier in mind as we continue our journey to accomplish our educational goals.

Success Goal	Universal Education
Learn Core Academics at a Success Level	Prepare students academically to a **demonstrable success level** for all core requirements at a minimum for each grade level. Academic rigor should prepare students to function well in society and/or move on to higher education if that is their plan. Students must be allowed to come to their own conclusions based on the facts and evidence provided, particularly for History, Social Studies, Civics, and Sciences.
Practice Critical Thinking	Students <u>must</u> be taught "**how**" to think, not "**what**" to think. The information age is an amazing phenomenon, but it also opens the door to a world of influences (*both good and bad*) from sources known and unknown. Our children must leave K-12 with the training and the skills needed to: • **analyze** this bombardment of information, • **think** about it critically from all sides, • **probe** for the truth, • **ask** the right questions, • **debate** others effectively (*a lost art*), and • **make informed decisions**. This is one of the most important skills goals we can hope to achieve for our children.
Access to Special Interests and Skills	Students have a broad set of aspirations, goals, skills, and abilities. Once the Core Academics are dealt with, schools could provide additional opportunities to explore mental, physical, and social growth through activities such as: • advanced academics in all categories; • sports and athletics; • business, agriculture, and trades; • politics, public service, military; and • vocation or technology pursuits.

LOOK!

Success Goal	Universal Education
	The level of access to these opportunities will of course be driven by available resources (funding in particular) to enable these activities. **Chapter 13** discusses how the next generation of education could be funded throughout the entire universe of public education – regardless of socio-economic circumstances.
Be Prepared for Higher Education	Currently, around 60% of High School graduates enroll in college, resulting in a 30% college dropout rate in Freshman year.[58] Students need to be better prepared to move on to higher education if appropriate. We must provide them with the planning tools, study tools, and proper counseling to help them succeed (and hopefully improve the retention and success rate).
Be Ready to Work and Prepared to Become Economically Self-Sufficient	Today, roughly 40% of high school students go directly from high school to the workforce. Another 18% drop out of college during their Freshman year and move to the workforce. That means 58% of students need the tools, training, and skills to allow them to succeed and prosper in a work environment and to develop a life independent of their childhood homes. **Chapter 10** discusses how to reach this and other success goals.
Be Responsible Citizens	Citizenship in America is a privilege that must be preserved through the education of our children to understand how to be good citizens and caretakers of our country. They must develop a solid understanding of political issues, civic life, the Constitution, and be prepared to protect our rights and freedoms. Above all, they must be taught to love our country and our people – all people. This is our home! **See the "Extreme CAUTION" box below.** These softer goals present special dangers to our children's education.
The Public Good	As we learned in the historical chapters, community schools were often provided for the public or common good. They understood that education, especially for the poor and middle class provided a population that was better prepared to work, less prone to commit crimes, and allowed for upward economic mobility.

Success Goal	Universal Education
	Horace Mann stated that, *"Education, then, beyond all other devices of human origin, is **the great equalizer of the conditions of men**—the balance-wheel of the social machinery."*[59] Great words. But **caution is warranted** here as well. See the "Extreme CAUTION" box below.
Common Culture	We are a **Nation of Immigrants** and much stronger for that amazing blessing. However, in order to **unify a diverse population** such as ours, we must bask unabashedly in the glory of our **Common American Culture.** That culture, supported by the United States Constitution, has made our magnificent country a land that is the envy of much of the world. The cultures of all immigrants should be appreciated and protected, but **ALL citizens should first and foremost be proud Citizens of the United States** – their birth or chosen nation. Immigrants should celebrate their own historical culture, but *LIVE the American Culture.* The mission of promoting cultural **unity begins at home**, but should also be **reinforced in the public school environment**. Teach students from all ethnic, religious, and racial backgrounds to respect each other as individuals AND as part of the American whole – the *Great Melting Pot* we are so proud of. Embrace our common language, American culture, American values. Learn to love our home. Be ready to fight for our home. This is how nations become strong, joyous, and One Nation. This is how we become civil, become one, become a United Nation – land of the free, home of the brave. [*Sorry, got a little overwhelmed there. Can you blame me?* ☺ *I'm not ashamed to say it, I love America!*]

LOOK!

Extreme CAUTION is warranted here.

LOOK!

As we will learn in Chapters 5, 6, and 7, we must exercise **extreme caution and vigilance** when addressing the educational goals identified above. We cannot allow any of these to wander into the realm of teaching students "***what***" to think.

With softer goals such as "*Be Responsible Citizens*" and "*The Public Good*", it can be exceptionally enticing and effortless to stray into teaching children what to think rather than "*how to analyze the facts they are being taught.*"

This can be especially dangerous when the "*what*" is being taught from a **single perspective**. Purely one-sided "*what to think*" verges (*to put it nicely*) on indoctrination and is perilous and counter-productive to students learning to be free and critical thinkers.

In the early 20th century, **many students in public schools were taught that it was okay to be racist**. Sadly, those were the social values and political dogma of the day.

→ We understand today that those teachings were utterly wrong, destructive, and dangerous. **For many decades now we have wholeheartedly condemned those in no uncertain terms**.

Yet now, in the early 21st century, we are doing this again and teaching children "*what to think*" regarding **fluid social values**, **political dogma of the day**, and **disputed/ unsettled sciences** that are based purely on the beliefs of one segment of the population.

These teachings are contradictory to the beliefs of much of America and delivered WITHOUT the benefit of presenting any input from opposing or contrary viewpoints. In fact, **those opposing viewpoints are brutally discounted and treated as misinformation, disinformation, fake, and dangerous**. No contrary discussion is allowed in today's educational environment.

In the near future, many of these teachings will likely come to be understood as utterly wrong, destructive, and dangerous by the general population. No matter what our thoughts on these matters are today, they are fluid, changing, and opinion-based and **should never be taught to our children as absolute truth designed to foster a specific mindset**.

Because we have strayed into teaching *"what"* based on the current beliefs of some, **we have done great damage to several generations of children**. We cannot allow this to continue in other generations!

Now, back to our regularly scheduled program…

The **foundational educational goals** presented in the previous table are critical in taking us to the next level of universal personalized education for ALL students in America who wish to take advantage of the public school system.

Success metrics can easily be determined for each of these goals and must be required as a minimum certification for all education providers. **Chapter 10** and **Chapter 11** discuss quality of education, quality of providers, and how to ensure educational success metrics are met throughout the system.

———————— ♦ ————————

To step back just a little bit, I poured through numerous stories, studies, and polls trying to define and refine what the purpose or mission of public schools is believed to be. There was wide variance based on who was polling, how the questions were framed, and who responded. But at a very high level, there was some general agreement that is in line with the Educational Goals I had set out above.

A PDK Poll on the *"Public's Attitudes toward the Public Schools"*[60] reflected that only 45% of parents stated the purpose of education was to *"prepare students academically."* While 51% were nearly evenly split between *"prepare students for work"* and *"prepare students to be good citizens."*

This is part of the reason why I believe the Goals approach is much more effective and useful than a specific curriculum approach. The specifics will be up to the education providers (whose customers are the parents) to ensure that they meet or exceed all goals. This will **foster innovation, competition, and continuous improvement** of the school system as a whole.

Intrigued? Wondering how we can do that? Can't wait to get to **Chapter 10**? Hang in there, you don't want to miss the ride to the top of this roller coaster.

———————— ♦ ————————

There is one more controversial topic that needs to be addressed before we move on. This has been at the core of many of the debates that have dominated the news during this period.

> ### <u>WHO</u> should be shaping our children's morals, social values, political opinions, and other personality-molding belief systems?

In 1963, **45 Communist Goals** were read into the Congressional Record by Congressman Albert S. Herlong, Jr. of Florida.[61] If you have not read these, **it is imperative that you do**. You will be amazed at how many of these goals have been achieved in America or are in active combat in today's society.

Goal Number 41 is so on point and exceptionally evil, I have to share it now:

LOOK!

> "**<u>Communist Goal #41</u>**. *Emphasize the **need to** raise children __away__ from the negative influence of parents. Attribute prejudices, mental blocks and retarding of children to suppressive influence of parents.*"

If that doesn't scare you, it should.

Over the last 50 years or so, a visible schism has developed between our public school system and the parents of children using that system. The Gubernatorial race in Virginia highlighted that the public school system has taken on a larger and more dominant role in "Shaping" our children's beliefs, **rather than teaching them how to develop <u>their own belief systems</u>**.

Although all elements of public education should embrace basic moral and positive values, ***it is my belief*** that it is NOT the public school's job – or within its goals, purpose, or mission – to teach our children <u>*specific*</u> morals, societal values, sexual orientations, politics, religions, or other belief systems that will shape, or reshape, who they are.

Parents should be the primary moral and value compass and if any indoctrination in religion, politics, or other beliefs is believed necessary, it should come from the parents to THEIR kids based on their values.

- That is the nature of family.
- That is the nature of a culturally diverse nation of immigrants.

We should never impose one universal set of beliefs (*fleeting and changing according to the whims of those in power*) on children in a setting intended to serve all children from all backgrounds. We should assiduously avoid this, particularly in a mandatory attendance setting such as public schools.

———————— ♦ ————————

I really am working to be as politically neutral as I can in this book, but I'll come flat out and say this, even at the risk of offending some readers; **the government does <u>*NOT*</u> own our children** and has no right to indoctrinate them in anything.

Even if I should happen to agree with the indoctrination topic, it is never right.

It is important that teaching children *what* to think remains out of the realm of our goals-based education. Children must understand how to think openly, clearly, and critically. They must be taught how to ask questions, to seek answers, and to come to conclusions for themselves.

They must <u>never</u> be given someone else's conclusions, then <u>provided curated material</u> to support those conclusions.

Now… *let's take a breath and shift gears a bit.* This seems like a good point to move on to a more foundational topic.

DO OUR PUBLIC SCHOOLS WORK?

> *"Education is the passport to the future,*
> *for tomorrow belongs to those who*
> *prepare for it today."*
> — Malcolm X[62]

Have we as a society delivered on our obligation? Do ALL children have access to that *"passport to the future?"*

If our K-12 public schools were working well, there would be very few people reading this book (*in which case, I would happily give up this manuscript and toss it on the burn pile*). If we were doing everything we could to ensure our children were receiving the best possible education, this book would be a waste of time. Therefore, by simple logic…

**We as a society must believe that
there is something wrong**.

What is it? In the following pages I lay out numerous issues **hindering the success of our school system**. Taking this journey together adds to the **tapestry of understanding** that will lead us to understand we *must* do something. To get there, we need to walk through a bunch of **dark and disturbing detritus**.

———————— ♦ ————————

The good news is that there is a brilliant light burning at the end of the tunnel, **drawing us nearer to intersecting a glorious future** for our children and those that come after them. The hard work of putting this together for them will be well worth the effort – as are the battles that will stand in our way if we choose to pursue this difficult path.

So where do we start on this daring journey?

Let's start with **our continued insistence on using band-aid solutions** to try and "**fix**" these problems. That path can only doom the system to continued failings in the future. Dare I say, even to **the point of extinguishing the Sacred Fire of Education and diminishing the great light that is America.**

If we do not change the trajectory of where our schools are headed now, **most will likely devolve into warehousing institutions that barely prepare our kids** for minimum wage entry level jobs. It will fail entirely in helping them reach the broader promise inherent in America.

Parents must regain their trust in and love of the public school system or more and more of them (*who have the ability to do so*) will seek out alternative methods of schooling – **leaving the rest of our children behind**.

> **If we do not move beyond band-aids, those left behind will settle into a downward spiral as the system devolves.**
>
> **We must accept that band-aids do not work any longer.**

Children from households who cannot take advantage of alternative methods of school will have to endure in a dying system that will become incapable of educating them to even the most basic standards. Throwing more money at this will not stop the deterioration (see **Chapter 9** for proof). This decay is evident in many school systems today, particularly in the inner cities.

Our children deserve a better future than that.

There can be no doubt that there are many fine public schools out there. Unfortunately, that is not the case everywhere. And the problems continue to escalate within most school districts – sometimes from **internal factors**, sometimes from **external forces** with agendas.

The problems become exponentially worse as we move into more and more densely populated urban areas that suffer high levels of poverty, increasing crime, desperation, and daily violence. **As the community declines, the schools get worse. As the schools get worse, the community declines. All in a self-perpetuating circle of decay**. Despite all the political promises, we never seem to find a path to resolution.

In fact, by all measures the decay in education and environment seems to be accelerating.

Some **external factors** that impact the quality of a school system include:

- Bad community and school environments,
- Lack of community connection and opportunity,
- Single-parent and/or disconnected or abusive households,
- Crime, gangs, and drug usage,
- Poverty and lack of jobs or other opportunities,
- Lack of community involvement in youth,
- Lack of parental involvement in schools, and
- Improper (**not** "*insufficient*") funding.

Those are all challenging external factors that **tend to drag kids away from an aspirational mentality and towards survival existence**. We only need look at some of the school districts in the inner cities of New York, Chicago, and others to see the visible challenges our children face in these environments.

It is chilling to see from the outside. Imagine how it must feel for a child to live in that environment day in and day out. It is no wonder that **many kids turn away from traditional familial lives and support systems and gravitate towards unsavory, dangerous, criminal, or alternative ways of living**.

———————— ◆ ————————

We now come face-to-face with the classic "**chicken-and-egg**" conundrum. Does education fail because of the **external environment**? Or does the external environment fail because of a **bad educational system**? In reality, it is a self-destructive feedback loop that grows exponentially through numerous failures within the closed system.

Consider this theoretical conceptualization on how this might work in the **extremely simplified cycle** I define below (*did I*

qualify that statement enough?). This feedback loop creates a downward spiral that sucks our children into a **vortex of fear, uncertainty, hopelessness, anger, resentment, and anti-social behavior that seeks irrational shortcuts to a way out**.

1. A borough in a large city sees a rise in crime due to population pressures.

2. Businesses leave due to crime losses and jobs are lost.

3. Money gets tight in the community and more businesses fail or move to greener pastures.

4. Crime increases as opportunity declines.

5. Families stay because this is the home they know. This is where they grew up, where extended family is. I call it the "**momentum of stasis**."[63]

6. Financial and opportunity stress at home leads to abuse or family breakups.

7. Stressed or abused children lash out at school and in the community, creating hostile environments.

8. Better teachers leave for safer school systems or retire early.

9. Education in the borough loses passion and purpose.

10. Students **lose aspiration** for a better life due to stress and fear at school, problems at home, a lack of opportunity, and an absence of hope.

11. Crime, drugs, gangs, and negative influences increase.

12. More businesses leave, properties deteriorate, community environment declines.

13. The "**Broken Window**" theory[64] becomes reality.

14. Youths drop out of school and seek false opportunity where they can find it: gangs, crime, prostitution, drugs.

15. Single parent household numbers increase dramatically.

16. Lack of supervision leads to truancy, bad influences, gang involvement, more single parent pregnancies.

17. School environments dramatically deteriorate, driving away more good teachers. Sapping the will to excel from those who remain.

18. Education becomes less about education and more about pumping students through the grades and out of the school system to become someone else's problem.

19. Students lose faith in the school and are there only because they have to be – until they decide to quit coming.

20. Lack of education leads to lack of opportunity and a defeatist, victim mentality.

21. This lack of aspiration, hope, and dignity feeds back into the system locally and the cycle repeats and deteriorates over and over again.

The self-destruction of the system becomes inevitable at some point. The problems must ultimately reach critical mass and, like a black hole, it becomes harder and harder to escape the event horizon. **The momentum of living in an environment like that destroys all personal belief that one can escape** without some extraordinary event.

Irrational belief in an easy out seems like the only way to succeed for many – winning the lottery, being drafted by a major sports league, becoming a hit singer/rapper, or making enough money through drugs or prostitution to buy their way to a better life.

Others just accept that this life is just how it is. A failing school system and the Momentum of Stasis combine to blind many to the possibility that there might even be another way. **These are poor**

> **"Momentum of Stasis"**
> **is a mindset that seeks the easiest path – even in the face of hardship. This often means that families stay in deteriorating areas because that's where they've always been. It's what they know.**

substitutes for living a life of true aspiration where many levels of success can be earned. Where success is not some magical solution available only to the lucky few. Success can be defined in many ways and is available to anyone who is prepared to recognize it.

Sadly, **our current educational system fails miserably** in feeding an aspirational life and a positive view of self.

———————— ♦ ————————

Unfortunately, **we have a few more misapplied band-aids to rip off** to get where we need to be and some of those bloody patches conceal gaping wounds in the system that may be infected.

Before we can accept that **we need fundamental foundational reformation rather than band-aid solutions**, we need to fully understand the internal and external factors that infect and influence our current educational system.

Internal factors have negatively impacted this system for generations, slowly reshaping and retargeting our educational system to accomplish social and political agendas that may not be in the best interests of our children and of America as a whole.

Some of the internal factors we will discuss such as government/political influence, teachers' unions, education associations, and others may *seem* like external factors at first glance but are really a part of the **systemic makeup of the educational universe that controls the system holistically**. These influences must be examined as a part of the corporate body to **understand how they can be adapted or excised during a foundational reformation**.

The rest of this chapter is focused on a deeper look into those internal factors to fully understand why **foundational reformation is necessary** and why we must step up and fight for it. Be prepared, there's going to be a lot of dramatic band-aid ripping, viewpoint tugging, and maybe even a few tears.

Ready?

GOVERNMENT-RUN SCHOOLS

"What the Government Giveth, the
Government Can Taketh Away!"
     — Broadly paraphrased from Thomas Jefferson[65]

Now that we have a sense that there are fundamental issues with how we handle public schooling, let's take a peek under the hood to see what issues might be caused by reliance on a school system run by the government.

> **Spoiler alert** → *by this point you may be getting a sense of where this is headed. Hang in there and your patience will be rewarded.*

Some readers may bristle at use of the term "***government schools***." But I am of the belief that a "***public school***" system that is funded by all levels of government (through taxation) – **where Federal and State governments have tremendous quid pro quo power and control** over the entire educational system – is by definition **a government school**. However, being the affable and charming character I am, you will notice that I have been referring to our K-12 Public School system as "*public schools*" or "*community schools*" for the most part. I will continue to do so.

--------------- ◆ ---------------

Schools that are subject to the direction, control, and direct influence of the Federal Government – as most are now – must be considered "**arms of the Federal Government**."

However, there is **no U.S. Constitutional authority** giving the Federal Government any control, authority, direction, or funding power over any school system in any state. Without that specific Constitutional authority through an enumerated power, the right falls "***to the States respectively, or to the people***" according to the **Tenth Amendment of the Constitution**.[66]

All 50 states in the U.S. include language related to the creation and maintenance of a **public education system in their State Constitutions**. Some incorporate specific provisions, others offer vague guidance such as providing "*a suitable and* *efficient system of free public schools.*" But all felt at some point that it was important to include education in their State Constitutions. Furthermore, **county and local governments** have given themselves varying levels of authority to administer, finance, and manage public schools.

LOOK!

WHY is this important?

The closer to the people that educational authority comes, the closer it will be to the desires of the parents and the needs of the students.

This point becomes evident as we examine the problems we face now in our educational framework. The **centers of power have moved so far away from the people** they serve that students and parents no longer have a true voice.

———— ♦ ————

One clarification is needed before we move on. I have used the term "**K-12 Public Schools**"[67] throughout the book. This refers to our publicly funded primary and secondary schools in grades Kindergarten through 12th grade. "**P-12**" is also sometimes used and refers to Preschool through 12th grade.

We are now also seeing "*Preparatory Preschools*" designed to prepare our children to attend Preschool. Fortunately, as of this writing, "**PP-12**" has not made it into our public school system. *But I think we can all guess where this is headed.*

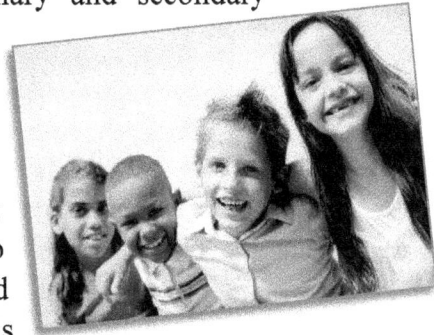

There is significant debate about the **long-term value or detriment of preschool and kindergarten** and whether they should continue to be incorporated in the K-12 public school system. However, **that debate is beyond the scope of this book** so I will leave that discussion for the future as it has minimal impact on our new school model.

IS A GOVERNMENT-CONTROLLED SCHOOL SYSTEM BAD?

There are of course many who will argue that **ONLY** the **government can provide a service as vast and integral to our society as the school system**. They will contend that "**only the federal government** itself can truly direct and control a massive nationwide program such as this to prevent that system from falling into chaos."

The argument will be that federal oversight and standards are necessary to unify state oversight and standards, which in turn is needed to unify the services directed and provided by county, district, and local educational systems.

This is **a compelling argument on its surface** and has been used to justify numerous large, powerful, and arguably intrusive agencies that impact all aspects of our lives. I have no doubt that most who espouse these beliefs truly have faith that this type of oversight and control is the ***only way*** it could ever possibly work.

– *But this is a misguided argument.* –

This type of systemic governmental control has **utterly failed our children time and time again**. *Case-in-point…* have our inner-city school systems improved over the past 50 years?

If they have not improved, why?

We have been complaining about them for 50+ years. Countless children's lives have been damaged. Where our children need our help the most, **the government has failed.**

We continue to push **used band-aid solutions** that do not stem the bleeding. In fact, through our **ineffectual actions and blindingly conspicuous inactions**, we encourage the wounds to broaden and fester into **life-threatening systemic diseases of the entire school ecosystem**.

———————— ◆ ————————

If we are truly honest with ourselves, it would be hard to name any government agency or organization that is effective, economical, operates at peak efficiency, and fully serves the purpose and people it was designed for. By their very nature, **government agencies are like living organisms**. They need to grab more and more power and money in their natural quest to grow in influence.

> **Living Organisms**
> Government agencies are living organisms that must grow larger and exert more dominance to validate their existence and to prove they are worthy of more funding and more power.

If these organisms want to grow (and they do), **they cannot achieve a point of stasis** where they are simply performing the function they were designed for. **It is not in their nature to work within that governmental framework** to innovate to be more efficient and effective at stasis level. They must **seek new avenues to stretch into as their tendrils forever expand** into broader powers, impact, and influence. They must grow the body (*staff*) and ensure more access to food (*funding*) to survive.

As the story of the scorpion goes, **that is just their nature**.[68]

The problem for us is that as we move farther away from smaller local control and into a vast bureaucracy, **we also move farther away from the desires of the parents and the community and into politically driven management, commandment, and micro-control** from a distance. This creates numerous problems.

COMPULSORY (FOR THE PUBLIC GOOD) GOVERNMENT-RUN SCHOOLS

Later in this chapter and in **Chapter 6**, we will discuss the *"indoctrination"* and *"politicization"* nature of government-controlled schools. At this point though, we want to examine the **foundational obstacles** that are inherent in an education system built upon government control and influence.

Note that, although this is a discussion of "**government**" organizations, many of these traits also apply to related **Educational Unions and Associations**. As (*generally*) non-profit organizations tied to the school systems, they tend to operate very similarly to the government organisms they emulate.

My goal here is to help you build a solid understanding of why **the current system cannot be "fixed"**. It must be **built upon a <u>new foundation</u> that promotes adaptation, innovation, and actually serves the customer**. We cannot build on a large government system managed by bureaucrats and politicians and expect it to be any different. Why? Because all government systems eventually become:

- extremely expensive and loose with money;

- exceeding in scope and over-expansive;

- overstaffed and administered;

- budgeted incorrectly; and

- **subject to the whims of** *current* administrators, government officials, unions, lobbying interests, and other outside influences.

In fact, **it is the nature of government agencies to spend more and more money** to justify getting more and more money in their next budget round. It is an endless cycle.

These problems are especially true for any **compulsory participation government program**. With a guaranteed user base that has little option but to participate, the agency has no incentive to operate competitively or with the user's best interests in mind. A government program is, by nature, a monopoly that has no need to compete in the free market. It has no incentive to innovate or change.

And **no need to put the primary focus on the users or intended beneficiaries** of the monopoly. End users become pawns in the battle for more money and power. **There is only the body that must grow and prosper.**

The **Users** (in this case, parents and their children) simply become a means to an end – with the end being the **continued expansion of the organism**. The more users drawn into the system, the larger the organism and their related budgets grow.

Multiply this philosophy downstream through all levels of government – federal, state, county, city, town – and we begin to see that **many dependent organisms have a vested interest in growing their control** of the schools, the children, and what/how they are being taught (*a later topic*).

As mentioned earlier, we must also take into account the vested interests of **Unions**, **Associations**, and other parties drawn in by this vast monolithic system with a captive audience.

> *How can public education EVER*
> *be what it was intended to be*
> *under those conditions?*

———————— ◆ ————————

What the Government Giveth, the Government Can Taketh Away

That title is an old adage, but there is much truth to the saying. **If we become dependent on the government** to provide a service, benefit, protection, regulation, or money… **we become, well… dependent**. As this government benevolence (using our tax dollars) takes on a bigger role in our life, it becomes harder and harder to believe in our own minds that we can do without it.

> *We go beyond dependence into addiction.*

Consider Social Security, Medicare, Medicaid, Health Care, Welfare, Unemployment Insurance, the Postal System, and the **Public School System**. There are many other large government programs we can become dependent upon on a daily basis, but you get the idea.

We pay taxes at all levels, then bureaucrats and politicians devise ways to use our money to provide us services at a societal level – with conditions. **Always conditions.** Those in power get to choose who those services are doled out to and who will benefit, many times arbitrarily based on the political whims of whoever is in power.

There are many examples of this throughout our history, but I want to highlight just one current example that is highly relevant to federal government influence in education and why they should NEVER be allowed to provide funding to schools.

- The **U.S. Department of Agriculture** (USDA) and the **Food and Nutrition Service** (FNS) under the USDA announced that they were redefining sex discrimination to include discrimination based on equity, gender identity, and sexual orientation.[69]

- This announcement built upon President Biden's Executive Order on *Preventing and Combating Discrimination on the Basis of Gender Identity or Sexual Orientation.*[70]

- In order to comply, **Public, Private, and Religious schools** across the country who make use of the **National School Lunch Program** and **School Breakfast Program** MUST incorporate and abide by these new rules or the USDA-FNS will **PULL ALL FUNDING** intended to feed the children.

- This **comply or deny** demand will cost schools billions in funding used to feed disadvantaged children across the nation **unless they adopt the social agenda commanded by the government**.

- Expect other agencies who fund schools to follow suit and withhold funds for compliance.

This decision by the Federal government to **withhold Federal funding from schools is intended to force them to comply** with a political agenda. It is appalling and exactly what we have been talking about here. The government addicts schools to money for specific purposes, then they threaten to pull the funding out from under them if they don't do exactly what the government demands. It does not matter if any of us agree with the demands, they are holding schools hostage with the money they themselves hooked the schools (*and parents*) on.

Now, *at first glance* **it may seem that I am attacking this action and demanding the Federal government** continue paying for school breakfasts and lunches without conditions.

Exactly the opposite!

The **Federal government should never have been sending money to local schools** to pay for anything. Besides the **lack of a Constitutional construct** to authorize this, we see a perfect demonstration of what this **Play-for-Pay**[71] is about. *What the government giveth, the government will take away…* **unless you do exactly what they say** based on current political winds.

───────── ♦ ─────────

LOWEST COMMON DENOMINATOR (LCD)

As with all of our discussions here, **none of this is intended to disparage any teacher, school, or district**. There are a many wonderful teachers and schools who truly want to properly educate our children. However, **they face tremendous headwinds and pressures** to accomplish that mission.

Because our school system is a massive government-run institution, there are internal and external pressures to operate as an education mill. Schools are being pushed towards pumping children through the program while **trying to ensure they all** (*within a singular system*) **receive the same education**.

As with any government program, this means that **the schools must run sub-optimally and cater to the Lowest Common Denominator (LCD)** to meet all equality, equity, and fairness doctrines driven by social, societal, and political mandates of the day.

What this results in is that **we must make it easier and easier for our children to fail by passing**. Rather than focusing on

> **Lowest Common Denominator**
>
> *Defined*:
> Simplified to appeal to, or be accessible to, the largest number of people in order to level the playing field.

exceptionalism and mental expansion, our current system focuses on the LCD. This system must ensure that no student feels inferior or is left behind in a strictly structured grading system that functions under this **equal outcome methodology**.

> *There appears to be little to no room for adjustment, modification, or adaptation to different skills, abilities, talents, intelligence level, maturity, or mental competency.*

Rather than **pulling children up and pushing them to explore** their boundaries, we hold them down to keep them all on a level playing field. This suppresses the natural inclination to improve and compete against their peers for higher achievement.

Remember our discussion in early education where **play was a foundational form of self-education** for children? In that play, there were always winners and yes… **losers. That is our nature**.

Now, I am **not** suggesting for a moment that some of our kids must be "losers". But I am saying that there may be a better way to approach this massive educational environment that allows everyone to win based on **their own scales of success**.

Note that I did NOT say "everyone wins" the same.

Today's version of the "**win**" game is to inflate grades to ensure that those who are failing *feel* like they are winning – *or are at least equal to everyone else*. That is a false "win" that is simply a disguised failure leading to bigger failures.

What I DID say is that each could win on "**their own scales of success**." We are not all equal. I can write (*I hope you agree with that one*); I am terrible at math. Others are good at science. Others at mechanics. Some are artistic. Some are academics. Many do not know what they are good at yet. We are all different, which is what makes our world so grand and wonderful.

Education is NOT a zero-sum game.
All students can win at their own levels –
if we allow them.

BUREAUCRACY VS. MERITOCRACY

I wanted to touch on one more fundamental issue regarding our government-based educational system. Our public school system exists exclusively as a government-structured and managed institution. As with all government institutions, schools operate under a **bureaucratic system that primarily values time-in-service, checkboxes, degrees, and tenure**. As long as a teacher or bureaucrat doesn't commit a **major fireable offense**, they essentially have a job for life.

This is clearly demonstrated by what have been deemed "**Rubber Rooms**". There are many variations of this throughout the U.S., but the most infamous were the **New York City School System Rubber Rooms**.[72] Hundreds of teachers were parked for long periods of time at these

NOT an actual Rubber Room! No Teachers were harmed in the making of this picture.

"*Temporary Reassignment Centers*" while **awaiting the final outcome of investigations** into misconduct, incompetence, hurting children, and more. Teachers were sent to these Rubber Rooms (seven locations in NYC) for **an average of three years** where they would sit and do nothing – **while getting full pay** (some earning over $100,000 a year), pensions, and benefits.

**A system that allows this is
broken beyond belief!**

It was **nearly impossible to fire any of these teachers** for any reason – *often due to the power of the Teachers Unions*. Systemically, there is little consideration for the quality of work, capabilities, competence, self-improvement, increased skills, or other business considerations for the retention of employees.

This level of job security is virtually impossible to find outside of government and educational systems (both private and public). **This structure can only survive with endless money and resources** (your tax dollars).

Without endless money and government legislation and protections, private sector businesses must operate under a **merit-based system**, a "**Meritocracy**," in order to attract and retain the most highly qualified personnel and remain competitive.

Why is *Bureaucracy* vs. *Meritocracy*
important to our discussion?
– I'm glad you asked. –

The difference between these systems is the major factor in how quality, cost, effectiveness, and customer service delivered to end users is managed. **This is foundational to the solution I will detail in Chapter 10.**

A comparison of the operational structures of the two systems is provided below – at a very high-level (*not universal of course*):

- **Bureaucracy** – A *qualified* teacher is hired.
  o The teacher joins one or more unions.
  o The teacher is a union member and has tenure after a few years and can never be fired (*except for extraordinary circumstances*).
  o Knowing their job is safe till retirement, **the teacher has little motivation beyond personal desire** to improve their skills, become exceptional, work for a promotion, or to strive for higher ratings.
  o They are generally set for life once hired.
  o Administrative personnel work under the same conditions – though they may be a little more focused on promotions and money.

- **Meritocracy** – Qualified prospects compete for the better jobs in the better education organizations.
  o They interview and provide proofs of their exceptionalism, skills, and growth.
  o **If** they get the job, they work and train for promotions, raises, and better jobs and pay.

- o **If they fail to retain quality or performance standards, they can be terminated**.
- o The best employees rise to the top and build a career just like everyone else.

As we can see, the **bureaucrat teacher** just has to <u>not mess up</u> too badly and they get to keep their job till they retire. This creates **a culture of minimal motivation** to go beyond the basic requirements. Why should you work harder than others?

On the other hand, the best **merit-based employees are highly motivated** towards continuous improvement, career growth, more money, skills enhancement, better customer service, and more. **They must please the customers** (students and parents) or their job may be at risk. Imagine that motivational mentality as a driver for all of our children's teachers. What would education look like then?

Easier said than done of course, but that's why I wrote this book for you.

———————— ♦ ————————

PROBLEMS FACED IN PUBLIC EDUCATION

*"Educational institutions created to pass on to the next generation the knowledge, experience, and culture of the generations that went before them have instead been **turned into indoctrination centers** to promote whatever notions, fashions, or ideologies happen to be in vogue among today's intelligentsia."*
— Thomas Sowell[73]

Most people agree that **some form of community-funded, easily available common community schooling is necessary and desirable** in today's society. Even though we have always had access to private schools, parochial schools, homeschools, and other alternatives, the convenience, ease, and continuity of community placed schools makes them highly desirable for most people.

Shared cost with the entire community, shared facilities, bussing networks, competitive sports, music programs, and pooled resources – all within a self-contained system – is very attractive. **The self-containment makes it extremely easy** for parents to have their kids participate in the public school system. In fact, if you don't participate, you must generally notify the government that your kids will be educated elsewhere – or they will come looking for you and your children.

With a captive user base and high participation rates, **it was an easy reach to evolve this desire for a community resource into a too-big-to-fail government-run program** whose cost was shared through everyone's taxes. The population grew, the need grew, and it was only natural for this government program to grow larger and more powerful over time.

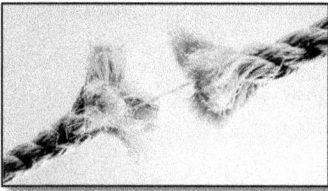

But the <u>promise</u> was always that these schools would provide all of our children a proper education.

BROKEN PROMISES IN EDUCATION

I could write entire books on the broken promises and inherent problems in our public K-12 system today, but that is not our purpose here. My intention is to **lay out a foundation to help us understand <u>what must be avoided</u>** at all costs in a reformed system… if we are to truly commit to foundational reform.

To do less would be a waste of time. We cannot go through a major reformation and ultimately end up making the same mistakes. There will not be a second chance in our lifetimes.

What we must fully accept is that we have not managed to solve the major problems within the educational system over the past 75 years or so. In fact, **most of these issues have gotten worse** – some terribly worse. To get us to where we need to be, we will concentrate on just a <u>couple of those major topics</u> here as **pointers to a greater understanding of WHY a major foundational, ground-up reformation is required.**

The next two chapters will wrap up our look at what has gone wrong and why we cannot allow this to happen again. We are nearing the payoff but, to fully grasp how fundamental the change I am proposing MUST be, **it is critical to understand the depth of the failures of today's educational system**. Bear with me a little longer as we take a look at:

- The failure of educational standards;
- The politicization of education and schools;
- Political and social indoctrination;
- Radical political activism in schools;
- Crate training of students;
- Racism, anti-racism, CRT, etc.;
- Sexualization of young children;
- The impact of Unions and Associations;
- The political takeover of School Boards;
- Attacks of traditional education; and
- The War on Parents.

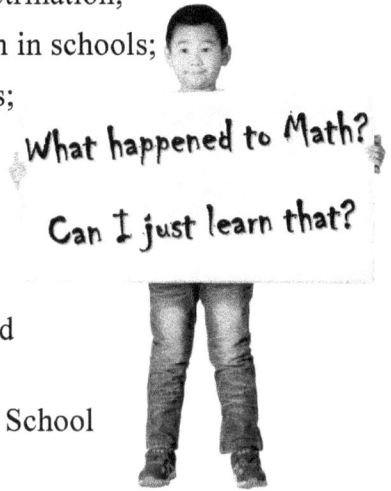

What happened to Math?

Can I just learn that?

From the beginning I had intended to make this book light and positive throughout, but as it progressed, and as my research went deeper, that became harder with every page. I could not leave these topics untouched and unexplored. **The true depth of the attack on our educational system** became more evident in its appalling, destructive, and dangerous nature.

> *If a foreign power had set out on a campaign to change the very nature of America by destroying our education system, we would have rightly looked upon that as an Act of War.*

LOOK!

But the attack is mostly from within. Powerful forces in our own nation have been pushing and pulling on the strings of our educational system for decades, molding it to drive our future towards specific sociopolitical goals. **Our children have been used as pawns and experimental cattle**, caught in the middle of this mission to change the face and future of America.

We have been wounded as a nation.

And the wound has become infected.

CHAPTER

6

SUFFOCATING THE SACRED FIRE

Things to consider:

➤ Are we suffocating the Sacred Fire to the point that education must die in order to live again?

➤ Are politics eternal?

➤ Who do our children belong to?

➤ Is this all just hysteria and overreaction?

"People are all born ignorant but they are not born stupid. Much of the stupidity we see today is induced by our educational system, from the elementary schools to the universities."

—Thomas Sowell[74]

CAN OUR EDUCATIONAL SYSTEM BE "FIXED"?

What we have seen so far is that our current K-12 public school system is broken. We have also seen that **there are options to exit the public school system** for something better. But what we have also come to understand is that **our public school system is here to stay**… at least for the foreseeable future.

So, can we in good conscience **leave nearly 50 million children in a failing system** that can only get worse over time as those who have the ability to exit the system, do so?

How do we know the system will continue to fail and even get worse?

We know this through the evidence of the last 50+ years and our many failed attempts to *"fix"* the system. By the end of this chapter, my hope is that you will understand in your heart and mind that a **foundational reformation from the ground-up is the ONLY path to fundamental change** that will return the focus of education back to the children who must remain in the public school system.

I urge you to continue reading externally, researching, and **thinking critically about every point I make in this book**. I have provided an abundance of end notes for your research, but **please go out on your own** and really dive into the points I lay out here. Build your own conclusions.

LOOK!

Ultimately, understand in your heart that the sickness is so systemic that the patient is terminal. No amount of medicine can heal it.

It will become clear that the infection is so deep that **nothing short of <u>death and rebirth</u> can truly resolve our K-12 public education system into what we want it to be**.

Before we get to that point though, we still need to walk through some of the **dark and disturbing aspects of today's educational system**. You are likely already aware of many of these issues, but this chapter brings them together for a holistic look at the influences that drive today's schools. This is a necessary medical examination of the patient to understand why **death and rebirth are absolutely necessary**.

———————— ◆ ————————

Parents have entrusted their children to the public school system for the purpose of educating their children. That public service is supposed to be a proper academic education to prepare our children to succeed. Unfortunately, **return on investment has diminished greatly** as the system turned away from traditional core education and more towards social indoctrination, politicization, and an actual animosity toward parents and the children themselves.

This **infection of our school system** has been growing steadily for decades, but has **accelerated exponentially in the last 20 years**. In my opinion, what we are experiencing is the **product of a so-called "progressive" program to control what our children learn and believe** in order to further an agenda designed to reshape our nation and our futures.

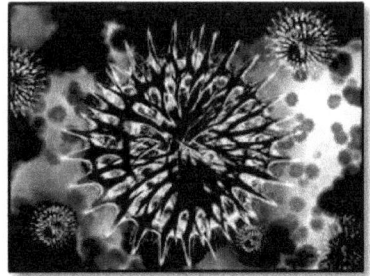

Why would someone do that?

I have many opinions on *why*, but let's take a closer look at one thought – the **Communist Goals** I mentioned earlier. These goals were derived from *"The Communist Manifesto"*, written by Karl Marx in 1848.[75] You may be shocked at some of these. Most have already been firmly established or accomplished. You may even recognize some of these from news stories today.

Selected **Communist Goals** *related to our discussion*:

- **#15**: Capture of one or both of the **political parties** (*indoctrinate students toward the chosen one*).

LOOK!

- **#17**: **Get control of the schools**. Use them as transmission belts for socialism and current Communist propaganda. Soften the curriculum. Get control of teachers' associations. **Put the party line in textbooks**.

- **#19**: Use **student riots** to foment public protests against programs or organizations that threaten the agenda.

LOOK!

- **#25**: **Break down cultural standards of morality** by promoting pornography and obscenity in books, magazines, motion pictures, radio, and TV.

- **#26**: Present **homosexuality**, **degeneracy** and **promiscuity** as "normal, natural, healthy."

- **#28**: **Eliminate prayer** or any type of religious expression in schools on the ground that it violates the principle of "separation of church and state."

LOOK!

- **#30**: **Discredit the American Founding Fathers**. Present them as selfish aristocrats who had no concern for the "common man." (*Recently, present them as slave owners so they can be entirely discounted and ignored. Tear down their statues.*)

- **#31**: **Belittle American culture** and discourage teaching American history on the grounds that it was only a minor part of the "big picture."

- **#32**: Support any socialist movement to **give centralized control over any part of the culture**– education, social agencies, welfare programs, mental health clinics, etc.

LOOK!

- **#36**: Infiltrate and **gain control of more unions**.

LOOK!

- **#40**: **Discredit the family** as an institution. Encourage promiscuity and easy divorce.

LOOK!

- **#41**: Emphasize the need to **raise children away from the negative influence of parents**. Attribute prejudices, mental blocks and retarding of children to the suppressive influence of parents.

- **#42**: Create the impression that **violence and insurrection** are legitimate aspects of American tradition; that **students and special-interest groups should rise up** and use "united force" to solve economic, political or social problems.

As you can see, **13 of the 45 Communist Goals center around the U.S. educational system and our children**. You will surely recognize many of these in the activities we see going on today related to our educational system. Again, *why*?

> *Early **indoctrination as youths** creates future **adherents as adults**.*

LOOK!

Which is a great lead-in to our next section. [*I love it when a plan comes together.*]

———— ♦ ————

POLITICIZATION AND INDOCTRINATION

> *"The education of all children, from the moment that they can get along without a mother's care, **shall be in state institutions.**"*
>
> —Karl Marx[76]

> *"Those who control a people's opinions control its actions. Such control is established by **treating citizens, from infancy, as children of the State.**"*
>
> — Paul Johnson, *Intellectuals: From Marx and Tolstoy to Sartre and Chomsky*[77]

LOOK!

We need to start with the foundational question of *"**who gets to indoctrinate our children**, i.e., form their minds, and manage their innocence?"* Is that the parent's job? Or the government's job... ostensibly for *"The Greater Good"*?

We seem to have come down to a battle between **Cultural Marxism**[78] **and American Values of family, individuality, and freedom**. Our current educational system has become an **experiment in a petri dish** to see how far the system can move away from core family and towards a **homogenous, compliant society** that is **ready and willing** to be fully monitored, managed, and controlled by our political class.

By plan, **the K-12 educational system has become an effective incubator for higher education** to enhance compliance and group think in students. If K-12 students are properly indoctrinated and prepared they will willingly accept societally approved "*absolute knowledge and truth*" from authority figures in Colleges and Universities as undeniable reality that deserves NO dissent or discussion.

Students will not challenge approved thought and theory fed to them. In fact, they will defend what they are told to think with vigor and use peer pressure, alienation, and cancellation to ensure classmates think in line with *currently* acceptable political and social values and philosophies.

> *As students embrace full indoctrination, they become more authoritarian in their world view until THAT view becomes compulsory for anyone who wants to participate and succeed in their world.*

In just a few decades, influential power centers have transformed K-12 and institutions of higher learning from **exploration and expansion of human knowledge** into **political activist centers of brainwashing**. These centers incubate the next leaders of our society – who then move on to positions of power to enforce further indoctrination in all educational systems. **This indoctrination cycle self-perpetuates**, resulting in what we see in our educational system today.

> *But is this all true? CAN it be true?*

It seems too fantastical… too conspiratorial. But if we think about it systemically, we realize that **the system is self-perpetuating by nature and designed to embrace this type of indoctrination**. To participate in these environments as a Teacher, Professor, or Administrator, you would need to conform to approved philosophies in order to get and retain employment positions within those systems. **All others need not apply**.

The same goes for those external to the system who want to participate. If you want the schools to adopt and buy your curriculum, books, software, etc., then you had better adhere to the current approved social new-normal.

An indoctrinational[79] **system naturally culls out those who disagree** with the system through hiring practice bias, peer pressure, hostile work environments, lack of growth opportunities, and frustration with the system. Those who are not of the correct "**right think**" will self-choose to move on to environments that are less antagonistic. Leaving only those who "*believe*" in the new normal to now exist in an intellectual silo of "**same thought**." Qualifications no longer matter… only that you think the same.

Conversely, a **NON-indoctrinational system will naturally accept all qualified participants** without regard to their socio-political beliefs (*within reason*). The point is that **participation is generally controlled by *reasonable* societal boundaries**, NOT the personal or political beliefs of those currently in power within the system.

Our educational system was never meant to be politicized as it is today. **We used to celebrate our differences of opinion** (*particularly in higher education*) as an opportunity to debate, discuss, and explore different beliefs. Spirited debate and discussion used to engulf classrooms, coffee shops, and the town square.

> **WHAT HAPPENED?**
>
> We used to celebrate differences of thought. Today many treat it as a call to battle and a reason to segregate and destroy those who disagree with us.

Today, true debate is not possible. It has become acceptable to just sky scream absolute beliefs at "others" without allowing a response of any kind from those who disagree with their approved "same thought."

All counter-discussion is shut down, denied, and removed from consideration. Alternate thought is not allowed because it is not considered "sane" and/or "truth". It is not worthy of discussion. **YOU are not considered worthy**.

What happened? What Changed?

Part of the problem is that our entire educational system has become politicized and is geared towards **indoctrination as a function** of that education. We teach our children today that authority figures such as **Teachers and Professors speak only absolute truth** – especially when expressing social or political beliefs. Therefore, that truth cannot be challenged.

> *Once this **authority of truth is fully implanted in the student's psyche** it is only natural for them to think in absolute terms of "**Us**" and "**Them**".*

In their minds now, **"Them"** ignore truth, discount *"established" or "settled"* science, disregard facts, snub common sense, and **are just plain being ignorant by choice**. If "Them" cannot or will not accept truth as presented by authority, then they are willfully choosing to disregard reality.

> *"Them" are no longer <u>worthy</u> of debate and discussion – only derision and cancelation.*

How could we have produced such a divisive education for our children? **Why would we?**

Unfortunately, the evidence of this is all around us and demonstrated in news stories nearly every day. The next few sections of this chapter will focus on how this came to be. This is important in **understanding why band-aid solutions don't work** and how to prevent this same failure in the future.

———————— ♦ ————————

Those with certain socio-political persuasions have gradually *transformed* our educational system without much dissent. For decades now, schools have pushed core academics lower in education priorities and have concentrated more on anti-American values, anti-nuclear family, pro-authoritarian, pro-sexuality of youth, and more recently focusing on promoting racism through the guise of "anti-racism" teachings.

This **poisoning of education goes way beyond those headline topics** and to the very core of who we are as a nation. Again, I point back to the **13 Communist Goals** we discussed earlier as **they are so on target** with what we are seeing today.

We cannot afford to lose yet another generation to this poisonous environment, yet change will not come without pain. First, **we as a nation of parents must understand the genetics of that poison** and learn how to *permanently* purge it. It is critical that we understand how to **prevent it from being introduced into our newly reformed educational system**.

The various poisons of politics in education seems like a good place to start.

RADICAL POLITICAL ACTIVISM

Political activism is rampant throughout our educational system and spreads like a virus. **Our educational body is primarily a singular governmental system** that is connected internally to many different systems.

The political virus has systemic access to the entire organism allowing the poison to spread quickly through the whole body.

This poisonous activism comes in many flavors. In recent years it has involved significantly more government, organization, and school sponsored or advocated **activism** focused on <u>one-sided political or social agendas</u>. These activities are promoted by teachers and the organizations they support and are often highly organized.

This type of activism does not represent educational opportunity or value, but in fact draws away from core education. Forced participation in these activities—through requirement, authority pressure, and/or peer pressure—is employed to ensure maximum participation.

———————— ◆ ————————

This is where "**Action Civics**"[80] comes in. It is a fairly recent phenomenon that gives physical form to indoctrination through activity-based civics – particularly protests. Much of this activism focuses on **using children as political props** to support causes those children (*some as young as 5 years old*) may have little or no understanding of.

> ***This is all designed and promoted***
> ***to foster a feel-good/do-good aspect***
> ***to entice children to participate.***

Why wouldn't children want to help save the planet from *imminent destruction through global warming*? Why wouldn't they want to fight against *"institutional racism" that is dividing our nation*? Why wouldn't they want to support ***anything*** their authority figures tell them is important?

Students are taught that **their first duty as a good citizen is to participate in these activities to save the world**. If they don't (*they are told*), they are complicit in these bad things and become bad people themselves.

Many may understand at a high level ***what*** the issues are, but **they are not taught or prepared to analyze and debate alternative viewpoints**. Nor are they as children prepared with the information needed to understand the full impact of the activities they are promoting. They are taught only what the authority figures believe they need to know in order to promote happy compliance and participation from the students.

> *Without that **full understanding and analysis**,*
> *students cannot make an **informed decision***
> *and, as a result, **will happily participate in***
> ***order to please their classmates and teachers.***

"What kind of activities are you talking about?" you might ask. Probably at its most benign are the classroom **letter writing campaigns**. Even when I was in school long ago, we were tasked with writing letters to our Congressmen about various causes.

You might think, *well, that seems like a good way to learn about civics and how we communicate with the people who represent us. That seems okay.*

True… except for one thing. **<u>We were NEVER offered both sides of an issue</u>.** We never debated or discussed the conflicting points of view to come to our own opinions about what we would ask of our Representatives. The teacher always instructed us what the topic was and how we were to present it.

One example from my own ancient past (*paraphrased a bit from old fuzzy memories*). **Teacher**: *"Students, today, we're writing our Congressmen to help them understand that nuclear weapons are bad. Kids, you do NOT want your parents to burn in a nuclear blaze, do you?"*

To which we would **dutifully reach out with shaking hands and take the pre-addressed card** from our teacher and, **through tears of terror over our impending doom**, proceed to tell our Representatives how all nuclear weapons are bad and we don't want to burn in a hellish ball of fire or lose all of our hair from radiation.

> POSTCARD
>
> Dear Mr. Senator,
> My teacher says I
> should tell you to stop
> making nuklar bombs.
> I do not want to die in
> burning fire ball or
> have my hair fall out.
> Please remove all bombs
> from the world so I can
> keep my hair.
> Sincerely,
> Little Billy
>
> Senator
> U.S. Congress
> Washington, D.C.

Today, **Action Civics has become much more aggressive and singularly focused on specific social and political agendas** by the teachers, schools and particularly, outside organizations.

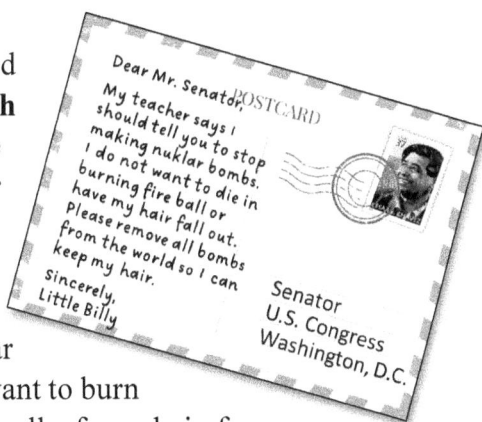

———————— ◆ ————————

*"Many of today's 'educators' not only **supply**
students with conclusions, they promote the idea
that students should spring into action because of
these **prepackaged conclusions** – in other words,
vent their feelings and go galloping off on
crusades, without either a knowledge of what is
said by those on the other side or the intellectual
discipline to know how to analyze opposing
arguments."*

—Thomas Sowell[81]

Examples abound throughout our nation and can be found all over the internet with simple searches. Just a couple of fun examples of biased action civics include:

- The purely propagandist **Obama Songs** taught to elementary school students;[82]

- A simulated **Protest Rally** in a school auditorium with signs that included "***Jail Trump***";[83]

- Advice to **10-12 year olds on how not to get arrested** at a protest;[84]

- An annual nationwide "***Week of Action***"[85] to perform purely one-sided social activist, politically driven, mandatory actions and activities for **children as young as 5-years old** that have included single-sided sociopolitical themes such as the **positively-framed disruption of Western Nuclear Family Dynamics**.

Let me be very clear, I am **NOT** taking a stance against civics education, action civics, or any type of student action in public schools. There are important things to learn and experiences to be had in these areas. However, **they should never experience the political and social bias** children are experiencing today through teachers, administrators, and external forces such as teachers' unions, educational associations, and the Department of Education (ED) itself.

> *Political indoctrination and biased activism, <u>no matter the persuasion</u>, should never be allowed in our schools.*

Teaching our children ***what*** politics is, ***how*** our political system is structured, ***how*** the system functions, and the ***history*** of government and politics is desired and expected in a traditional curriculum. Teaching them ***what to think*** regarding specific politics, social values, and political agendas is NOT! **Period!**

In the right context, at the right age, it is a good thing to present children with different political ideas. However, **those ideas must be presented from all sides equally, fairly, and without ascribing any bias to one way of thinking or another**. Present all sides to the children, teach them to think critically, ask questions, explore, and research… then allow them to make up their own minds.

In today's environment, do we really believe this is what students are experiencing?

———————— ♦ ————————

You get the idea. Action Civics, sometimes called "**Project-Based Civics**" or "**Civic Engagement**" is prevalent throughout our K-12 educational system. No matter what it is called, it is often subject to significant corruption by those who would indoctrinate our children.

How "realized" is the methodology of Action Civics now?

Advocates of Action Civics are poised to force widespread adoption through many K-12 pathways. Tremendous amounts of money and influence are **pouring gas on the fire to ignite the flame of a wholly integrated government element in schools across the nation**. This will engrain the methodology deep into the bloodstream of education giving direct access to students through numerous government interventions.

You may be wondering at this point **why I am spending so much time on Action Civics**. During my research, I kept running across various discussions about the power, prevalence, and potential of Action Civics. Two things became obvious.

1. The **government is almost always involved** and uses this connection at every step to reach deeper into the schools... *"for the greater good."* You will understand why this is incredibly important in **Chapters 10** and **11**.

2. By all research, beliefs, and opinions I encountered, the consensus seems to be that overall, the activities related to **Action Civics are currently around 90% left leaning or hard left progressive** focused.[86]

Those trying to control the public schools are aware of the power of this approach and are working hard to expand its reach and permanence. The following two examples are just the tip of the needle being used to weave government influence irrevocably into public schools.

- In 2021, the **National Education Association** (NEA) held their 2021 Annual Representative Assembly. At this meeting it seems they approved funding for promoting CRT in K-12. This resolution appeared to **commit to using public schools as platforms for political activism**, with a particular focus around issues of equity and social justice.[87]

- On March 11, 2021, the **Civics Secures Democracy Act (CSDA)** (*117th Congress, S.879*)[88] was introduced in the Senate. Early efforts to pass the bill were unsuccessful. A revised version crafted by progressive lobbyists was reintroduced on June 14, 2022 that attempted to cloak the built-in ideological agenda. Fortunately, it too failed.

  o On its face, *as usual*, the bill seemed like it had good intentions. Its stated purpose was to expand access to and strengthen civics education. **Sounds good, right?**

However, I believe this was just **institutionalized Action Civics** at its worst.

o The CSDA would have budgeted **$1 BILLION annually for 5 years ($5 Billion total)** to allocate these funds **under the direction of the Secretary of Education** in *whatever way they deem appropriate*.

▪ **States would have to participate in the National Assessment of Educational Progress testing** for civics and U.S. history and make the testing data public to qualify. (*Remember our discussion about "conditional money" from the federal government*?)

▪ Certain recipients would have been required to meet *undefined parameters* to receive grants. **These "strings" attached to the money would ensure that only groups and organizations with the "proper" mindset would prosper.**

▪ Money would be focused on the promotion of CRT studies and action civics.

▪ The bill would have provided **$30 million in grants to activist organizations** to support grassroots activism aimed at innovative and evidence-based civics. These activities would likely include lobbying and protesting.

▪ The bill would introduce **formalized political activism to elementary school students**.

o There is much more to the CSDA, but you get the picture. With billions in funding being doled out at the whims of those who control the purse, favored groups could entrench their power even more. Fortunately, the CSDA itself seems to be a lost cause at this point. But expect to see more in the future.

As Donald Trump and the Republicans take over the Federal government in 2025, it is unlikely that this (or similar) bills will pass anytime soon. But **political fortunes change**, and we could face this or worse again as administrations come and go.

There is much for us to do to secure our children's futures in this window of potential sanity. THAT is the point of this book.

Without fundamental foundational changes to our public school system, we will always face danger from those who have ulterior motives for our children. When we get to **Chapter 11**, you will see that there *is* a pathway to prevent most government interference with the public schools. It won't be easy, but it will be powerful if we implement it.

First, we need to turn our attention to some of the most powerful **external organizations** that could have negative impacts on our children's health, wellbeing, and futures. These organizations were **meant to protect our children**'s education.

But we have to ask… **have *they* failed our children while in pursuit of their own goals**?

———— ♦ ————

UNIONS AND ASSOCIATIONS

> *"Normally, our kids have been off-limits. But in modern history, since the huge desegregation battles, kids have been off-limits. Now, they are the battlefield."*
>
> *"My gut reaction [on Betsy DeVos] was, oh, my God. We are now back into the education wars."*
>
> *"*[In response to the Florida Parental Rights Bill] *This is propaganda. This is misinformation. This is the way in which [education] wars start. This is the way in which hatred starts."*
>
> —Randi Weingarten, *President of the AFT* [89]

Education-related unions and associations would at first glance appear to have our children's best interests at the core of their very existence. If you read their websites, their passion for education and children is extremely compelling. All the right words are there. How could you argue against any of it?

Once you scratch the surface though, there
are fundamental issues that seem to be at
odds with those words.

Over recent years these groups (along with the School Boards we'll talk about shortly) have begun to show where their real beliefs lie. **The crack in the veneer has widened to shed light on the nature of the policies and activities within these organizations that are harmful to our children**.

As always, there are no absolutes in this area. I am sure there are some great organizations and some very fine people within that have only the best intentions. But even there, **those intentions may be colored by a darkness that blinds them to the larger picture**.

A full **understanding of the threat that is inherent in the nature and intent of these organizations is critical** to protecting our new reformed educational system. *Why is this so important?*

The activities of these organizations
demonstrate that the purpose and intent of
their mission has been corrupted. Their
power and influence will continue to
overcome any system they control.

This is all opinion of course, so I invite you to review the material I provide and then do your own research to come to your own conclusions. **When you are done, ask yourself this**…

- If we have a new pure and pristine educational system focused on the lifelong success of the students, *will the existing unions and associations allow the system to run under its own design?* **Or** *will they be compelled by the power they wield to return the educational system to their* vision, *their* agenda, and *their* social beliefs?

You may not understand the significance of this now, but **Chapters 10 through 12** will substantiate this belief.

Our shiny new educational system **must be allowed to operate under its own rules, constraints, and vision**. If we leave power with external organizations who may be corrupted by socio-political influences of the moment, the system will quickly return to what we have today.

> *Everything we had fought*
> *for would be undone.*

WHO ARE THESE ORGANIZATIONS?

Educational unions, associations, and other organizations are numerous, bountiful, and extremely powerful. Their influence is felt in every aspect of our educational system and their tentacles reach deep into the schools themselves. These include:

- Teachers Unions and Associations

- Administrators Unions and Associations

- School Board Unions and Associations

- Lobbying and Political Organizations

Seeing the list, you might ask what the difference is between a Union and an Association.

- ***Associations*** are not union based and generally are formed to help develop skills and career growth of particular groups of people such as teachers. But don't let that simple mission fool you. They are very powerful and have tremendous influence over how their members think and act. They have no codified power over the schools, but their influence cannot be understated.

- ***Unions*** on the other hand are *extremely powerful* and possess several tools of influence. One tool in particular allows them to flex that power very effectively – the **Collective Bargaining Agreement (CBA)**. The CBA gives them tremendous bargaining power with the school systems through the ability to demand concessions and to strike. They also retain vast amounts of money to buy influence and lobby effectively. This gives them the ability to speak with **One Voice**, even if many members do not agree with them.

———— ◆ ————

WHAT KIND OF POWER DO THEY HAVE?

The two largest teacher unions, the **National Education Association (NEA)**[90] and the **American Federation of Teachers (AFT)**,[91] represent roughly **4 million members**. Their massive power is evident, but statistics vary depending on sources used. The numbers look a bit like this:

- Just these two unions represent about **three quarters of all public-school teachers** in the U.S.

- They represent ~**40% of all unionized public employees**.

- **NEA is the largest labor union in the U.S.**

- Their combined **revenue is over $1.5 Billion** per year (*depending on how they calculate national vs. state and other sub-level parts of the organization*).

- They employ approximately **6,000 personnel**.

- **NEA and AFT almost exclusively support the Democrat Party (*the Unions, not necessarily the members*) at an <u>astounding rate of 95% to 97%</u>**.[92]

Now THAT is some real **powerhouse clout and influence** condensed into just two of the many unions, associations, and other organizations that are influencing our schools. The power of these and other organizations is built upon a **60+ year campaign of integration, intimidation, influence, and power grabs** supported by governmental interference.

Remember our previous discussion about how government-based organizations must grow? It is in their nature. Although Unions and Associations are not governmental, they do live and operate under a similar philosophical belief…

"Growth Promotes Power"

"Power Promotes Growth."

Unfortunately, that philosophy is **also deeply steeped in a single sociopolitical belief system** as demonstrated by their 95%+ support of a single political party and their agenda. Their direct influence and power throughout the entire educational ecosystem is a **dangerous and lethal combination**.

With educational unions and even nonunion associations, **we can see the direct impact of their actions throughout the system**. They influence, direct, or manage what teachers teach, they influence and guide the social agendas, how schools are operated, when the schools are open, course curriculums that are used, books that are promoted for classes and in the libraries, action civics, and much more.

Only **educational organizations possess this kind of world-altering power**.

HOW DID THEY LOSE THEIR WAY?

I don't think most of these organizations (*at least many of the people within them*) believe they have lost their way. I think they honestly believe they are doing what's right – it's just that **what they believe is "*right*" is not necessarily in alignment with the best interests of the students and their future success**.

Of the many differences between us, the biggest irreconcilable difference is **the question of whether children belong to parents or to society**.

In some societies around the world, children are treated as **property of the state**. The parents are allowed to care for, feed, clothe, and protect the children from harm, but the children's minds and beliefs belong to the State. **The State must keep the minds of the children untainted to ensure continuity of their belief system** for the next generation of leadership. They must perpetuate the State for it to survive. Parents cannot be allowed to infect their children's minds with impure thought.

> *There can be NO compromise on this issue in the United States. <u>All children belong to their parents</u>... body and mind.*

I highly recommend that anyone interested in the sickness facing our educational system watch the documentary, "***Whose Children Are They?***".[93] It is quite a riveting romp through the illness that is killing our public schools and changing how our children's view the world.

This book, that movie, and plenty of research will help you **understand how critical this question is**. And how fundamental it is to everything that is driving modern public education.

Fair Warning! Language is powerful.

If you go to the websites of these educational organizations and read through their content and postings, *you may walk away with the unimpeachable feeling that they are good, true, and faithful servants of our children, parents, and schools*. **You may even wonder why I have been saying all this mean stuff**.

If you have these feelings, take a few aspirins, lay down for a bit, and let the feelings pass slowly. At some point, the confusion will pass and a deeper analysis of their actions, associations, activities, articles, bylaws, and mission statements will begin to belie those feelings, and a bit of warmth will slowly spread to the affected areas.

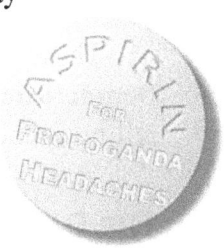

As you analyze what you read, a much darker picture will begin to emerge that **begins to show a tight alliance with leftist and Marxist ideals, education organizations, and agendas**.

You may remember our discussion earlier in this chapter about the **45 Communist Goals** read into the Congressional Record? Fourteen of those directly impacted our educational system and many are now woven into the pretty words put out by those organizations. These two Communist Goals stand out in particular.

- **#36**: Infiltrate and **gain control of more unions**.

- **#15**: Capture of one or both of the **political parties** (*indoctrinate students toward one political direction*).

When you finish reading this chapter, I urge you to **go back and read all 14 relevant Communist Goals** I provided there. You might see them in a different light now. At the very least, you will see how closely they tie to everything that is going on in Today's public educational system.

──────── ♦ ────────

The **corruption of mission seems obvious to me**, but these organizations do not seem to recognize that the corrupted values they embrace are antithetical to the values of the U.S., our Constitution, our Founding Fathers, and the ideals that this country was built upon.

Operating under the guise of "*for the children*" or "*the greater good*," they latch onto all the latest agendas that focus on anti-racism, DEI (diversity, equity, inclusion), CRT, and more.

The failure of this approach is most evident in the downward spiral of education in our inner-city communities.

These organizations have **donated over $100 Million to the Democratic Party**, yet there has been zero improvement for our failing schools. In fact, they appear to get worse every year.

THE DANGERS OF UNIONS AND ASSOCIATIONS

Unions and associations in general are not all bad, but we have some special issues related to educational organizations.

Other unions and associations do a lot of good in many industries. For instance, the American Petroleum Institute (API)[94] is an association that provides important guidance, specifications, manuals, and research throughout the oil industry. They are a major lobbying group and yes, politics are deeply embedded in API. However, there is one major difference between organizations like these and educational unions and associations.

LOOK! *Educational unions and associations have <u>unique access to our children</u> to shape their futures and the very nature of our country. No other organization has that kind of power.*

Educational unions and associations **as they stand now** have a direct impact on what our children learn, what they think, how their minds develop, what sociopolitical thoughts they form, and who they will be when they grow up.

This should NOT be the case.

These organizations have gone beyond their missions and have significantly expanded their original scope. We have to ask:

- Why is a teacher's union determining what curriculum my child will be subjected to?

- Why are they promoting activist organizations into my kid's school to push them towards a specific social agenda?

As dangerous as this overreach is now, the danger from their power will become more pronounced in the coming years.

If we intend to have true reformation, **our reformed educational system cannot tolerate the interference and control represented by today's unions and associations**.

Be warned though, that kind of power does not let go easily. Remember, entities like these must grow to survive. **The organism feeds on power and their ability to influence and control others**.

And speaking of the drive and hunger for power, let's talk about School Boards for a bit.

———————— ♦ ————————

SCHOOL BOARDS

> *"They had come to a time when no one dared speak his mind, when fierce, growling dogs roamed everywhere, and when you had to watch your comrades torn to pieces after confessing to shocking crimes."*
> —George Orwell, Animal Farm[95]

We have always known that it is man's nature that, given a just a bit of power, we will often take advantage of that power in the quest of more of it. Once in the unique position where we have control over others, power **acts like a drug, draining inhibitions against seeking more control**. Even those who have good intentions at heart may become blinded to the things that do not advance their power.

Yes, that is a dark assessment, but we have seen it play out again and again in all aspects of society. This need certainly does not apply to all people – which creates a conundrum.

> *Of those who gain a bit of power, those who seek <u>more</u> power may gain it. Those who seek only to help, but not power, may not achieve either.*

LOOK!

Those seeking to control the minds of our children eventually **realized how much power and influence the school boards have** in every aspect of our school system. **There are no guiding philosophies or system of guardrails**, yet a school board...

- Establishes a vision for the school district;
- Develops the policies the district operates under;
- Develops and adopts tax requirements and budget;
- Sets spending priorities at all levels;
- Negotiates with the unions;
- Is in charge of buying, selling, building, and maintaining school buildings and property;
- Initiates construction of new schools;
- Hires and fires the School Superintendent;
- Sets goals for academic achievement requirements;
- Approves curriculum, textbooks and library books;
- Directs emergency and health protocols (such as closings, mask requirements, etc.;
- Provides oversight of school operations and success.

As we can see, **tremendous power rests in the hands of these elected servants of the community**. By the way, salaries across the country run from $0 to $125,000+ per year. Most who get paid generally earn between $50,000 and $90,000.[96]

Seems like decent income (*for those who are getting paid at all*), but those getting higher pay ranges are generally living in larger urban school districts. Is the income alone worth the campaign cost of **$1,000 to $15 Million** that is being spent to land a public servant school board seat worth it?

You read that right... $15,000,000[97] *for a single campaign to fill a school board seat. Why?*

LOOK!

Most school board candidates spend $20,000 to $200,000 or more for these positions. The larger the district and the school population is, the higher the budget and the pay. **But it can't just be about the pay. There is much more to this.** That $15 Million was an unusual number, but there are many campaigns that go into the millions. They are funded by nationwide organizations to place candidates with the right agendas on these school boards.

This is because school boards control more than $600 Billion in spending annually and oversee the education of over 50 million children. We begin to see now how important these school boards are when we encounter numbers like that.

What we are seeing today is that educational unions and associations, non-profit organizations, large businesses, and certain wealthy individuals have **taken an interest in controlling the school boards**, not just to further social agendas, but **to control vast sums of money and power**. Remember, the school board handles union negotiations, building projects, and massive budgets for everything from curriculum to furniture and more.

This brings in massive donations from external sources that **dwarf what Mom and Dad can afford to invest** in a campaign for a local seat. Result?

Mom and Dad no longer have a voice in the school boards.

The intended outcome is that school boards may now be populated by politicians or bureaucrats who are only beholden to those external powers who put them in those positions of power.

Why? The answer is simple. Those trying to control the educational system **understand the power of these local positions**. They understand that controlling the foundational elements of society at the lowest levels makes it easier to protect and control the higher functions of society. This was the most effective pathway into our K-12 to accomplish several things.

- Control the school board.
- Control the money.
- Reward those who support the agenda.
- **Punish those who speak out** against the agenda.
- Control the curriculum and textbooks.
- Control what the children see, hear, and learn.

Parents!

It is quite powerful – especially if you can limit parents from getting involved. **Keep parents isolated and afraid to speak up for fear that it will affect their children**.

The school boards (not all of them) learned how to control the discussion and the parents. This freed them to expand their agenda to **hide critical elements from parents**, push agendas like CRT, propagandize curriculum, introduce sexual orientation activities, allow medical interventions, and much more.

Not all school boards act in these ways, but these agenda-driven, externally supported boards seem to be prevalent in more heavily populated areas where the boards have more power.

THE FUTURE FOR SCHOOL BOARDS

> *"No one believes more firmly than Comrade Napoleon that all animals are equal. He would be only too happy to let you make your decisions for yourselves. But sometimes you might make the wrong decisions, comrades, and then where should we be?"*
> —George Orwell, Animal Farm[98]

Aren't school boards elected positions? **Yes**. Don't they represent the desires of the people in their districts? **No**, not always. And it seems less and less every day.

How did we come to this contradiction?

We may lay that largely on our own complacency. For most people, living day-to-day life is sufficient enough for us. Life is busy. There's always too much to do and too little time to do it. The last thing we want to do is get involved in politics.

So, we leave something mundane like school boards to those who want to spend time on that (*remember the power seekers we talked about above?*). **We assumed people in these positions would have our children's best interests at heart**. When we chose where to live, we did the research and sources said the schools were great. So, we left it to "others" to keep it that way.

> ***We were wrong. Our children are
> now suffering for that complacency.***

Due to recent events such as the pandemic, government schooling at home, and parents' awakening we are just now starting to understand the scope of what has been happening to our children under the guise of education.

Is it too late to do anything?

Since these are elected posts, we do have some power and things we can do now. First, we must vote. Every election, every time. Recalls have also been fairly effective, but we usually end up with similar people in those positions until the next election.

------------ ♦ ------------

Again… we *know* things are bad in the schools. **Why am I spending so much time on these topics here**?

It is **not** enough to understand that there are problems with the schools. It is **not** enough to know we need to fix them.

But **it IS critical to understand** that negative influences come from many directions and we need to do much more than just "*fix*" things. We need to understand HOW they can get broken again and **put guardrails in the system to prevent this from happening again**. We need to fully understand and accept this before we get to **Chapter 11**.

One of the things I find most interesting is what I believe to be the main driver that awakened us to the full scope of the damage that was being done to our educational system. The semi-undeclared **War on Parents** bubbled to the top of our societal consciousness.

———————— ◆ ————————

THE WAR ON PARENTS

*"They're all our children. And the reason you're the teachers of the year is because you recognize that. They're not somebody else's children. **They're like yours when they're in the classroom**."*
—Joe Biden, President of the United States[99]

*"So, part of it is we have to break through our kind of private idea that kids belong to their parents, or kids belong to their families, **and recognize that kids belong to whole communities**."*
—Melissa Harris-Perry, Ad Campaign on MSNBC[100]

The most telling aspect of all these incredibly outrageous things we've discussed is the not-so-secret **War on Parents**. When parents themselves became an **impediment to the indoctrination and social formation mission** of the educators, the educational system itself declared war for the very souls of our children.

> *Unfortunately, for a very long time, it has been a secret war waged behind closed doors in the classrooms.*

Most parents really just want to concentrate on raising their children, advancing their careers, and living their lives. **They don't want to be involved** in the minutia of politics or the nuts and bolts of public services.

Parents move (if they have the means to do so) to the districts that supposedly have the "best" schools and then leave it to those in the educational system to "educate" their children. **They are supposed to be the professionals, right**?

Unfortunately, most Americans do not have the luxury of just picking up and moving to better school districts. They are captive to their situations for various reasons and must accept what they are offered. **This is a critical situation that has resulted in the devastation of generations of children** who are living in some of the worst school districts in America.

Whatever the case, most parents never realized that there was a war being waged against them.

They went about their lives, assuming that the differences between the left and right were just that... differences. Right vs. Left. Political differences. **Differing degrees of understanding** about what America is and who we are.

How could we have been so wrong? So blind?

We assumed everyone had the same goals for our children – **education and success**. However, the veil began to fragment due to COVID, shutdowns, shifts in ideology in our leadership, and changes in the power structure at all levels of government. We witnessed a fundamental change and the awakening began.

What became clear was that **psychological warfare was being waged to destroy the bond between us and our children**.

The focus of our schools had become to create compliant citizens of the state for the Greater Good.

Parents woke up to the existence of this war and became an inconvenient **speed bump slowing down the state's momentum** in altering the fundamental beliefs of our children.

For them, educating our children had become secondary, tertiary, or worse. Everything within **the educational ecosystem became tainted** with the agenda and the mission of those who were now in charge.

Looking longer term, the system's success grew over the years and the product of these schools (our children) stepped out into the world. With strong beliefs installed, they added to the ranks of those who believed the state had a right to our children. Their ranks grew and a new front in the war emerged.

A broader attack on the nuclear or traditional family emerged and took hold.

I urge you again to review the Communist Goals we discussed in **Chapter 5** and earlier in this chapter – especially numbers **40** and **41**.

- **#40**: **Discredit the family** as an institution. Encourage promiscuity and easy divorce.

- **#41**: Emphasize the need to **raise children away from the negative influence of parents**. Attribute prejudices, mental blocks, and retarding of children to suppressive influence of parents.

Is this not exactly what is going on throughout our educational system today? If you look under the hood of nearly every policy, every program, and every curriculum, you will see that **these anti-family, anti-parental themes saturate the entire system**.

Whether or not our politicians and educational leadership are even aware of these specific goals is irrelevant. What is relevant is their actions and their tight focus on meeting the intent of these and other philosophies put forth by generations of Marxists, Communists, Socialists, and others.

They are all **tightly aligned on the separation of our children from family bonds** so that they may be more easily manipulated, swayed, and controlled to be useful to the state. There is nothing new to all of this. It is a tried-and-true method for building a willing army of followers who will provide little resistance.

Why would they do this?
Aren't we all Americans?

Yes, we are. However, we have come to a place where **there are very different visions taking hold of what America should be**. This could be yet another book, but it comes down to the difference between two fundamental beliefs driving politics, policies, and social agendas today.

1. A **Constitutional America** where *"all Men are created equal, that they are endowed by their Creator with certain unalienable Rights, that among these are Life, Liberty, and the Pursuit of Happiness."* An America built on free market systems that provide opportunity to ALL Americans, regardless of their color, background, connections, or political beliefs. A country where justice is blind and government is limited to the powers given to it by We the People in the U.S. Constitution. *Or...*

2. An America where **the Constitution is a dated fluid concept that can be reinterpreted** as needed by the powers in charge for *"the greater good."* A country that has no borders because we are citizens of the world who may be beholden to powers outside of our Constitution. A country where one can achieve power, wealth, and privilege, but only by serving the will of those in power at the moment and in advancement of the needs of the government.

Harsh? Maybe... **Simplistic**? Perhaps... **Biased**? Certainly... However, the fundamental beliefs of the two sides of the scale cannot be denied.

———————— ♦ ————————

"How does this constitute a War on Parents," you might ask. You might think that this is just a difference of opinion and approach that the two sides haven't reconciled yet. Sadly, there is significant evidence to the contrary demonstrating that the state

has been actively pursuing the second belief. Knowing that parents would never accept this approach:

- They hide their actions, agenda, curriculum, and student interactions from parents.

- They actively encourage students to hide activities, thoughts, and even medical changes and procedures from their parents.

- Most recently, they have openly and aggressively attacked parents who would dare even to question what is going on.

Although the war is obvious now, it is not something that has just come on the scene recently. The forces behind this push have been hard at work for many years.

For one such instance we can go back to none other than **Mrs. Hillary Rodham Clinton**. She is just one small cog in the giant anti-family machine that has been ramping up their efforts for many years to prepare for a time such as now.

In 1977 the **Carnegie Council on Children**[101] established a panel to address a claim by sociologist Uri Bronfenbrenner that the Soviet Union was superior in child rearing to the United States. Hillary Clinton joined the panel that ultimately produced a book-length report called, *"All our Children."* (This might bring to mind her much later book, *"It Takes a Village,"* but **her earlier work is much more egregious**.)

To develop this report, this panel is reported to have started with an assumption that **the *"universal entitlement state"* is inevitable**. From this they went on to conclude that American parents could best serve their children by hastening the arrival of this state. They (*including **Clinton***) made the determination that:

WOW!

Just as the educational system (back in the 1970s) had been turned over to the state, the government could lessen the cultural impact of the <u>demise of the nuclear family</u> and the <u>normalization of divorce</u>.

Scary stuff indeed. In the 1970s, they had already determined that:

- public schools were owned by the government,

- divorce would be the cultural norm, and

- the nuclear family would eventually be recognized as an outdated concept that was no longer necessary.

This was obviously not the only report, study, or other activity that our government, colleges, universities, and think tanks were involved in over the past 50 years. It was a popular topic and has fed the thinking and beliefs of generations of people who are now in power.

———————— ♦ ————————

Sadly, one of the strongest proofs of their success against the family is the **proliferation of fatherless homes**, particularly in minority communities in our cities.

Fatherless homes have been identified as one of the most important factors in driving the problems our youth face in areas such as school dropouts, unemployment of teens and young adults, participation in criminal and gang activity, drug use, violence, unwed pregnancies, and other failings.

> **Fatherless homes tend to take our children down *self-destructive paths* that lead to <u>more</u> fatherless homes.**
>
> **A vicious cycle that creates generational failure.**

Fatherless homes may only be *partially* a result of the War on Parents. However, the school-centered promotion of anti-family sentiment, victimhood mentality, sexualization of our youth, and self-centered teachings do **create social constructs that tend to lead our children down self-destructive paths**. The normalization of sex without consequences and a distaste for the traditional family ultimately creates a culture that must predictably results in fatherless homes.

Nearly 18.5 million children grow up fatherless according to U.S. Census Data.[102]

That is an appalling number that clearly demonstrates **the nuclear family is truly in danger**. So too are our children. In a nation where **70% to 85% of children and teens** who suffer behavioral disorders and drug and alcohol abuse are from fatherless homes, we begin to understand the critical nature of "family". Structure, predictability, discipline and other factors also factor into the equation.

Why is this important to our discussion here? I believe that a culture focused on family and community can break that cycle of failure and give more children the opportunity to grow up with a broader sense of self-worth, empowerment, hope, and a desire to be better. This requires a **fundamental, foundational, reformation of our educational system** that centers on learning, opportunity, and a focus on their futures.

This will not be easy, but it is necessary for us to stand up for our children. Many educational leaders have recently implied, and even openly stated that *"parents should not have a say in their children's education."* That is unacceptable.

ARE THESE OUR CHILDREN OR NOT?

The answer is, of course, yes! Parents have every moral right in the world to have **full visibility into all curriculum, books, teaching plans, and other materials that are presented to our children**. As the parents, we are responsible for their safety, security, and physical and mental health.

*I will cede that **some caution** is necessary* regarding control of environment, curriculum, and books to avoid chaos within the schools. This could easily become mired in confusion from too many direct voices. **Chapter 10** and **Chapter 11** address resolutions for this concern.

However, there can be **NO question about our parental obligation** to achieve access to ALL information regarding our children, especially in the schools we pay for.

Would we allow our young children to go to unknown movies, read unknown books, go to unknown places, see doctors, have unknown medical procedures, participate in radical protests, and more without some understanding and validation of what they will be doing and what they will be exposed to? **Of course not**.

Then why would we allow them to be exposed to unknown information, activities, and even medical procedures for 12 formative years without some visibility to it all?

It is an absurd concept.

Yet, we have done exactly that for generations. **We believed that the schools had our children's best interest in mind**. It never occurred to us that the schools would engage in the activities that we've discussed so far (with more to come).

I would ask, "*what are they so afraid of?*" But the answer is obvious. The schools do not want parents to be aware of the level of indoctrination and social engineering that is going on. They know that the more parents know, the more of an obstruction they will be to the agenda.

In general, people hide things because they know what they are doing is wrong, or they want to hide their true agenda.

> *By allowing this to continue, we*
> *will be complicit in the continued*
> *degradation of our educational*
> *system and our country.*

Required by law or not, the moral imperative of providing information and access to parents should default to "**the child belongs to the parent and the parent has full responsibility for the proper care of that child**." Unfortunately, our current school system operates under a "**need to know**" moral code that allows teachers and administrators to decide for themselves what a parent "*needs* **to know**."

In fact, many in the school system do not believe parents have a right to know *anything* and **must "earn" the right to receive**

carefully curated bits of information from the schools. The following is from an <u>equity training program for teachers</u> in Wisconsin...

Insane!

"Remember, parents are <u>not</u> entitled to know their kids' [sexual] identities. That knowledge must be earned." [103]

The audacity and arrogance of that and other themes contained in equity (and other) training programs encapsulates the essence of their War on Parents. **Parents are the enemy and the only thing standing in the way of them shaping our children's minds in their own image**.

I think the counter to that is expressed quite elegantly in the following quote regarding who our children belong to.

"If you question whose children these are...
***they are MINE.** You may try to take them*
when I run out of ammo."
—Unattributed

Lest you think that sentiment is a bit too strong, do a quick search online and you'll find thousands of examples... so many that I didn't even try to fit them in this book.

———— ◆ ————

CAN WE EVEN FIGHT THIS WAR?

Obviously, my answer is going to be, "see **Chapter 10**" for how we win the war. But the important thing to remember is that **we should NOT be in any war like this to begin with**. When did our educational system decide that we, the parents, were the enemy?

In any modern society, parents
<u>should</u> be the primary determiner
of what our children are being
taught or exposed to.

One critical point to remember if we are ever going to break out of this cycle is that **the students of today will grow up**. As these indoctrinated children graduate from these new "progressive" programs, **many of them become members of the educational ecosystem** (teachers, administrators, politicians, organization leaders, etc.) and push education farther into the realm of shaping, indoctrination, and agenda perpetuation.

Perpetual ➤ *Our children may grow up to be the next generation's enemy in this war on education.*

It is sobering to realize that in 10 to 20 years, **we could be battling against the K-12 and college students of today** to reform our educational system. They will have been indoctrinated into the very system that we are trying to fix.

We cannot "win" the War on Parents on a battlefield designed by our opponents and manned by zealots. To win the educational war we face, we must **design the battlefield ourselves** and set the stage for generations to come (see **Chapter 10**).

Our schools have been **operating under the cover of darkness** for decades. It is time to pull back the curtain and expose the inner workings of our educational system to parents and students everywhere.

———— ♦ ————

SNUFFING OUT THE SACRED FLAME

"Whenever people talk glibly of a need to achieve educational 'excellence,' I think of what an improvement it would be if our public schools could just achieve mediocrity."
— Thomas Sowell[104]

It is no longer just a difference of opinion about what we "*believe*" is right. **The evidence of the failure of our educational system** is out there in abundance. Raw data and statistics, coupled with daily stories that reinforce this educational disease, make it impossible to honestly deny that the system is in serious decline – functionally and in size.

> *Which brings us back around to the point of this book – the Mass Exodus from our public schools. What will those who are left behind be left with?*

Public schools are projected to **lose around 16 million students by 2030.**[105] That is roughly a 32% loss over the next five years or so. A lot of factors could drive that number significantly higher or lower, but the fact remains that public schools will lose a lot of students and a lot of funding. Why?

A big part of the exodus comes simply from a **loss of faith** in our public school system. Decades of neglect and now obvious disdain for parents have taken their toll and, no matter how much it hurts, parents are looking for alternatives.

Parents are seeking out alternatives that better aligned with their beliefs and desires for a stronger education. They are looking outward from the convenience of public schools to homeschooling, private schools, and others. The biggest winner by far has been homeschooling. It had been growing strong in recent years, but experienced a big boon during COVID. **The trend to exit public schools has not abated since then**, and doesn't look like it's going to anytime soon.

So, what does this mean to us here?

The impact of this exodus from public schools will **reshape the educational landscape in profound ways**... most of them will not be healthy for public schools and their students.

- As student populations decline, funding from state and federal sources will also decline, forcing the schools to make tough financial decisions.

- The loss of scale may have an impact forcing program cuts. Some art, music, and extracurricular programs may no longer be feasible.

- Reduced resources may force students into larger classes, reducing the effectiveness of teachers. Additionally, special needs students may be impacted more heavily.

- Socioeconomic disparities may become more prominent as those from lower income families may not have the ability to exit, forcing disproportionate numbers to remain in public schools.

- Perceptions of decline may create a negative feedback loop that forces further exits of students and teachers.

- Fixed costs such as buildings will remain, even as the student population declines. This will force even more cuts to critical programs to the students.

- The psychological impact on remaining students may have a negative impact on their self-esteem and motivation.

There are many other potential impacts, but I think we get the idea. The **downward spiral could be catastrophic** if we don't get ahead of this. And who will take the brunt of this decline? The students of course.

This future decline is why a major reformation must happen.

Once again, I urge you to do your own research on all sides of these issues and **use your amazing analytical powers** to come to your own conclusions. Don't just take my word that a reformation must happen.

Check out multiple sources **from all sides** and build your own consensus. *Be cautious though*, those who are fighting for the status quo are very, very good at using **language as a weapon**. Look deeper than the pretty words they offer. **Look at the actions and the actual implementation** of what they say they do.

In the meantime, we have a few more issues to explore to fully understand what we must do to prevent recurrence of this situation in the future.

———————— ◆ ————————

ONE final thing… You may have been asking yourself, "*Self, why in the world hasn't he talked about the* **Department of Education** *yet*?" Yet another good question.

I wanted to save this to close out our chapter on the Sacred Fire as the **Department of Education**[106] **(ED)** is one of the biggest failures of our educational body and deserves some limited special attention. To begin with…

The Federal Department of Education has NO Constitutional authority to exist!

Education is not mentioned anywhere in our U.S. Constitution and is **NOT an enumerated power of the federal government**. Yet, this federal agency has its fingers in every aspect of our state school systems – down to the classroom level. You can find no aspect of public schools that the ED is not involved in at a fundamental level.

Interestingly, as I was writing this book, the **educational landscape** has been in continuous flux as the **political landscape** has gone through massive changes. When I started writing, it seemed that the elimination of ED would be one of the biggest hurdles we would face. However, with the massive changes in the political landscape, the entire picture may have changed.

At the time this book was published, the Trump administration was pushing hard to entirely eliminate the ED. By the time you read this book, the Department of Education may already be eliminated or severely curtailed. **Keep that in mind** while reading this section as the situation may be fluid.

HOWEVER, the unfortunate aspect of the current push to eliminate the ED is that **they plan to shift many of its responsibilities, actions, funding and other activities out to other federal agencies**. Although the ED might be gone, many of it's powers and tendrils may remain. This is still counter to everything noted in this book regarding federal involvement.

Therefore, whenever I talk about the Department of Education, just assume I mean that to apply to either the ED or to any other federal agency that has taken on any aspect of previous ED functions.

The underlying problem with federal involvement is that **is their massive powers**, including receiving federal tax money and doling it out to states and school districts with conditions. Remember discussions of "**conditional money**" in **Chapter 5**?

> *Federal Agency involvement is one of the*
> *primary reasons "Public Schools" are*
> *really "Government Schools."*

Also remember from **Chapter 5** that the farther the educational decision makers are from the classroom, students, and parents, the **farther the schools drift from the needs of those students and the parents**.

The ED works side-by-side with educational Unions and Associations to directly shape the nature of our educational system and the curriculum. **They are fully intertwined** – the organizations provide guidance to the government entities, then the government entities build directives, regulations, federal government guidance, and laws that are then passed down to be implemented and enforced in the schools.

> This circular feedback loop between ED, Unions, and Associations creates a <u>closed environment</u> where only certain ideas <u>approved by an inner circle</u> can be advanced.

To make matters worse, many of the State-level Department of Educations are **attached at the bellybutton to the Federal ED**. They act in concert with each other and the bureaucrats *with the right agenda and connections* get promoted up through the system **to perpetuate "correct thought" throughout that system**. There is no room for those with differing thoughts or ideas.

A case can be made that "**State**" Department of Educations should exist depending on each state's Constitution. However, these state agencies, *if implemented*, **should be independent of**

any federal government influence and act primarily in an oversight function of the educational system. They, or the **bureaucrats that run them, should NOT be managing and directing every activity of the schools** in that state. They should only provide oversight to ensure state law is followed and to possibly set some minimum standards (see **Chapters 10** and **11**).

Much caution should be exercised here though. **Even a State level Department of Education is alarmingly distant** from the students and parents it is designed to serve.

> *What works in dense urban areas may*
> *be entirely destructive in rural areas.*
> *And vice versa.*

Other than providing oversight and guidance to protect teachers, students, and parents, state-level agencies should be very small and mostly hands off.

From the above discussion, **we begin to see how the web of agencies, unions, and associations deepens and how the tendrils reach into every classroom in America**. It is no wonder that the system is poisoning itself and contaminating its own environment.

————— ♦ —————

The good news is we are getting closer to understanding why a foundational reformation is needed to resolve most of these problems. Reformation is necessary to allow us to turn education into something profoundly beautiful that will **help our children attain the glorious futures that they deserve**.

Now, sit back... take a deep breath... and relax as best you can. We still have a few nasty webs of intrigue to wade through before we get to the meat.

CHAPTER

7

TRANSFORMING SOCIETY ONE CHILD AT A TIME

Things to consider:

➤ What is the best way to transform a society?

➤ When is it too early to sexualize our children?

➤ Should we attack racism with counter-racism?

"The aim of public education is not to spread enlightenment at all; it is simply to reduce as many individuals as possible to the same safe level, to breed a standard citizenry, to put down dissent and originality."
—H.L. Mencken[107]

USING CHILDREN TO FUNDAMENTALLY TRANSFORM SOCIETY

Unfortunately, Mencken's words ring true today and the *"future guardians of the liberties of the country"*, as George Washington once called our children, are instead being groomed to be the **guardians of the prevailing sociopolitical philosophies** of those who hold power.

It may be cliché, but **our educational system has devolved into teaching children "*what*" to think**, rather than providing them with facts and knowledge so they can learn "*how*" to think and develop their own philosophy of life.

The problems go way deeper than that though. Schools today have become indoctrination mills where **students are encouraged to embrace blind obedience to current authority figures**. This happens while at the same time, the system is tearing down the nuclear family and any authority vested to the parents by traditional cultural norms.

◆

Massive power, influence, and an unending war chest of money (*much of it our tax dollars*) is marshaled to stop parents and watchdog groups from having any visibility into our educational system. Why do they fight so hard to blind us?

We have voluntarily turned our children over to this system for six to eight plus hours a day, five days a week, for 12+ years. Yet **we are not allowed to monitor or evaluate** the system and the teachers. Why?

Consider this. Would you leave town and turn your home over to be completely remodeled without providing a plan, guidance on what you want, instructions, approvals, progress reviews, walkthroughs, or a budget? **Would you blindly accept that it will all come out alright in the end**? Would you be okay with zero visibility into what was being done to your home and what shape it was taking until it was done?

> **This vast empire we call our educational system does not want YOU to see into the empire. Why?**

Of course not! So why do we do that with our most important possessions in the world?

We accept that it is natural for our children to come home from school so very different from how we raised them. Too many are angry, combative, secretive, distrustful of us, and hating everything we stand for. They display **massive personality changes that include embracing values and social agendas so vastly different** from how they were raised that we barely recognize them. The change is often incredibly profound.

"Oh, they're just teenagers," we rationalize.

Parden my language, but "Bull!" Yes, there are hormonal changes with teenagers, body changes, a bit of rebellion, and even some mental changes and challenges. **It is a chaotic time for them. Which only makes it easier to open the door to external influences** that can do unimaginable damage. The resultant harm is then claimed to be natural and normal.

> **Our educational system takes advantage of the chaos of children's teen years to reshape them to conform to artificial cultural agendas.**

However, most parents who provide alternate education (homeschooling, etc.) for their children will tell you **it doesn't have to be that way**. Even more telling is that parents who work dynamically to counter the indoctrination and are actively involved in the daily lives of their children understand that something has gone very wrong.

The fundamental changes we see in our children in public school today are not "natural and normal".

This *"angry, combative, anti-parent, anti-family, hyper-sexualized teen stage"* is **a construct designed to hide the infection** that is being **intentionally injected** into the core personality of our children.

You may also notice this injected personality of self-destruction always leans towards chaos. Teenagers do NOT come out of public schools screaming at their parents:

> **"NO, Mom and Dad!** *I don't care what you say. I am going to build my career, get married, raise a nuclear family, and live a happy and fruitful life; and* **you can't stop me***!"*

◆

Okay, I kid a little, but the point is that **these changes in our educational system are designed to fundamentally transform society into something different.** We see the rotted fruits of that today as indoctrinated children grow up and move into positions within or adjacent to our educational system – **perpetuating the transformation**.

The brainwashing, indoctrination, training, and grooming of the next generation has been ongoing for ages. I believe those who have **succumbed to the infection** generally tend to fall into three classes (*with many exceptions of course*):

1. **Victim Class**: The weaker of those transformed become the *"victims of society"* and/or wards of the state with the inability to function in normal civilization.

2. **Influencer/Activist Class**: Some move on to career or college and continue to transform society based on the agendas they were indoctrinated with. Many become next generation teachers, administrators, and politicians.

3. **Functional Class**: These grow up to be normal functional citizens. However, they can always be counted on to reliably vote for school boards, politicians, and others who will perpetuate the same political values that they were indoctrinated with.

What better way to grow, control, and transform future generations than to create current generations of activists who will promote, support, and fund the policies and actions that will strengthen the efforts to transform our society.

Today, our children are useful pawns in a massive social engineering effort to **reshape America into a conforming member of a worldwide society** that thrives on dysfunction and chaos. Anarchy, crime, and disaffection create a ripe field for those in power to remain in power. This is not a new concept and is common throughout the world.

Still not convinced? Then let's take a look under the hood to see what's really going on.

SOCIAL ENGINEERING – AN ATTACK ON EDUCATION

> **These new ideologies are fertile feeding grounds to open the door to the total deconstruction of classical education.**

So, *how does that get us to where we are now*? One of the most devastating attacks on education comes through **attacks on traditional education itself**. We have moved so far away from classical education now that the true meaning of the word *"education"* in America begins to come into question.

America's schools have been breaking down traditional barriers that aligned schools with parents for many years. Declining test scores, comprehension, critical thinking skills, and independent thought have all fallen victim to this assault. **Political correctness evolved** into **"woke" ideologies** and then expanded into **open hyper-sexuality** and so-called "**anti-racism**" or **CRT**.

The rest of this chapter will focus on the damage dealt primarily from attacks on these three fronts:

- **Loss of Classical Education**

- **Sexuality of Children**

- **Loss of "Self" and "Individuality" to the "Greater Good"**

———————— ♦ ————————

Before we move on to those weighty subjects, we need to address **four high-level Attack Theorems** that are the underpinnings of most of the activities that support the attack on education.

1. Homogenized Education Factories
2. Death of Traditional Literature
3. Erase Western Values of "Individualism"
4. Grade Inflation

Each of these methodologies piles onto the other changes that have altered the focus of our modern educational system. They are designed to prepare our children to be malleable and easily absorb the propaganda and alternative focus of a system that pressures them away from traditional education. Let's take a quick look at each of these attacks.

1. HOMOGENIZED EDUCATION FACTORY

Our educational system has always maintained a strong leaning towards **homogeneity in application**. We discussed teaching to the *"lowest common denominator"* back in **Chapter 5**. In an effort to ensure that no student is left behind or is made to feel inferior, we try to make them all equal. **Now take that concept and put it on steroids**.

Some of our school systems are now moving towards an **"Equal-Results"** approach to how children are managed, educated, and graded. This approach stems from the tenets of CRT (*discussed later in this chapter*) as well as **DEI**. In this circumstance, the "Equity" equation is simply codeword for bringing high achievers down to **equalize resources and outcomes** with the lesser achievers.

Conversely, **"De-Leveling"** (i.e., universal learning) targets children with learning disabilities and who may be in an Individualized Education Program (IEP). They are artificially leveled up to a norm that they may not be capable of achieving.

This denies everyone the possibilities of greater success based on their accomplishments.

> ### *Merge Equal Results and De-Leveling together and you have a <u>Homogenized Education Factory.</u>*

The result is that all students, regardless of ability, circumstance, or capability are treated the same and provided the same education plan, resources, books, lectures, and *outcome possibilities*. **Individualism is not allowed to flourish**.

Individuality is further discouraged through **authority- and peer-shaming**, as well as strictly enforced political correctness **to entrench homogeny in our children's psyche**. They learn (*falsely*) that "equity" is the only true path to fairness.

In reality, those who could have excelled are artificially held down to lower standards. Those who may have learning and application challenges will not receive the specialized help they need and will have a higher fail rate. → *Equity at work.*

2. DEATH OF TRADITIONAL LITERATURE

Gone are the days of *"The Adventures of Huckleberry Finn"*, *"To Kill a Mockingbird"*, *"Of Mice and Men"*, and many historical accounts of George Washington, Abraham Lincoln, and most of our Founding Fathers. In fact, much of American history is in the process of being erased. Claims of racism, sexism, slavery, false white histories, and more are used to remove cultural context and actual history from our children's education. Why?

To make room for more contemporary writings that **incorporate woke ideas of sexual ideologies, sexual identity, (supposed) anti-racism, white privilege, and alternate false histories** (*more on the 1619 Project later*). This is all part of teaching children "what" to think rather than "how" to think.

If actual history and past cultural norms do not support the agenda and propaganda goals of our new educational ecosystem, then **the past must be erased and replaced**.

3. *ERASE WESTERN VALUES OF "INDIVIDUALISM"*

Do you see how this is all starting to tie together? If you homogenize and equalize everyone... then erase contrary cultural memory, you **chip away at individualism in favor of the collective**.

Those with influence on our educational system have **rejected the Eurocentric Worldview of Individualism**. They see it as an **impediment to the fundamental transformation of our society** into one that functions under a compliant, complacent, collective worldview. **The self, the individual, must be sacrificed** for "*the greater good.*"

Our **individualism**, our **freedom to be ourselves**, to **think for ourselves**, and to **explore our individual natures** was the **genesis for all the great innovation** that made America so unique in the world. Look to our Founding Fathers if you want to see the greatest example of this. Our uniqueness boils down to **a simple American thought**...

LOOK! ➡ ***When everyone says it
cannot be done, I must find
a way to do it.***

This sums up the **soul of innovation in America** and our cultural need to be individuals. Let's look at just one.

───────── ♦ ─────────

There are many stories of truly amazing American individuals, but there is one in particular that spoke strongly to me about the possibilities of being exceptionally human *if we are not homogenized into doubt and obscurity*. Let's sidetrack just a little bit if you don't mind.

The Incredible American Story of Kevin Cooper[108]

Kevin Cooper (also known as Cole Summers) was saving money to build a new house for his parents; he was working on a movie script and a series of children's books teaching business literacy for kids; he was breeding heritage turkeys; looking for a celebrity to endorse his line of luxury toiletries made from the milk of his award-winning goat herd; all while writing guest essays for notable political bloggers and finally publishing his autobiography; he had two other books in progress – when he tragically died in a kayaking accident **at the age of 14**.

> *"Don't ever take 'can't' as the answer*
> *unless you've verified that it is against the*
> *law or against the powers of physics."*
> — Kevin Cooper (from his autobiography)[109]

There is an undeniable agent in the **American Spirit of individualism, innovation, and amazing accomplishments** that prompts us to do great things. This remarkable young boy was the epitome of that greatness and consequence we aspire to. **Not because of any single thing he did**, but because he saw the needs of the world as bigger than himself.

Kevin was *not* a boy of privilege. His family was incredibly poor. They were also all disabled. His father is a disabled veteran in a wheelchair. His mother is partially blind. His older brother is autistic. Despite that, Kevin believed that we are capable of doing anything; and he set about doing just that.

In addition to the accomplishments in the bio box above, he purchased a 350-acre farm when he was nine (*remember, his family was literally dirt poor*) and set about developing regenerative animal agriculture with landscaping and earthworks to increase water retention and prevent soil erosion.

Kevin was writing other books beyond the autobiography he published just before his death. He was working on a movie; started his first business at seven years old; did all the work on the home and farm for his disabled family; and much more. All by the age of 14 when an accident ended his adventure.

Why am I sharing THIS story here? Beyond just being an amazing tale of exceptionalism and tragedy, I thought this was on target to our discussion on homogeny in education.

For consideration as relevance to this book, Kevin was a **homeschooler**, or more specifically an "**unschooler**", who developed his own curriculum and educated himself well beyond others of his age. He was studying Warren Buffet at age six to teach himself about business and finances.

He never attended a day of public school in his life. Now, I cannot say if homeschooling drove any of his exceptionalism, there were many factors he faced in his short life that could have driven his ambition. And he was obviously incredibly intelligent.

I wonder though… *if he had been forced to attend eight years of Public Schools as they are today…* **WOULD HE HAVE DONE ANY OF THIS**? Would today's public-school environment, starting at age 5 or 6, have *equalized* him down to all of his peers? Or would he have brought some of them up? Would peer pressure to conform and fit in have stifled him? We will never know of course, but I'm glad his family did not take that risk.

Kevin Cooper is an **incredible American story of individualism, selflessness, and service to family and society**. I am glad society did not impose limits on him, but must wonder how many others have been lost to our education mills and their push to conform to equity and erase individualism.

I encourage you to read more of the inspiring story of this amazing American kid who touched so many people before his untimely death at 14.

———— ◆ ————

Considering Kevin's story (as well as many others) one has to wonder why "*individualism*" is such a threat to those who have been remaking our schools? Don't we want *that* to be the core of who we are? The answer is in the **45 Communist Goals** we talked about in **Chapter 6. Individualism is NOT conducive to the implementation of those Communist Goals** and must be crushed to allow for the full transformation of American society.

4. GRADE INFLATION

Our last theorem revolves around a process called *"Grade Inflation."* This was a *thing* long before "woke" and "equity" came on the scene. For the older readers here, you may remember many years ago when "**self-esteem**" was all the rage, and **we were afraid that bad grades would make kids unhappy and stifle growth and their desire to succeed**. That's how it started to be broadly used. Although I suspect individual teachers were doing that long before it became common.

There are many reasons that grade inflation is still being used today and it ties quite nicely to all the **equity factors and manipulation** of children and parents we see today. A few of these reasons include:

- Conforming with the equity agenda;

- Continued belief that having grades lower than other students devastates self-esteem;

- Low grades are racist somehow;

- Grade inflation supports chaos and confusion;

- Teacher's desires to inflate student success levels to appease parents; and

- Sadly, as a means to **move kids through the system** and out into the world quickly **to make them someone else's problem**.

The problem with this? By artificially inflating grades we create *"Failure Through Success"* (a common, but sometimes misunderstood term). Artificial success created by grade inflation creates in itself an environment of **false security**.

By helping a child "succeed" *without* them earning that success, **we set a <u>much lower bar</u> that might not be realistic in the real world**. When the child goes out into the world, they are ill equipped to participate, much less succeed. As a result…

Grade inflation feeds the cycle of chaos,
failure, dysfunction, and promotes a higher
potential for becoming wards of the state.

———— ◆ ————

Those were just a few broad strokes of how **our children are being molded into tools to transform society**. These relentless attacks on education come from all corners of the educational environment. As a result, our public schools have **descended into academic mediocrity** and centers for "**woke**" **indoctrination**.

Our children are being groomed and prepped to become adults who will be malleable, disenfranchised, unhappy, and easily manipulated by propaganda and indoctrination. As adults, they will be more than happy to continue this self-destructive cycle when they move into the workforce and become teachers, administrators, and politicians themselves.

I know that sounds dark and dystopian, but it is undeniable if you look at the totality of everything we've discussed so far.

Unfortunately, **some of the worst is still to come** as we work through the transformation process.

———— ◆ ————

SEX AND SEXUALITY OF CHILDREN

> *"This is the Marxist global revolution – it's the Cultural Revolution – and this is what is coming into our schools. It is Marxist propaganda. It's designed to divide the kids from their parents, divide the kids from their country, divide the kids from their culture, and even in many cases, divide them from their very selves."*
> —Florence Thomas[110]

One of the vilest attacks on education and the youth of America is **using our educational system to inspire and promote the sexualization of our children**. This sexualization has reached down to children as young as five years old. Will it go younger? *Has it already gone younger?*

The real question though is, **why do this**? Why introduce sexuality to children at such young ages? Why do this against the parent's will?

There are many answers to this. My belief is that **it is yet another piece of the larger puzzle** in promoting chaos, dystopia, and government reliance that is necessary for a government to rule **without <u>effective</u> interference from the people under their rule**. The proof of this is borne throughout history.

My hypothesis only accounts for those in positions of power. What about all the others **who believe that early sexualization is a good thing**? Do they *really* believe that it is beneficial to a six-year-old child to learn the various places where a man can stick his penis? Do they believe this promotes a healthy and happy childhood?

I can't read their minds of course, but my belief is that **this is NOT about the child** at all. It is more likely about a misguided sense of "*societal health*" to advance DEI (diversity, equity, and inclusion). **The mental and physical health of the INDIVIDUAL child may not even be a consideration**.

Lest you think this is an exaggeration, a short exploration of this educational environment of hyper sexualization of children is in order. It is sad we need to go here, but necessary if we are going to understand why the system needs **foundational reformation**.

--------------- ◆ ---------------

Comprehensive Sexuality Education (CSE)[111] is a term used to address many levels of youth sexuality from practical health understanding to exposing 6-year-olds to multiple ways sex is performed (*to put it gently*), alternate sexual lifestyles, sexuality, and much more.

> Promoting hyper-sexuality as the functional and societal norm to children as young as six creates mental chaos and confusion.

Some will promote it as **enabling young people to protect and advocate for their own health, well-being, and dignity**. That sounds wonderful, but it is clear to see that today's educational system has taken that concept and **perverted it into programs to instill hyper-sexuality as the norm** in the youngest of students.

I doubt that few parents have a problem with schools providing classes on anatomy, health, safety, and normal bodily functions. That has been educational fair game for a long time.

Where we have gone off the rails though is expanding into a world of exposing young children to actual sexual content, methods of fornication, sexual ideologies, and much more.

LOOK! ➤ *Just a few years ago, anyone exposing children to what they are seeing now in public schools would have received 5-10 years in prison.*

There is ZERO reason that any child in K-12 needs to have an authority figure (or a delegate) **exposing these children to pornographic imagery**. Nor in my opinion should they be talking about personal sexual activity, or teaching sexual lifestyles, providing explicit descriptions of what happens when two naked people of any mix of gender have sex, or providing any other training, encouragement, or exploration of sexual activity of any kind.

———— ♦ ————

How has this come to be the standard within our educational system? Part of it is that the schools operate at the whims of those in the **educational power circle** of politicians, government organizations, associations, and unions. **This circle-of-power is pushing hardcore** (*pun intended*) **social agendas** without any external checks and balances.

Parents have lost nearly all influence in their schools. They are fighting back now. but it will be a long and bitter battle with a questionable outcome. However, there is hope.

- Numerous states are passing parental rights bills.

- More and more parents are running for and winning School Board seats.

- The public is starting to recognize what is going on.

- Polls show sentiment is growing in support of children and parents. An APP poll[112] at this time showed that 60% of those polled supported stringent laws related to sexuality in public schools.

But the battle will rage on as long as the schools are operating under the influence of the **circle-of-power**. The chain needs to be broken and power returned back to parents (see **Chapter 10**).

——————— ♦ ———————

The argument has been made (*ad nauseam*) that parents have regularly failed when it comes to **teaching children about the birds-and-the-bees**. Therefore, *they say*, it is up to the schools to take up the slack.

I agree that it is sometimes hard for parents to step up and address this issue. BUT it is still **their responsibility**, **not the school's**. If parents were to abdicate their responsibility entirely and give this responsibility to the schools, it still would not justify what is being promoted in schools today.

> *Teaching alternative sexualities,*
> *transgenderism, homosexuality, and other*
> *hyper-sexual topics is a far cry from teaching*
> *children the "Birds-and-the-Bees."*

If parents are not comfortable providing a minimal level of sexual education, and they think it is important, there will be no end of **non-government free market solutions** that will pop up to serve the market at various levels of explicitness.

——————— ♦ ———————

EXAMPLES OF SEXUALIZING OUR CHILDREN

Sadly, there were thousands of examples to choose from, but I limited it to a random snapshot of just a few to drive home the point of this section.

You are welcome to skip over these examples. *If* it offends you so much that you wish to avoid these, then the point is made and need not be belabored. If you are offended, imagine what your young child feels. *There will NOT be a test afterwards.*

- **Drag Performers Reading Time**[113]
  New York City reportedly paid Drag Performers to read transexual, DEI, and anti-family books to young kids.

- **Librarian Defends Sex Work in a Book**[114]
  A school librarian apparently defended a book in the library with a chapter, *"Sex Work is Not a Bad Term"*. The librarian reportedly claimed that kids come to the library who do sex work and the book makes them feel validated. → *Yikes!*

- **Teacher Boasts of Adult-Themed Queer Library for Students**[115]
  A California teacher boasts of her *"queer library"* in the classroom with over 100 books, many with extremely sexual content.

- **181 K-12 Educators Arrested in the U.S. on Child Sex-Related Crimes**[116]
  In the first six months of a recent year, at least 153 teachers, 12 substitute teachers, 12 teachers' aids, and 4 principals were arrested for child sex-related crimes ranging from child pornography to raping students.

- **Teachers Union Promotes Ways for Teachers to Hide Pronouns from Parents**[117]
  It appears that the American Federation of Teachers (AFT) promoted pronoun cards to help kids (as early as Pre-K) change their pronouns without parents knowing.

- **Radical Gender Lessons for Pre-K Children**[118]
  One Illinois School District adopted a curriculum for Pre-K to 3rd grade to break the boundaries of gender, European Colonization, and sexual orientation. → *It's okay, they also learned how to make macaroni art.*

- **New Jersey Gone Wild!**[119]
  Under new state sex education guidelines, first graders could be taught they might have boy parts, but feel like

a girl, and second graders will learn about various gender identities. In fifth grade kids can explore opportunities to talk with a counselor, therapist, or doctor about feelings they have regarding gender. They may even be referred to an endocrinologist.

- **California Department of Education Advocates Books Promoting Gender Transitions for Kindergartners**[120]
  California now wants to be sure that your 5-year-old knows everything they need to know about sexual identity and transitioning to another sex, **just in case they want to transition when they turn six**.

More and more examples hit the news nearly every day. The ones I provided are just a tiny sampling of what our children are facing on a day-to-day basis.

———————— ♦ ————————

THE FINAL WORD ON SEXUALIZING OUR CHILDREN

Under the guise of equity, inclusion, and mental health, those who are attacking our schools and our children are **willfully choosing to introduce raw sex, sexuality, gender identity, alternate sexual orientations, and graphic images and descriptions of sex** to children as young as 5-years-old.

The innocence of childhood, once taken or lost, can never be regained.

LOST!

Have we forgotten that these ARE Children?

Times have changed and our moral values have shifted somewhat with those times, but **shouldn't it still be up to the parent to determine how much pornography our children are exposed to**?

It used to be (*that's code talk for I'm not young and hip*) that if a teenager was caught showing the **J.C. Penney women's lingerie catalog** (*okay, even I am not that old*) to the other boys at school, he would get suspended and his parents would have to come pick him up. Maybe that was a bit traumatizing, but NOT life changing.

Times have changed though and all kids have access to the internet, but **shouldn't we draw the line somewhere short of hypersexuality**? Should we institutionalize graphic pornography as we have and allow authority figures in the schools to teach young children about very adult sexual activities?

———————— ♦ ————————

The war over our children's innocence is raging fast and furious. It is hard to keep up with and we have to ask ourselves, **WHY are the schools themselves now pushing sexuality, gender identity/fluidity, alternative lifestyles, and all manner of sexual intercourse on our very young children**?

The answer is themed throughout this book and clearly demonstrates that we cannot have a school system that is subject to the whims of the current powers that be. There must be stability. There must be continuity. There must be trust.

We, the parents, need to achieve an unbreakable mandate to ensure our schools respect our **primary authority** on how we want to raise our own children. That is missing now.

———————— ♦ ————————

WHY DOES ALL THIS INDOCTRINATION WORK SO WELL?

"Destroy the imagination of a child, and you have taken away its chances of success in life. Imagination transforms the commonplace into the great and creates the new out of the old."
—L. Frank Baum, author of *"The Wizard of Oz"*[121]

LOOK! You see, the real tragedy is *not* in what children are being indoctrinated to become, but the *confiscation* of WHO they could have been.

Lying, **propaganda**, and **gaslighting** (*which we will call collectively "indoctrination" from here on*) are nearly as old as man himself. It is most effective when tapping into **deeply personal emotions** through:

- carefully curated words;
- slick and repetitive slogans;
- disseminating selective information;
- use of demagoguery to inflame emotions and induce personal decisions;
- censoring or manipulating facts, numbers, statistics, and even history to provide "proofs";
- employing authority figures and celebrities to push specific messaging; and
- driving powerful peer-pressure to diffuse any lingering doubts or concerns.

Then **multiply that by a million-fold** through social media. People, organizations, and governments have become masters at indoctrination, especially in today's **hyper-communication environment**. It comes at us from all corners, driven by a massive treasure chest of dollars.

The power of indoctrination has been proven throughout history. It is incredibly effective in fundamentally transforming a society *without war* – and generally without most of society even realizing it's being done.

———————— ♦ ————————

By focusing these forces on school age children (*whose minds are still extremely malleable*) these efforts become a **force-multiplier** that will self-propagate and deliver results for generations to come. The K-12 environment is a perfect incubator for this type of generational indoctrination.

And, of course, the most important tool of all in this environment → **full, unfettered, access to your child's mind** for six to eight plus hours per day, five days a week, *without* **interference from parents**.

What better place to create generations of believers than a environment **isolated from parents** and families, **unmonitored**, and led for hours every day by authority figures tacitly authorized by the parents themselves? Children really have no option but to accept what these *"authority figures"* **present to them as absolute truth**. A truth backed up by schoolbooks written by other *"authority figures"* who have similar beliefs.

> *Eventually, this mandated truth*
> *becomes "their" truth.*

Ultimately, peer pressure comes in to play to lock down this truth and ensure that all students believe in the approved narrative. **Our children never had a chance** against this onslaught.

———————— ◆ ————————

THE PRIMACY EFFECT

> *"What we **learn first** is the thing we tend to believe. Over time, that primary learning leads to '**belief persistence**' where it becomes very hard for us to change our minds about it."*
> —My adaptation of Primacy to Indoctrination

Traditionally, the **Primacy Effect** refers to how our memory works in something like the memorization of lists. We tend to remember the beginning of lists better than information at the middle or the end. What you hear first tends to stick easiest.

> *"The Primacy Effect" is one of the*
> *major challenges we face in the*
> *indoctrination of our children.*

Our children are taught at younger and younger ages about social and political agendas that are presented as **"truths" from authority**. By putting these truth agendas at the *beginning of the list*, they short circuit ongoing thought, debate, and analysis from peers and external sources. **These "truths" become the child's own beliefs**.

After first-in information is implanted, you add **repetition, reinforcement, and additional authority engagement** to harden these beliefs into "***belief persistence***". Once something is learned and fully engrained as a person's own beliefs, it is very hard for them to change their minds about it. In fact...

> *Once <u>Belief Persistence</u> has set in, those*
> *who challenge those beliefs are met with*
> *a lack of understanding as to WHY*
> *someone would believe differently.*

Does that sound familiar? Those who push indoctrination understand how this works on the young mind and how quickly it creates a **lifetime acolyte who will likely never stray from the approved word**.

One of the most powerful demonstrations of the effectiveness of this is how parents are often blindsided by the change in their children. They are at a complete loss to understand why their child *suddenly* has these powerful belief systems and **will not even discuss that there might be something different**.

In fact, their child – *who suddenly has a completely new belief system that is at odds with how they were raised* – will become **belligerent and intolerant of any other viewpoint than the one that has taken primacy and persistence**. The parents will feel that they have lost all authority over their 12-year-old and the connection they had before becomes strained.

> *We need to change the trajectory of*
> *indoctrination and ensure that persistent*
> *beliefs in our children are positive,*
> *forward-looking, flexible, and accepting*
> *of parent's views and beliefs.*

As parents, we need to teach our children truth BEFORE they are squirreled away in public schools to be inundated with lies, half-truths, and bias propaganda that will shape them. We need to give them the foundational tools to understand what is being presented to them and how to strengthen their own belief systems.

Today's educational system wants to teach our children certain concepts YEARS before we, the parents, believe our children are ready to process these thoughts properly.

A conundrum now exists that
endangers our children.

The forces that are driving our K-12 educational system reach down to younger and younger children **to use the primacy effect and lock in their beliefs <u>BEFORE</u> we parents are ready** to expose our children to them. This is NOT by accident.

———— ♦ ————

WHY USE THE CHILDREN TO CHANGE SOCIETY?

"Train up a child in the way he should go. Even
when he is old, he will not depart from it."
—Proverbs 22:6[122]

Children *want* to **DO good**. They *want* to **BE good**. They want the acceptance, approval, and recognition of their authority figures and especially their peers. This makes them **easy prey**, which is why **we must be ultra-vigilant** about what information is being fed to our children.

The reason for their focus on children is
that they are <u>not only</u> indoctrinating our
children today, but through belief
persistence they are <u>indoctrinating the next</u>
<u>generation of indoctrinators</u>.

It is a self-perpetuating cycle that multiplies the desired agenda exponentially. We discussed this earlier. These children will grow up to be, *among other things*, future teachers, administrators, and politicians **who "believe" with all their heart the agenda they were indoctrinated in**. They will easily accept whatever follows and push that as their inherent world view. There can be NO other world view because they don't understand how YOU can believe something different.

They become the indoctrinators.

THIS is the power of indoctrinating young children wholesale through our educational system. Once you have trained (indoctrinated) millions of children *"in the way they should think"* and reinforced that for 12-16+ years, it is extremely hard to turn them from the path they have been led down step-by-step.

And, *through no fault on our children's part*, it works very, very well. Part of the reason for this is what I believe is:

"Crate Training" for children.

We all know the old saying that *"you cannot teach an old dog new tricks."* The reality behind this for humans is that as we become older, our minds change, we become more set in our ways, and we already have our belief systems in place. The minds of puppies and young children are still forming, their belief systems are still developing, and they are **receptive to being taught without questioning authority**.

> **The puppy must be trained BEFORE it becomes brave enough to resist or strong enough to think on its own.**

By putting a puppy in a crate, it learns that it must learn and obey in order to get out of the crate. From there it learns that **there is an authority figure who will teach it what needs to be learned**. AND it learns how to learn from the authority figure.

Children are not puppies of course, but the training concept is somewhat similar. Today's schools are the crate and in order to maximize the effect of indoctrination (*training*), the students must be filled with the approved agenda and beliefs **BEFORE they are strong enough** to form their own worldview belief systems and have the strength of will (*bravery*) to question what authority is teaching them. AND it must be done before they are strong enough to even question the authority of that authority.

This is why we see indoctrination being driven down to younger and younger children (down to Pre-K and earlier).

The earlier you can <u>reduce the influence of the parents</u> *and* <u>promote the unquestionable authority of the indoctrinator,</u> *the more primacy and persistence you can lock in.*

———————— ✦ ————————

So, what about older children who did not have the "*advantage*" of early indoctrination training. That is where more traditional indoctrination comes in. The authority figures play on **emotions, anxiety, the desire to make a difference, and the need to belong**. All traits that teenagers have in abundance.

They are anxious to figure out who they are, what their place is in the world, and how they can go about making a mark. For many, **it is the allure of a passion they haven't felt before** that they don't understand how to channel.

Then, along comes someone with **a mission to save the planet**, or **end racism**, or **save democracy**, or whatever the agenda of the moment is. **They are shown a way to express themselves** and to make a difference in the world. Emotion and passion become all-consuming drivers and **they become receptive to the mission of the goals of the indoctrinator**.

Again, NOT the student's fault. They are what they are supposed to be. The fault lies in those who will take advantage of that and **forever change the trajectory of a child's life**, just to fulfill a political or social agenda.

> ***Parents need to be able to***
> ***short-circuit this process.***

Those who would indoctrinate children will NOT stop on their own, so parents need to be reinserted into the cycle in a position of authority that can counter these attempts.

———————— ✦ ————————

THE LAST WORD ON THIS SAD LITTLE CHAPTER

> *"It is the children the world **ALMOST**
> breaks who grow up to save it."*
> —Frank Warren[123]

This chapter has been a horrifying journey into the dark side of a sickness that has taken over our educational system. **These travels were a necessary evil to our goal of understanding that** THE SYSTEM **CANNOT** BE "*FIXED*". As you may remember from our earlier discussion, we are beyond any possibility of fixing the system and any attempt will be temporary at best – the cancer is too rooted in to excise.

In various parts of America, we have "patched up" some elements. The localized patches listed below are likely temporary and could be undone the next time power changes hands.

- Remove pornographic books from libraries.
- Make curriculum and teaching materials open and available to parents.
- Audit teacher's training and classroom activities.
- Get student-first parents elected to school boards.
- Expand School Choice to more states.
- Ban DEI, CRT, and other similar teachings.
  - **Note**: *At publishing date of this book, President Donald Trump had issued a nationwide Executive Order banning Federal funds from going to public schools that teach CRT or gender issues. It was partially effective, but this was enforced by using Federal tax dollars as a carrot to force compliance. I am in favor of the direction he went of course, but may not be when the next President comes along. There is no permanence, and you may remember our discussion of how bad Federal involvement can become back in* **Chapter 5***.*

NONE of this resolves the underlying systemic problems of a **government- and agenda-driven educational environment** that brought us to where we are today.

———————— ♦ ————————

We are at a **tipping point** now. A crisis point if you want to get dramatic. Those who seek to create **the next generation of faithful believers in this religion of indoctrination** are very close to reaching their goals.

Millions of children have been indoctrinated and have grown up and moved into positions of power where they willingly indoctrinate others.

Millions more are being deeply indoctrinated now to do the same in the future.

This may seem like hyperbole, but the proof is everywhere. That is why so many examples and references are included in this book.

Allowed to go unchecked, the destructive impact on future generations in America will be incalculable and our ability to overcome will become nearly impossible.

> *It is time for us to commit to a*
> *foundational reformation or a*
> ## *Great Educational Reset.*

Our educational system as it stands must pass into the dark night of our history if we are to remain America the Great and a Powerful Beacon of Light for the world.

The forces at play are already too entrenched for us to even consider heroic efforts to save what we have. **It is time for a new generation of education to rise from the ashes** and reignite the Sacred Fire of Education.

8

CRISIS IN EDUCATION

Things to consider:

➤ Are we really at a crisis point?

➤ Where are we headed without change?

➤ Is an exodus to alternative schools the answer?

*"And who are its enemies? It always appears that they are not only those who attack it openly and consciously, but **those who 'objectively' endanger it by spreading mistaken doctrines**. In other words, defending democracy involves destroying all independence of thought."*

—George Orwell[124]

A CRISIS IN PUBLIC EDUCATION TODAY

Our educational system is **the core of who we are now and will become as a nation**. Our children eventually become our educators, our industry leaders, our statesmen, and the leaders of our government.

LOOK! ➡️ *Today, our children rely on us.*
Tomorrow, our nation relies on them.

Yet, right now, our schools are being used to fundamentally change the very fabric of who we are and what the United States of America stands for. These changes are turning our children, as a society, away from the "***Great American Dream***" towards being just another nation-member of a greater world order.

We will fade from being the shining Beacon
of Hope for the people of the world into
simply becoming a piggy bank to plunder.

Our question here becomes, *what damage has been done to our children and what will it mean to theirs*?

If our goal is to **educate our children and prepare them for success and exceptionalism**, then there is no denying our educational system is in crisis right now.

In this chapter, we will wrap up our analysis of the systemic diseases infecting education, cross-examine what we have done to try and save the schools, and prepare everyone to finish their grieving and move on. In **Chapter 9** we will look at what we can do to prepare for the **Great Education Reset** that is needed to save our nation.

In **Chapter 10** and beyond, we will do a post-mortem and begin **our journey into a new, reborn educational life** that is full of promise and potential. One that is forever inoculated from the ravages and corruption of the old educational system.

———————— ♦ ————————

Our focus so far has been on **indoctrination, propaganda, interference, manipulation, and other external factors** driving agenda in the "thoughts" of our children. All of that is bad enough, but the one major factor we have not really examined is, *"how well are students learning traditional competences in today's educational environment?"*

There is no end to books written, and being written, about the poor state of today's education and how our children are doing. Endless information can be found on the internet through countless sources. Here are just a couple to whet your appetite if you *really* want to dive down that rabbit hole.

- National Center for Education Statistics (NCES).[125]
- The Nation's Report Card (government).[126]
- National Assessment of Educational Progress (NAEP).[127]
- United States Census Bureau.[128]
- Research.com Education Statistics.[129]

The point of this book however is *not* to dive into the morass of statistics and numbers that exist. We *know* something is wrong. Even for those who doubt this is a crisis, it is indisputable that **we can do better!**

We are America, damn it! **We are *the* great innovators.** Yet the approaches we use for public K-12 education have not really changed in a hundred years.

We need to understand the widespread failure in the system itself so that we recognize **that foundational problems are NOT just the indoctrination and other issues we've been discussing**. The crisis is compounded by an education system that is failing to properly educate our children.

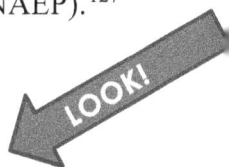

In a word, the State of Education is –
<u>*Not Well.*</u>

Okay, that was two words, but the point is clear. **We are failing our children throughout their educational journey** on top of the efforts to indoctrinate them and shape them into someone else's vision. Merge these two foundational points and you have a recipe for disaster. **This is not acceptable**.

As recently as 30 years ago or so, the United States was ranked <u>Number 1 in K-12</u> of the ~35 industrialized nations of the world.

But what does K-12 education look like these days? **Pretty bad compared to the other industrialized nations of the world** where we rank near the bottom in nearly all research studies. I had originally incorporated a bunch of statistics, numbers, and other data here, but quickly realized much of it was conflicting to nail down, changing constantly, and sometimes biased.

Then I realized, **the actual numbers are not the point of this book**. Suffice it to say that K-12 education is not healthy.

In fact, American Millennials **TIED FOR LAST** in the workforces of all industrialized countries on tests in mathematics and problem solving according to the **Organization for Economic Cooperation and Development**.[130] Indicating by these reports that we have one of the worst-educated workforces in the industrialized world.

HOW is that even possible?

If you do your own research (*as you should*), you will find data that supports this **as well as data that contradicts to some degree**. This is only natural in today's hyper-informational, hyper-confrontational environment. If you dive into the contradictory rankings, you will find much of it is opinion- and perception-based. Also, make sure that your research is based on data related to K-12. Rankings based on higher education are significantly different.

> *Whatever level of failure we might*
> *attribute to K-12, there can be no denying*
> *that our schools are failing to educate.*

Approximately **50 million students** currently attend America's public schools.

This means that **tens of millions of our children are potentially being undereducated AND indoctrinated every year**. This is enough to build an army of acolytes that will indoctrinate the next generation, and the next, and so on. This is not sustainable if we want to remain America the Beautiful.

Part of the answer AND part of the problem is the **Mass Exodus of students from public schools**. Recent numbers show that roughly **15 million students** have exited the public schools to attend Charter Schools, private schools, and home-school.[131] These numbers are increasing significantly as the issues we've been discussing become more public and parents recognize the problems and dangers of the public school system. Which again begs the eternal question of this book…

> *What happens to those <u>left behind</u>*
> *in our public schools?*

Although I am an advocate of most alternative schools and have almost always seen the public school system as a failure, the fact remains that **public schools will remain as our <u>primary education vehicle</u> for the foreseeable future**.

If that is the case, **we have a moral imperative** to assure the successful educational futures of tens of millions of students per year who must remain in the public school system.

> *Keep reading to see how we can do that.*

———— ♦ ————

On a side note, these failures in education and the push for DEI are strong as well in our colleges and universities. Higher education continues the process to **reinforce belief persistence** of the indoctrination students received in K-12.

The **Wall Street Journal** noted from a study that at least *"one-third of college seniors were UNABLE to develop a cohesive argument, identify quality of evidence in a document, and interpret data in a table.*" The study also found that students graduating from prestigious universities have little to no improvement in their abilities to think critically.[132]

While higher education is not the focus of this book, one can imagine how much impact K-12 education has on students moving to their freshman year at a college or university. Because **we fail to lock down the basic foundations** of subject matter as we pump kids through the system to the next grade, they must struggle harder to succeed – or they fall behind or fall out.

Evidence suggests that high school seniors are not academically, mentally, or emotionally prepared for college.

———————— ♦ ————————

WHERE ARE WE HEADED?

The previous chapters have provided a solid backdrop of where we are headed **without** **fundamental foundational reformation**. I think we can safely say that we will always be faced with a crisis in education as long as our children are educated at the whims of whatever political and social forces are in control at the moment.

The rest of this chapter will examine the consequences of what we've read about so far.

After that, we'll touch on ways we can **reduce the bleeding** to try and slow down the decay of our public schools until we are ready to initiate a new model in education. We will also take a short look at some of the **alternate methods of education** that are being used today. This is a growing solution for many families, but is it what we need as a nation?

Then, in **Chapter 9** we will ask IF we can do better with what we have. Is there *really* no way to save the current system? Let's find out for sure before we give up.

———————— ♦ ————————

Part of the problem we faced for many years has been the push away from a "**meritocracy**" focus and towards "**equity education**" and "**equity economics**." As I write this book, there is a push to shift back towards meritocracy as but it will be a long road to get back to our roots in meritocracy in America.

The reason for bringing this up is that the movement away from meritocracy and towards equity was fundamental in leading us down the path of the "**lowest common denominator**" as we discussed in **Chapter 5**.

*If we are **not** raising people up based on merit and the challenge of competition*, the result will be that we must average down to level out to that lowest common denominator.

How does all this affect our current educational system?

- Students are presented with lower and lower expectations.

- They will be equalized so that all students have the same chance at success or failure.

- The brightest students are not given opportunities to expand their horizons and stretch capabilities.

- All students are averaged down to ensure **equal outcomes**.

- Discipline from authority figures is frowned upon as abusive, resulting in a loss of discipline applied and a growth in violence and abuse against authority.

- Teachers do not need to compete on merit and many will just plateau and stay at a level that is comfortable for them (whether it is good for the students or not).

- Excellent teachers will not be recognized or advanced and bad teachers will not be punished or removed.

Terminating this destructive pathway is part of the solution we will discuss in **Chapter 10**.

The previous rigors of a K-12 education have been dropped for a **soft touch and an inability to encourage excellence**. In fact, there is a push now for *"gradeless"* schools where teachers only provide subjective comments on work but no grades. The argument is that grades are abusive and somehow a symptom of systemic racism.

SCHOOL-TO-PRISON PIPELINE

This is nothing new, but the fact that it has not gotten any better over the years is telling of larger issues. The problem is particularly evident in the inner cities where violence, hatred for authority, and the prevalence of drugs have led to a large number of students hitting the prisons either while still in school or shortly thereafter.

It was originally theorized that suspending students for violent behavior resulted in them dropping out, getting arrested, and spending their lives in prison. The violent behavior was not the problem, some posited. The school's reaction to the violence was the problem.

As discipline from authority figures dissipated, the violence by students increased. The result is more students flowing through the school system straight to the prison system.

This cold conduit to prison needs to end
and the schools need to start preparing
our students to succeed, not fail.

Chapter 10 and **Chapter 12** address methods for discipline, security, and reducing violence in schools.

I do want to point out that ALL of this cannot be laid upon the schools. **Much of the blame belongs at home as well**. In particular, the rise of **Fatherless Homes** has reached epidemic levels. According to the Census Bureau, approximately **19.7 million children do not have active father figures** at home.

ONE in FOUR children live
without a father at home.

The poverty, health, and crime statistics for children who live in fatherless homes is shocking. I was not able to nail down a reliable single statistic for the *number of prison inmates who came from fatherless homes*, but **it seems to be as high as 70%**.

If we combine this with the loss of discipline, structure, and actual education in school we have a recipe for disaster. And it is only going to get worse in today's educational environment.

So, what does that have to do with our discussion? It brings us to the **chicken and egg dilemma**.

1. Are there more broken homes because schools are *not* preparing our children to be successful in life? OR...

2. Are broken homes making it impossible for students to succeed in school?

We can do nothing to *directly* prevent broken homes, so **I'll choose door Number 1. Chapters 10** through **12** lay out a plan for an educational system designed to **provide a success-focused education for all students**, no matter their socioeconomic position, race, color, or physical location. Education will **focus on life-success factors** and will be flexible enough that it could provide special structure or services for at-risk students, particularly those from broken homes.

If we do NOT do something to address this issue, **it will continue to be a self-perpetuating problem** that can only get worse.

TEACHER SHORTAGES

Teachers are bailing out of the system in larger numbers than at any other time in history. Part of this was COVID related, but that only aggravated an ongoing problem. Although the poll noted below was taken during the COVID period in 2022, it appears that *COVID has really just given many educators an excuse to leave*. The problems run much deeper than the pandemic.

According to a National Education Association poll, more than half of teachers *want* to leave the profession early.[133] This is more prevalent among minority teachers but the overall desire to leave is 55% for all groups.

DO ALTERNATE METHODS OF EDUCATION WORK?

It is clear from the previous sections that we are in an educational crisis. Our children are in crisis as well. So, what are we doing about it?

As we have seen, **band-aids will not work**. They may solve some specific problems for a limited time, but **they do not address the systemic brokenness that plagues our current public educational system**. They only push the can down the road for someone else to deal with later. Oftentimes, these band-aid solutions create other problems that endanger the system.

Until that happens, the only option available to parents is to pull their children out of the general population of public schools and embrace **Alternative Educational Schools**.

- Charter Schools
- Private Schools
- Homeschools
- Parochial Schools
- Online Schools

There are other alternative schools as well such as corporate-sponsored schools, Co-Ops, and more. *I know… you thought we were done with history*, but I want to touch on a tiny bit here. Before public schools, **children who were lucky enough to receive ANY education** were educated, instructed, or trained through a hodgepodge of arrangements.

- Church-supported schools (*with classes generally held at the church proper*).
- Tuition Schools set up by traveling schoolmasters.
- Local coop schools organized by towns and groups of parents for the good of the community.

- Charity schools for poor children, run by churches or benevolent societies (*intended to help poor children learn enough to benefit local businesses*).

- Boarding or Finishing schools that were only for children of the well-to-do.

- "Dame Schools" run by women in their homes.

- Private or home schooling done by traveling tutors.

- Work apprenticeships that included rudimentary instruction in reading, writing, and arithmetic.

These were generally arranged for the benefit of the community, <u>NOT for the benefit of the child</u>. For example, children were taught reading to better understand the Gospel and spread the Word. Businesses learned that children with *some* education tended to be better workers in the factories and workshops. Apprenticeships provided for cheap labor and any education provided was to make the child more useful to the tradesmen and companies.

———————— ◆ ————————

Fast forward to today and we see that, although education is *supposed* to focus on the child, the focus in today's public school system is more on making the child an obedient citizen for the greater good of society. **Where is the benefit to the child?**

That is where alternative education forms come in. Most alternates exist to focus more directly on the education and welfare of the child. Parents choose this path for many reasons:

- They can afford to choose a non-public path.

- They have lost faith in the public school system.

- They want a better education than they perceive they will get from public schools.

- They want a religious-based or less secular education.

- They have specific higher-education goals in mind.

- They are alumni of certain "connected" schools.

- They want a specific and more rigorous education for their children.

- They fear the violence, drugs, and bad influences in public schools.

Whatever the reason, the result is the parents want their child to receive an education outside of the traditional public-school environment. This trend has been growing in popularity over the past few years.

Does this solve our crisis in education? Unfortunately, NO.

First, not everyone has the money, time, transportation, or resources to choose an education outside of the public school system. Whatever it might cost them to choose an alternate method, **that is on top of what they are already paying to support the public school system**. And even though they are paying for the public schools, in most circumstances they are <u>not</u> allowed to make use of resources such as sports programs, gyms, pools, game fields, libraries, and more.

Second, many of the alternate education models are still reliant, dependent, and/or existent upon the whims of the government. For example, **Charter Schools exist at the discretion of the government**. If the government chooses to pull the plug on a Charter School, they can do so. See the Charter School discussion later in this chapter.

[*Sidebar*] ***Why do ALL schools need to be <u>independent of the government laws, regulations, and influence</u>?***

> This will be discussed in detail later, particularly in **Chapter 11**, but it is important to understand that government MUST be kept out of schools if those schools are to remain student-focused and parent-driven. It is hard to keep government out of schools entirely, but **ANY involvement by any government agency, power, or representative must be limited and controlled**. As we have seen, when the government has the purse strings and the legal authority to interfere with the schools, they **will** do so, *believing that they are doing a greater good.*

Consider this cautionary note. Because the government is not allowed by the U.S. Constitution to interfere with religion, **the Church is in essence a Free-Market Worship system of religious education**. Churches receive no government support, no government interference (*generally*), and are completely funded by the people who choose to participate.

The success of organized religion cannot be overstated. Most are well funded, some massively so, and they manage to do it without government control, mandates, or funding (*the exception being some tax breaks with caveats attached*).

If the government were allowed to "*help*" churches, they would immediately begin regulating, monitoring, assigning oversight, and delivering directives forcing diversity, equity, and inclusion (DEI) among other things. This "*help*" would be based on the whims of the government people in charge at any given time and would become more and more intrusive as time went on.

If education had the same protections as religion, our schools would be free of government influence and interference and could focus entirely on the welfare of students based on the desires of the parents. Unfortunately, it would take a Constitutional Amendment to provide directly delineated protections from the Government. That is not likely to happen in the foreseeable political environment.

However, we will learn later that, if we empower it, a **Free Market Educational system** would be free to operate by its own internal **Constitutional Protections** (**Chapter 11**) and **Guardrails** to prevent corruption and interference from corrupted government agencies. A significant portion of this book is dedicated to those protections... read on.

ALTERNATE SCHOOLS IN USE TODAY

There are incredibly wonderful and brilliant people out there working to provide and/or support an overwhelming world of school choices. Some of these are extremely effective, but we will focus on just a few to keep this book short (*I know, too late*).

Alternative schools are NOT the answer to educating all children, but I want to be clear that they hold a VERY important place in our educational environment now and **will continue to**

> Our reformed free market school ecosystem will partner with and share resources with alternate schools as part of their foundational charter of educating all children.

play a critical role in education after the foundational reformation proposed in this book is implemented.

Remember, we determined in our earlier discussions that there is a place for a public educational system in America, but **that does NOT mean it is the only place.** Just as it is today, not everyone will want to participate in the public school system, no matter how great it might be after reformation. They will seek out alternatives that address their personal needs and concerns.

Our new educational model should encourage, support, and provide assistance where needed and desired to all **education-positive** alternative educational systems.

> *After all, every educational system*
> *should have the same goal in mind…*
> *the education and success*
> *of ALL students.*

Our focus here is NOT which choices are the best ones, but primarily how they are affected by today's educational environment and how they might play into our reformed system. Let's start with one of the newest alternatives, Charter Schools.

CHARTER SCHOOLS[134]

The first Charter School was established in 1992 and there are now over 7,000 of these in the United States. Similar to typical public schools, Charter Schools are **free to attend** and are subject to many of the same government-driven rules as general public schools.

Consider Charter Schools a type of institutional hybrid. They differ in that they are independently run public schools that are focused by a "charter" to **obtain specific educational objectives.** These schools operate as a *"school of choice"* where the parents must submit an application to enroll their child. These schools are in demand and space is often limited.

So, what's the problem?

Charter Schools come very close to being the best of both worlds, but in the end, suffer from the primary failing of all public schools – they exist at the whim and control of government.

> *Charter Schools exist under the full control of multiple layers of government who can pull their charter to exist at any time.* **LOOK!**

In fact, the Department of Education and the federal government have been accused of *"waging war on Charter Schools"*. Many proposed regulations would tie funding to regulations issued by the prevailing government-of-the-day and give more power to people and organizations *outside* of the schools. One example of these proposed regulations would **provide regular public schools with veto power over any decision to locate a Charter School in their area**. Think *"monopoly"*.

Charter Schools are a great semi-alternative to public schools for that small percentage of students who have access to them. But they are NOT the answer to public schools.

PRIVATE AND PAROCHIAL SCHOOLS[135]

As we move outside of the government-funded public system, we come to Private and Parochial schools. These schools depend on their own funding (*tuition, grants, donations, endowments, etc.*). If associated with a religious organization, significant funding can come from there also.

However, as we move towards voucher systems from the state, we risk more and more conditions, caveats, and rules coming from government in order to continue receiving that voucher money. **When these private schools become dependent on government money**, it will be hard for them to step away and become independent again. It is the proverbial *slippery slope*.

Ignoring the voucher aspect, private and parochial schools have always been an enticing alternative to the public school system. As long as you have the resources to send your kids there. The cost for private schools range from $15,000 to $60,000 or more per year. Religious schools tend to be cheaper as they are substantially subsidized by the church, but still have tuition costs of $5,000 to $10,000 per year.

Even if you can afford it, **this is no guarantee of an indoctrination-free education**. Many of these schools failed at staying true to the mission of education and slipped into the realms of wokeness and indoctrination. The good news is that parents could choose to put their kids elsewhere if that happened. But where?

Parents do have more say here since **they are the customer of what is essentially a business**. They can take their children (and their money) to a competitor if the school doesn't deliver.

That's good for the parents who can afford it, but **this alternative only side-steps the public school system and leaves millions of children behind** in a failing system.

HOMESCHOOLS[136]

Before the introduction of compulsory public school attendance laws, most children who received *any* education were educated at home – either by the parents or by tutors. It is a proven method that is alive and well today.

Homeschooling should not be confused with the Public-School Virtual Learning that was forced on our children during the COVID pandemic. Virtual Learning in that context was still public education, but provided to kids at home over a computer by traditional public school teachers.

The COVID school shutdowns and virtual learning in the home were the **drivers for many parents getting involved** in schools again. They began attending more school board

> Interestingly, it was the COVID shutdown of schools that opened parents' eyes to the indoctrination and sexualization of their children.

meetings and **fighting for their children's rights and their right to be children**. Watching over their children's shoulders, parents finally got a glimpse into the secret world of what the schools were teaching their children.

And they did NOT like it!

Parents are now in a war to take back their children from an educational system gone wild. Refer back to **Chapter 6**, **The War on Parents** if you believe I am overstating this.

These events were the genesis for many changes during this period, but two massive movements in particular stand out.

1. A huge market boom in **EdTech** (**Educational Technology**). In particular. investment and growth in Virtual Learning programs/platforms and incorporation of AI has exploded.

2. A tremendous, sustained growth **spike in traditional Homeschooling**.

Homeschooling has maintained a strong and steady growth pattern for decades as an alternative to public schools. However, the shutdowns triggered an explosion in families choosing to homeschool rather than send their kids back to failing public schools. **The homeschooling population in the U.S. has tripled over pre-pandemic levels**.

Why are parents choosing the more difficult path of homeschooling?

- A total loss of trust in the public school system.
- To avoid indoctrination, sexualization, politicization, drugs, and other problems in the public schools.
- To focus their children's education on fundamentals of learning.
- Religious reasons.
- To provide flexibility in movement and travel.
- To spend more time with their kids.

- To provide a better education than the public schools are offering today.

- Simply because they want to.

Why do I tell you all of this? Because no matter what shape a reformed educational system takes, **homeschoolers will still be critical to the future of an educated America**.

Will homeschooling replace the public educational system? In a word, **NO**.

The majority of the general population will still prefer a public school system. However, **I envision a system that will partner with homeschoolers** and offer support, resources, and access to sports programs and facilities. After all, it's about education for <u>all</u> of our children, right?

———————— ♦ ————————

VOUCHERS AND SCHOOL CHOICE

There has been significant discussion and debate at all government levels in recent years about **Vouchers and School Choice to support certain alternatives to public schools**. This is great and would certainly help *some children*. I am all for that. The money should follow the child.

The problem as we have seen is that none of these alternatives do anything to fundamentally reform our current public educational system. Nothing will change in that system and millions of children will remain trapped in a substandard and dangerous environment that is focused on agenda, not on the best interests of the children or their parents.

Don't get me wrong. **Every kid we get out of the existing public educational system and into a real educational environment is a big win.** Yes, do all of that we can now. Save as many children from the system as we can.

But let's NOT kid ourselves into thinking that we are fixing anything. Long-term, the children left in the failing schools will still be left behind. A band-aid is just a band-aid.

———————— ◆ ————————

The real question becomes, *"If we continue on this path, how long will it take before we get to a point where recovery is nearly impossible?"*

These alternate methods of schooling do slow the bleeding a bit. **I wholly endorse any that are working for your children**. But I have to ask this: for the alternate schools that are succeeding much better than public schools (*and there are many*), why aren't we learning from that?

Why do we keep all of these alternate methods at arm's length? State and local governments even go so far as to say,

> *"Because **you chose to opt out** of the*
> *public school system you are paying for,*
> ***you cannot have access** to any resources*
> *in that public school system."*

Even though we still pay for everything in the public schools through our property taxes, *we* are not allowed to use any of those resources.

Where is the benefit to our children in that? **Is it even about the children any longer?**

Granted, most people who use alternative schools do not want anything to do with government funding and government-funded schools because they don't want government involved in the education of their children. As we have seen, they have valid reasons to be concerned.

———————— ◆ ————————

One last point on alternative schooling before we move on. We do not all agree on the purpose of education. We will examine some of the things we want out of education in **Chapter 9** and will see that parents do have different viewpoints on how their children should be educated and what they should be taught.

Disagreement is natural and healthy!

Because we disagree, and because all of our children are different and learn differently, **our current one-size-fits-all public educational system will continue to fail our children**.

Our current system cannot please all parents or all students. That is why these alternative systems are so popular. Those who are able or willing to make a choice will choose a system that works for them, not against them.

WHY DO WE ALLOW THE CRISIS TO CONTINUE?

> *"Children are not things to be molded, but are **people to be unfolded**."*
> —Jess Lair[137]

I love that quote. WHO will our children be if we **allow them to unfold themselves**, rather than forcing them into a mold of our making?

We made the assumption in **Chapter 3** that the majority of children will continue to attend some form of community funded K-12 public school system. More and more parents are opting out of public schools for other methods of education. Even so, **most parents in our society will remain with the public school system** because that is the *easiest path*, the *cheapest path*, and it is what we have always been taught is "*normal*."

If that is the case today and into the future, then I have to ask, *why haven't we done better*?

- Why do we accept the state of our public educational system as it stands today?

- Why haven't we learned from better systems and adopted **best practices** for our schools?

- Why haven't we implemented **true reform** that puts children and parents first?

- Why do we just accept it when educators say that children fully understand gender as early as 3 years old and where teachers use gimmicks such as a *"gender unicorn"* to teach very young children about all the various genders?

- Why do we allow the schools to teach our children beliefs such as that all white people are racist oppressors by nature and that people of color are all oppressed?

- *Can* we even do anything about any of this any longer?

Sadly, our educational system has NOT lived up to the standard of **American exceptionalism**. We treat our schools as just another **arm of the governmental body** rather than the frontline of education of our children.

In a country that was built on innovation, there has been no true innovation in one of our most important ventures – the education of our children.

On that note, let's move on to the next chapter where we examine *IF* we can do better.

- Is there hope?

- Can we do better *without* fundamental foundational reform?

- Are we going to leave all of these children behind in a failing system that we know cannot recover?

Let's find out!

CHAPTER

9

CAN WE DO BETTER?

Things to consider:

➤ Is it even possible for us to change?

➤ Why haven't we reformed before?

➤ Can't we just throw more money at it?

➤ What's different this time?

*"The greatest gift we can give our children are the **roots of responsibility** and the **wings of independence**."*

—Maria Montessori[138]

IS IT EVEN POSSIBLE TO CHANGE?

We have talked a lot over the last few chapters about how broken the system is... how *bad* the system is. Does that mean that we are doomed? That there is no hope at all?

Fear not, there is always hope!
We are Americans and have
overcome tremendous struggles.

The question for this chapter is to determine if we can rest any hope in retaining what we have now. i.e., Can we fix the current system **without** resorting to the extraordinarily difficult course of foundational reformation?

- Can we reverse the **mission creep** that has resulted in today's educational environment?

- Can we prevent more **corruption from outside forces**?

- Can we reverse the course of **indoctrination and sexualization** of our children?

Wonderful and dedicated people are working extremely hard to correct the failures in our behemoth educational system at this very moment. Some have been incredibly successful at doing this. They have accomplished great things.

BUT it always comes back to the fact that our public educational system (and many alternatives like Charter Schools) are beholden to a well-funded and powerful government, people, and organizations who have an *agenda other than the traditional education of our children*. No matter what our successes are, we are just moments away from having the rug ripped out from underneath us.

Homeschooling, *where tolerated*, is a successful alternative for educating without government interference. However, if you visit homeschool advocates such as the **Home School Legal Defense Association (HSLDA)**[139] and many state homeschool organizations,[140] you will see that there is a **constant battle going on to fight back government interference and regulation**.

> *The battle just to maintain the status quo*
> *is equivalent to death by a thousand cuts.*

Homeschooling is a perfect example of the effort and cost of **fighting back the monolith of government, politicians, associations, and well-funded individuals** in any effort to extract ourselves from the current educational system. HSLDA alone **spends many millions every year** in legal actions to protect homeschool families from government intervention and to advocate against anti-homeschool laws and regulations.

This battle is fought every day for most educational alternatives just to maintain ground. Sadly, the government has deep pockets that allow them to push indefinitely.

I know all that sounds very negative; my intention is not to sound apocalyptic. However, I wanted to be very clear about **the challenge that exists to maintain even the current state** of our educational system – much less try to improve it.

———————— ♦ ————————

ON A POSITIVE NOTE

As a result of the pushback from parents, conservative politicians, and other advocates, we are seeing some wonderful trends in the educational universe.

- **Downward Enrollment Trends in K-12**[141]
  We have seen **astonishing drops in public school enrollment** as many families opt for alternatives.

- **School Board Revolution**
  The pandemic pushed school boards into the public eye and parents did **not** like what they saw. **Uncaring and hostile school board members treated them like pariahs and**

criminals. Parents are getting more involved now and have taken many board seats.

- **School Choice Surge**

  As parents became more aware of the indoctrination, sexualization, and other challenges their children faced, the varied voices of school choice grow louder and louder every day. With the rise of **parents as a special-interest juggernaut**, pro-parent, school choice candidates grow stronger and the push for choice becomes bolder.

- **A Chorus of Voices**

  Not only are parents speaking out at school boards, but they are also organizing, coordinating, raising money, and learning. They have formed Parental Rights Groups, Political Action Committees, Associations, Forums, and other Outreach Groups focused on educating the public. They are a powerful block of citizens bent on forcing change and are now making their voices heard daily.

- **Political Winds**

  As I was writing this book, the wild winds of the 2024 elections blew through our country. What followed with the new administration in 2025 was a flurry of Executive Orders, administrative changes, and even actions to **eliminate the Federal Department of Education**. All great stuff, but at publication time all of this was all still up in the air and the final outcomes uncertain.

  One thing is certain though… Political winds will continue to blow in all directions and **none of this ensures lasting change** in our educational system. What will?

———— ◆ ————

If this pro-education movement continues to grow, as I expect it will, some great changes will be inevitable, and the growth of alternative schools will be quite impressive.

Unfortunately, **the underlying systemic problems will remain in public schools** as long as the vast resources of our government and the bottomless bank accounts of these associations and union exist. These improvements are only

emollients to make us feel better while the educational machine continues its march towards total domination of the system.

> *You may be wondering why I am addressing all of these <u>therapeutic actions</u> in a book about how to <u>replace</u> our public education system?*

The answer is simple. If we are to have any hope of lasting change, <u>we must fully understand in our hearts and minds</u> that **"band-aids" and "fixes" no longer work** for those children who must remain within our current educational system.

> We must understand that all the power, influence, money, and political investment in the current educational system *will not go quietly into the night*.
>
> It will never *"see the light"* and reform itself. It will **NEVER** bend into a system that is **forever** parent/child first.
>
> > *And what if the system did <u>bend</u> to our will? What then?*
>
> **What Then?**
>
> Do we just wait for the political winds to blow in the opposite direction again to corrupt the system... as it always has?
>
> **People in power have seen the potency of education** as an astonishing indoctrination tool that can mold generations of minds. They will not let go.
>
> We must **banish this educational system into the darkness of the past** and lead America into a new educational world that is focused on a generational success-oriented education for our children.
>
> We must build an educational system that **cannot be corrupted**. One that **cannot be influenced** by outside forces. And one that will **never use our children as political tools again**.

Chapter 11 explains how we can accomplish that permanence.

ATTEMPTS AT REFORM

K-12 education is arguably the **least-reformed institution in our great American experiment**. Since the establishment of the first American public school in 1635, we have done little to apply our exceptionalism and innovation to one of the most important obligations we have as a nation.

With over 300 years of American education under our belts, **we are not much beyond classrooms that were modeled to train industrial workers**. The biggest change is that the model is used now to train obedient servants of the state.

Additionally, most public schools still religiously follow long-abandoned agrarian cycles. The need for this practice passed long ago, yet we hold onto it because, *"that is the way it has always been done."*

> *We have abandoned even the pretense*
> *of innovation and evolution.*

Yes, we have added computers and a few other tools to the classroom. But they are simply bent to the way we have always done it. Just a new form of the same old thing.

Worst of all is the **one-size-fits-all approach** that we dutifully hold onto throughout the system, *and throughout every district no matter the socioeconomic makeup*. In fact, as we read in earlier chapters, **the current push towards "equity" and other imposed social constructs** forced us to dig our heels deeper and deeper into this one-size shoehorn philosophy.

Most changes that did make it into the system throughout the years amounted primarily to **band-aids held together with wads of taxpayer money**. This allowed various factions to lay claim to "fixing" or "improving" education.

REFORM ATTEMPT OF THE 1980S

Change of this scope is hard in the face of the **massive momentum of centuries of public educational history**. We have failed repeatedly at attempts for true reformation, but there was an interesting effort from the government in the 1980's to understand what the problem was and how they could fix it.

In 1983, the **National Commission on Excellence in Education**[142] produced a report titled, *"A Nation at Risk: The Imperative for Educational Reform"*.[143]

The Commission was established by the Secretary of Education, T.H. Bell. He had grave concerns that there was a *"widespread public perception that something is seriously remiss in our educational system."*

Doesn't that sound familiar? There are no viable recommendations in this report, but I do suggest reading it as they carefully lay out **contemporaneous educational concerns of 1983 that are unnervingly relevant today**... 40 years later.

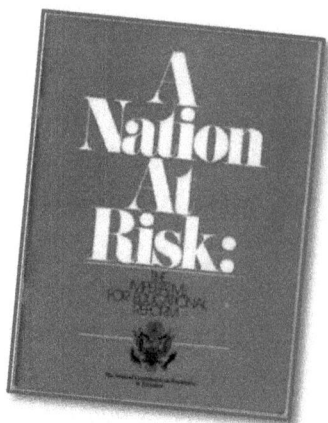

The **stated purpose** of the report was to identify and define *"the problems aflicting American education and to provide solutions."* They believed that the problems they identified could be corrected *"if the people of our country, together with those who have public responsibility in the matter, care enough and are courageous enough to do what is required."*

> Sadly, it seems that those who held public responsibility for the educational system were neither caring enough nor courageous enough to accomplish any real reform.

Even if they had enacted change – **without addressing the foundational problems** we have discussed here – I do not believe that they would have been successful in *permanently* reforming the educational system. If they had concluded with some actual reforms, it is likely that corruption and exploitation would have quickly overtaken the system again.

"Learning is the indispensable investment required for success in the 'information age' we are entering."
— "A Nation At Risk" (1983 Report)[144]

I was personally stunned by decades old list of "*educational dimensions*" documented from testimony given to the commission (copied below).

Remember that this was published in <u>1983</u>. 1983 Data

- *International comparisons of student achievement, completed <u>a decade ago</u>, reveal that on 19 academic tests, American students were never 1st or 2nd and, compared to other industrialized nations, were **<u>last</u>** seven times.*

- *Some 23 million American adults are functionally illiterate by the simplest tests of everyday reading, writing, and comprehension.*

- *About 13% of all 17-year-olds in the United States can be considered functionally illiterate. Functional illiteracy among minority youth may run as high as 40%.*

- *Average achievement of high school students on most standardized tests <u>is now lower than 26 years ago</u> when Sputnik was launched.*

- *College Board achievement tests reveal consistent declines in recent years in such subjects as physics and English.*

- *Many 17-year-olds do not possess the "higher order" intellectual skills we should expect of them. Nearly 40% cannot draw inferences from written material; only one-fifth can write a persuasive essay; and only one-third can solve a mathematics problem requiring several steps.*

- *Business and military leaders complain that they are required to spend millions of dollars on costly remedial education and training programs in such basic skills as reading, writing, spelling, and computation.*

Do you see now how dangerous it is to allow this to continue? The decline was in full swing well before the 1980s and <u>we have done NOTHING to stop the decline</u>, much less improve upon it.

We are Americans. We are supposed to lead the world in innovation, excellence, and the sciences. How appalling is it that these metrics came from a report in 1983! Why have we allowed this to continue?

Ah! Now that is the question, isn't it?

WHY have we done no better? I think we've seen that answer throughout this book. We have done no better because **there are powerful factions** that appear by all measures to want the system to remain dysfunctional. Why?

I could spit out numerous conjectures as to why, but a full exploration of that is beyond the scope of this book.

We only need to know that it IS, and that we need to find a way to **end this managed decline of American excellence**.

———————— ♦ ————————

Interestingly, **this report is a perfect example of why the government will NEVER succeed in a foundational reform of the educational system on its own**.

The commission did a decent job of identifying the problems. During interviews and testimony, they concluded that teachers were generally regarded (in 1983) as identical parts of an assembly line educational system that had not changed since 1958.

However, the commission failed
wretchedly in identifying any
actual solutions.

I was truly surprised at how *spectacularly governmental* their "findings" were. I had hope when I started reading the report, but that hope quickly faded when I realized that it was just the same old song and dance.

After more than **18 months of research** and **spending $785,000 in 1983 dollars**, these are some of the "findings" they arrived at (*note that there are a couple of decent thoughts, but most are terrible and none are solutions to the failing schools*).

Some Findings of the 1983 Report to Provide Solutions to the Problems in Education

- We conclude that declines in educational performance are in large part the result of disturbing inadequacies in the way the educational process itself is often conducted.

- We have a cafeteria style curriculum in which the appetizers and desserts can easily be mistaken for the main courses.

- The curricular smorgasbord combined with extensive student choice, explains a great deal about where we are today.

- Homework has decreased to less than 1 hour a night.

- The class time students in other industrialized nations spend in math and sciences is three times what American students spend.

- Only eight states require high schools to offer foreign language instruction.

- Students have too much freedom to choose their classes.

- Compared to other nations, American students spend much less time on schoolwork.

- Time spent in the classroom and on homework is often used ineffectively.

- Too few experienced teachers and scholars are involved in writing textbooks. The texts have been "written down" by the publishers to ever-lower reading levels.

- Expenditures for textbooks and other instructional materials have declined by 50% over the past 17 years.

- Teachers are not paid enough money and may need to supplement their income with summer employment.

Seriously, can we get our $785,000 dollars back? We'll even take it in 1983 dollars. Just make this insanity stop.

> Remember that the purpose of the report was to identify and define *"the problems... and to provide solutions."*

So now we have to ask if ANY of that was actually intended to solve the problems with education. Did any of those findings actually address the root challenges of the failing system?

Of course not!

There were <u>NO actual recommendations</u> in the report that I could find. Only the *"findings"* that *someone, somewhere* was supposed to *eventually someday* turn this information into some kind of *"action"*.

So, if we were to glean the intended *"solutions"* from <u>their</u> *"findings"*, those *"solutions"* to fix education would be:

1. Hire more teachers.
2. Pay teachers more money.
3. Throw more money at schools.
4. Give the students more homework.
5. Require more class time.
6. Do not allow students too much freedom in choosing their classes in high school.
7. Make all high school students take a foreign language.
8. Have more teachers write the textbooks and have the schools buy more of them.

What was the point of this exercise? Simply to demonstrate again that the government, particularly **the federal government, has no interest in changing the educational system** from what we have always had. That is why *they* must be removed from the equation of any true reformation.

MONEY IS ALWAYS THE ANSWER

Whenever we talk about *"fixing"* the schools, or reforming, or helping the students, the answer is almost always, *"We just need to spend more money."* *"If only we increased the budget more, we could fix everything."* All for the children, of course.

Money <u>seems</u> like the right answer, doesn't it? Simple. If something is broken, spend money to fix it. Right?

Well, it's not that simple. There are many more forces at play as we have seen throughout this book. Even if we were looking just at the money, we know it's not being spent for the children, but for the educational machine we have built.

All a politician or school board has to say is that "*it is for the good of the children,*" and we will spend the money. Where I live, I don't believe there has EVER been a school bond referendum that did not pass overwhelmingly.

Based on our increased spending over the years and the continued failure of our public educational system for generations, I think it is safe to say that...

More money does not equate to a better education.

This understanding is nothing new. Back in 1966, the National Center for Education Statistics[145] commissioned a report from James Samuel Coleman.[146] The "***Equality of Educational Opportunity***" report was commonly referred to as the ***Coleman Report***[147] and is still considered relevant in debates today.

Although their research was focused on equality, a major key finding of their research, **using over 650,000 students**, was that **school funding had *little* effect on student achievement**.

Below are a few relevant findings of the report related to funding. Keep in mind as you read these that **this report is from 1966** and was focused on racial equality of education.

- The report noted that a **significant gap in the achievement scores** between black and white children were already prevalent in the first grade.

- They determined that the differences in scores in each racial or ethnic group were **driven by one consistent variable** – the *educational* and *economic* attainment of the parents.

- The key factor that stood out for educational success was **the *attitude towards education* by the students, their peers, and their parents**.

- This informed their conclusion that **a student's background and socioeconomic status** was one of the most important determining factors in the educational outcomes of the student.

- They did find that quality of schools made a difference, but **the impact was negligible** compared to the other factors.

The KEY Factor was not money... it was the "*attitude towards education*" by the students, their peers, and their parents. I would expand that further to include the educational attitude of teachers and administrators.

We learned all of this 50+ years ago through a mass study, yet nothing has changed. The narrative is still twitching on the skeleton of **more money to fix the problem**. Per student spending increases EVERY year, yet the problems only get worse. I believe the report has proven itself – even 50 years later.

> ### *It is time to try a different pathway to success!*

With revelations in recent years from sources such as the Department of Government Efficiency (DOGE)[148], it has become clear that government cannot be trusted with Other People's Money (OPM). **Our government tends to forget that those dollars represent real dollars** that people worked hard to earn.

This is the case at federal, state, and local levels. It is easy to spend OPM. When there is a lot of it, people tend to spend very willingly with very few real checks and balances. Nowhere is there a more rampant example of this than in our government.

Our educational system is rife with waste, abuse, and maybe even fraud and payoffs in the guise of public service and "*for the children.*"

THE PRESCHOOL PROMISE PROGRAM

There are way too many examples, but for our purposes, we'll stick with just this one. This was so astounding that I doubted what I was finding but I'll do my best to interpret and summarize this as best I can. The Oregon Department of Education decided they were going to *help* low-income families access preschool. Their shiny new **Preschool Promise Program (PSP)**[149] launched in 2016 was designed to publicly fund (state-level) preschool to families at or below 200% of the federal poverty limit.

Sounds like a very worthy effort, doesn't it? But as with most government efforts, insanity quickly set in.

The essence of the program was that the state would award slots to expensive childcare facilities that would then be kept available for preschoolers of families below the poverty limit. The state would then pay these facilities approximately $14,000 per year to hold those slots open just in case any qualifying family wanted to use the facility at state expense. This is paid **whether any child used the slot or not**.

Do you begin to see where this could go wrong? Imagine for a moment what would happen if these childcare centers didn't fill those state-held slots? Well... we'll just call it wasting a lot of taxpayer money. They however like to call it *"an unfortunate side-effect of the funding model."*

The program is still active today and there are continuing reports of mismanagement within the PSP. But let's step back just a bit and look at reported numbers for school years 2020-2021 (year-1) and 2021-2022 (year-2) – a fairly recent **2-year span**.

- Oregon awarded approximately **$90 Million** dollars to childcare centers over this 2-year period.

- At ~$14,000 per seat HELD, that amounts to about **6,428 seats** held and paid for over the 2 years.

- ~**2,100** students were enrolled in the PSP program in year-1 and ~**3,300** were enrolled in year-2. For a total enrollment of ~**5,400** students.

- That left **~1,028 seats empty**. Paid for, but empty.
    - By my math, that looks like **$14,392,000** for seats that were never used.
    - It gets worse when you break it down to certain centers.

- One childcare center was awarded $600,000 dollars over the 2-years. During that time, they reported <10 students in the program. **Cost <u>per student</u> to the taxpayers = >$60,000 each**.

- Another center was paid approximately $224,000 dollars. They reported just TWO students enrolled. **Cost <u>per student</u> to the taxpayers = $112,000 each**.

- Yet another center was paid about $818,000 dollars. They reported just 10 students enrolled. **Cost <u>per student</u> to the taxpayers = $81,800 each**.

$520,000 per Student

- And the grand award winner was paid about $520,000 dollars. They reported **NONE** in year-1 and **ONE student** enrolled in year-2. If my math is correct, the **cost per student to the taxpayers = $520,000 each**.

- And the list goes on and on.

I'm sure that preschooler who got the **$520,000 dollar seat** received an **AMAZING education**. After all, *if more money equals a better education*, that kid should do well in life. Right?

How did Oregon justify this? Apparently, they wanted to hold the seats just in case and *they could think of no other way to manage the program* to eliminate the waste. Right off the top of my head, the simplest fix would be to **require a cutoff date for enrollment and a subsequent award adjustment**. \/ *See below*.

You see, the biggest insanity of all of this is that the childcare centers who were being paid for these slots were **required by law to hold those seats open** for program users. Often **<u>the centers had to turn away PAYING parents</u>** to hold empty slots for these Preschool Promise students – **even when those students never materialized**. An enrollment cutoff date would resolve that.

> ***This insanity was driven by the usual***
> ***government spending theology pumped up on***
> ***steroids to spend Other People's Money with***
> ***ZERO market sense or oversight.***

I am not sure if any of this has been corrected by the time you read this, but if you are a glutton for punishment, you can visit the **Oregon Office of the Auditor**[150] and dig through their audits of educational programs to learn more. However, I think I've made my point here.

———— ♦ ————

That was only ONE example of many that are easily found. The point is that the powers that be insist that *the only solution is more money*, yet they do nothing to ensure your money is audited, cared for, and used to educate children properly.

WHAT DO WE WANT OUT OF OUR SCHOOLS?

> *"True education reveals self-potential, more than just sows ideas." "In school we learn to think alike, but true education is to learn how to think differently."*
> —Toba Beta and Debashish Mridha

We have talked a lot about what is wrong with our educational system, but we have *not* really taken a deep dive into the "*Quality of Education*" portion of the equation.

I believe this continuing **decline goes hand-in-hand with the introduction of institutionalized politics, agenda promotion, sexualization, and propaganda infiltration that has yanked the focus away from a classical education**.

We will focus intently on building in quality of education in **Chapters 10-12**, but first, we need to have a solid idea of what we believe "*quality of education*" means.

———— ♦ ————

As we get closer to a reformation solution, we must understand what it is we **actually want** out of our schools *if* we are successful in fundamentally reforming the system.

We will never agree.   LOOK!

The one thing we can be sure of is that **ALL parents will NEVER agree as to EXACTLY what a perfect education looks like**. However, we can come up with an *Educational Framework* (**Chapter 10**) that the system must operate within and set up *Guardrails* (**Chapter 11**) that will prevent us from straying away from that Framework. Within that, the schools can provide numerous offerings that will allow parents and students to focus their education into exactly what the student needs.

The next several subsections relate general thoughts, concepts, and methodologies on what a more **student-centered** and **parent-driven** education of excellence would incorporate. This is not an exhaustive list. Nor is it THE list. But it is a start to the Framework and Guardrails we will examine as we move into **Chapters 10-12**.

Here are a few **very high-level concepts** to prime your mind for what a true American education should look like.

- Students should be prepared to **experience and take advantage of American life** – no matter what their socioeconomic background looks like.

- They should be prepared to **move into career, college, and/or parenthood** – whichever they choose.

- They should be **taught to TRUTH** – the good, the bad, AND the ugly – no matter how painful.

- We should help children understand the **greatness of America** and **to love their home and their people**.

  - **No country in the world other** than the U.S. teaches their public-school children to hate their country and despise their fellow countrymen.

This is Weird....

- Teach them to love the **United States Constitution** – a document so powerful that it has held together a fractious and tumultuous country for 250 years.

- Teach them to **think critically**, to **think for themselves**, and to **question authority**.

- Teach them that **they CAN succeed** in America – no matter their background, race, color, religion, or orientation. The pathway is to want it, work for it, earn it, and sometimes even sacrifice for it.

- Teach them to **love themselves** and **respect all others**.

- Give them the **tools to connect with people**, to engage with each other, to create together.

- Teach ALL children that **they are NOT victims**, downtrodden, irreparably oppressed, forgotten, or lost. They are ALL valued citizens of our amazing society.

- Focus on developing a **positive and enthusiastic relationship with learning** and seeking out truth.

- Promote **positive** and **productive engagement** with the community, businesses, and organizations that surround them.

If we refocus education on truth, a positive outlook on life, a love of learning, and student success, much of the rest will take care of itself. Remember the findings of the **Coleman Report**…

A <u>Key Factor for Educational Success</u> is
the attitude towards education by
students, their peers, and their parents.

———— ♦ ————

PARENT-DRIVEN EDUCATION

In **Chapter 6** we took a deep dive into the **War on Parents**. We learned that many educational organizations have determined that **parents are an impediment to the mission and objectives** of those driving the educational agenda.

There are endless examples on the Internet of how parents' rights are viewed by our educational system. Here is just one.

A member of a School Board stated on Facebook:

> *"The purpose of a public ed is not to teach kids what parents want. It is to teach them what society needs them to know. The client is not the parent, but the community."*[151]

Of course, the first question that always comes to mind is **WHO** gets to decide *"what society needs them to know"*?

Parents were rightfully outraged. This came from an elected School Board member who was supposed to represent the parents who elected them. When the pushback was loud enough, the School Board Member then posted what in my opinion is a condescending clarification that read in part [*emphasis mine*]...

> *"What it says is that public education is an ecosystem. Our community is the <u>collective</u> for which it* [public education] *exists. Not for any one parent, any one student, or any one person, but rather for us all. <u>The only agenda</u> of public education is to educate everyone, <u>for the benefit of everyone.</u>"*

I'm not sure which is more telling of the state of educational thought, the original post OR the follow-up clarification.

Let me be absolutely clear on my stance. Public education can NOT be a tool of government to develop common-thought citizens for *"the collective"* or *"for the benefit of everyone"*. We are not bees living in blind support of our Education Queen. We are individuals who will choose different paths, different ways, and have different thoughts. THAT is what made America so amazing – individualism, *not* homogeny.

Most parents don't want their children to be raised as part of the *"collective"*. **They want them to be the best individuals they can be.**

One of the primary objectives of a reformed educational system must be to **return the mission and objectives of education to the parents**. Parents must determine what is in the best interests of *their* children. *However*, **some caution is warranted**.

As I stated earlier, *all* parents will never agree on exactly what a great education looks like. That is why we need the framework and guardrails coming up in the next few chapters.

> *Parents' voices must not only be heard, but they must also have effective influence over what an Education of Excellence looks like.*

In our reformed educational ecosystem, parents will have a voice that can be heard, and they will have influence on the objectives of the schools. BUT → *for reasons that will become obvious later in this book*, **they may not have direct control of the specifics** of the educational system. Parents must have influence; visibility into the system; the ability to choose schools, programs, and course focus for their kids; and to vote with their dollars, safeguarding their ability to ensure **THEY control the trajectory of *their* child's education**.

———————— ◆ ————————

STUDENT-CENTERED EDUCATION

Students want what they've always wanted... to succeed and be prepared to step out into the world and start their own lives. Unfortunately, in today's educational environment, many may not think that is the case. They are focused through culture, indoctrination, and peer pressure to push back against education and treat it as counter to their desires.

This attitude is heartbreaking to those on the outside and self-destructive to the children on the inside. Anger and rejection of family and societal norms are understandable considering everything that our children face in today's educational environment (*see every page of this book*).

The disappointment is not just for those students who are pushing back, but also for those who truly WANT a useful education. They are stuck within **a system that seems to stifle their growth and suppress success at every turn**. It will take more than just fixing the STRUCTURE of education.

> *A correctly structured educational ecosystem*
> *must be accompanied by a*
> <ins>*CULTURE of Educational Excellence!*</ins>

We need to work culturally to **develop a positive ethos towards education** in parents, children, educators, teachers, administrators, community, and everyone who is engaged in the **educational ecosystem**. *But can we possibly do that?*

Part of the solution is focusing on students and their real needs. We must move away from the emphasis on agenda-driven programs calculated to "*help*" students further that same agenda. We must focus on helping students understand and believe that **they all have value within themselves**, that **society values them**, and that **there is value in society <ins>FOR</ins> them**.

It will not be easy considering how far down the social wasteland we have gone. **It might even take generations of success** in some societal environments to prove that this is the right path before it is accepted and promoted by those with the most external influence on children.

Chapter 14 and **Chapter 15** provide some focus on engaging family, church, community, business, and other societal elements in this positive growth for all children. **Chapter 12** provides guidance on delivering a student-centered education.

———————— ◆ ————————

A CULTURE OF ASPIRATION

You may remember our previous discussion about **Dunbar High School** that "Aspiration" is an important element of education. This ties directly into our discussions about a **student's desire to gain an education** being a **critical factor** for success.

In his **Rooftop Revelations,**[152] Pastor Brooks (from **Chapter 4**) noted that we had lost our connection to aspiration in the 1960s and began the move towards a culture of dependency that is still prevalent today.

> *Aspiration drives self-growth,*
> *whereas dependency stifles*
> *self-worth.*

Attitude!

This further circles us back to the **Coleman Report** findings that *"attitude towards education"* is a **Key Factor for Educational Success**. It does not matter how much we reform the educational system if it is not accompanied by a **Culture of Aspiration by the students** and a **Culture of Educational Excellence by all stakeholders in the system**.

Without those two elements, the system will decay and devolve over time. It would still be better than what we have today, but it cannot reach the full potential of what an educational system is capable of without those elements.

———— ◆ ————

A CULTURE OF LEARNING VS. A CULTURE OF KNOWING

To fully capitalize on the Culture of Educational Excellence we discussed above, we also need to develop a *"**Culture of Learning**"*, as opposed to a *"**Culture of Knowing**"*. The difference may seem subtle at first, but it is a foundational concept that makes all the difference in taking us to the next level of our educational adventure.

I'm going to get a bit into the weeds for a moment, but I believe **this concept is core in transforming our to-be public school system** into a powerful educational experience for every child in the system.

The following table compares some of the high-level elements of the difference between a "**knowing education**" and a "**learning education**".

KNOWING	LEARNING
➢ Taught a version of **facts**.	➢ Taught to **think critically** and **challenge** unsubstantiated claims.
➢ Taught **what** happened.	
➢ Provided a **timeline**.	➢ Provided topics and **given parameters** for learning.
➢ Told **what to think** about it.	
➢ Instructed to **respond with these facts** and serialized information.	➢ Provided facts sourced from **different viewpoints**.
	➢ Taught how to **question the facts** and dig for the how and why.
➢ Rewarded for "**correct**" **answers** that match the information provided.	
➢ Rewarded for **memorization**, not analysis.	➢ Rewarded **for unique responses** or **challenges** to "known" information.
We know things, but does that translate into success in life? Does it help us grow, evolve, and prosper?	*Learning mindset allows us to adapt to changes in what we know and what we don't know. We expand and grow.*

What we have now is, of course, the culture of knowing. Children are taught from textbooks page-by-page and are expected to memorize the chosen highlighted information as directed by the educator. Testing demonstrates that **we "know" these directed things and can repeat them back.** How many times did our teachers tell us, *"This will be on the test"*? How does that help our personal growth?

Knowing only means that *we know stuff.* How we understand it, build on it, and use it is what makes the difference. We must learn beyond what we are told. There are many potential ways to incorporate a Learning Culture into our educational system.

- Make "learning" itself a **skill** as part of the student's personal success toolkit.

- School and homework should include researching multiple sources outside of the classroom textbook.

- Encourage students to ask questions and challenge responses that are unsubstantiated.

- Textbooks should be a guide for self-learning, not a recitation of single-viewpoint facts.

- When "facts" collide and contradict each other, challenge the children to analyze sources, viewpoints, and veracity. Then have them logically debate one side or the other if they cannot be reconciled.

- Frequently challenge children to learn something new outside of their schoolwork and potentially present or teach that learning to the class.

- Grading is important, but we should also promote competition among the students to compete in their learning skills. Possibly competitive identification of "Most Interesting Facts", "Most Conflicting Facts", "Providing Proofs of Actual Misinformation", etc.

- Promote student's maintenance of a learning diary and learning goals.

- Most importantly, Teachers must be trained to understand the difference between knowing and learning. They must understand at a fundamental level how to integrate a culture of learning into every curriculum and every class.

Given the chance, **we are learning creatures**. Unless stifled, we are always seeking to evolve our understanding of the world around us. If we **give our children the ability and desire** to constantly learn and grow as is their nature, they will be capable of doing so much more than they are doing in our current educational environment.

Today's education mill is designed to pump enough "knowing" into children's minds to allow them to pass **the next test**, then **the next grade**, then **pass out of school**. This one-way road fosters **memorization and movement** through the system, but not expansion of the mind.

——————— ◆ ———————

WHAT HAVE WE LEARNED?

"It is nothing short of a miracle that modern methods of instruction have not yet entirely strangled the holy curiosity of inquiry."
—Albert Einstein, 1949

Albert Einstein **captured** the problem with how we approach education way back **in 1949**. None of this is new. What is new is the **acceleration and implementation of propaganda and indoctrination** applied to children in United States.

The children of China, Russia, North Korea, and other socialist, communist, and despotic states have faced this for many decades. These tools of educational domination are necessary to keep the population in lockstep with the collective and unquestionably loyal to the leadership of those countries. Without **the weapon of education in hands of these nations**, they could not remain in power as long as they have.

That is the **political aspect** of the message I have been addressing throughout this book, but the bigger picture is, well… so much bigger.

> ***We must ensure that our children learn to think for themselves so they can never be mentally enslaved through the application of these weapons.***

Weaponized Education

Chapter 10 will begin our discussion on an approach to fundamental foundational reform of our educational system. Before we jump to the solution though, we should do a quick recap of what we've learned over these last nine chapters.

It is important to pull it all together so that **we have a firm grasp of WHY this must be done.** It's not enough to know that something is bad and that it should be replaced. **We need to understand deep in our psyche that a fundamental,**

foundational change MUST happen if we are to avoid going back to the same old ways. This is an important point...

Changing the system will mean nothing
if we do not also implement controls to
PROTECT the system from corruption.

With that in mind, let's do an level-set recap of what we've read so far. This will ensure we are ready to absorb the next chapter.

Chap.	Title	Important Takeaways
1	A Pesky Little Premise	In **Chapter 1** we discovered that formal public education began in 1635 and has not fundamentally changed since that time. We also learned that this is not intended as a "political" book, but as a guide to how we can apply our exceptionalism to our educational system. **My ask of you was to read this book with an open mind** and an absolute belief that we can do better for our children and our society.
2	Why Read This Book?	By now you should have a decent understanding of WHY we need "**Fundamental Foundational Reformation**" of K-12. We learned that band-aid solutions only stem the bleeding, but do not resolve structural systemic problems. We also learned that education is a natural element of survival, and that growth of the collective body is fed by learning-to-learn and passing on true knowledge and experience. **My ask of you** was to step back and reimagine how we can do this.
3	How to Read This Book (*This is an important chapter. Please go back and review if necessary*)	We made some assumptions that were necessary to keep focused on the mission. No matter your feelings on these issues, I asked you to **temporarily accept these assumptions** so that you could keep that open mind we talked about earlier. **Important Assumptions**: • A major fundamental reformation is needed. • "Community Schooling" is necessary. • Some form of taxation is currently necessary to help support any form of public education. • We as a society want to retain some form of social and extracurricular activities in the schools.

Chap.	Title	Important Takeaways
		Our children's futures are their fortunes, so I had a couple of asks for you here. • Remain open to the possibilities of reform. • Apply Critical Thinking and fairly Challenge everything I have presented. • But temporarily <u>assume it CAN be done</u>. • Quit stressing over "*how*". Our greatness is to recognize something needs to be done, determine to do it, THEN figure out what to do to accomplish it. Much of the *what* and *how* is described in the chapters that follow.
4	A History of Public Schools	***When man understood that a sense of history and future <u>created a sort of collective immortality</u>, everything changed – the age of education had begun.*** The freedom to learn is critical to our growth as a society. **Chapter 4** dove into a bit of history to understand how our issues have existed since the dawn of American education. We also learned more about why **we cannot "<u>fix</u>"** what exists today and that only foundational reformation will provide lasting change.
5	Current state of Public Schools	We explored today's educational system and what the real purpose of education is. We also defined "**core academics**" and explored nine high-level success goals. This chapter also explored the **21 steps to failure** of a community through failure of the schools. Finally, we examined the government's role in public education.
6	Suffocating the Sacred Fire	We built a factual conclusion that the systemic problems are so ingrained that the system **cannot be "fixed"**. It must face death and rebirth in order to bring about fundamental foundational reform. This chapter addressed politicization of the school system, school boards, unions, associations, and other external influences on local schools. Finally, we explored "**The War on Parents**".
7	Transforming Society One Child at a Time	This chapter took a deep dive into the social engineering that drives our educational system. Rather than focusing core academics as the primary function of the schools, the focus has been on the **deconstruction of classical**

Chap.	Title	Important Takeaways
		education. Our schools have become **Homogenized Education Factories** that focus on whatever the current social agenda is as the schools de-individualize and equalize the students. **The self is sacrificed for society**.
8	Crisis in Education	We discussed how the U.S. educational system dramatically fell in rank on the national stage. We used to rank #1, **now we rank 15th to 30th against the 35 industrialized nations of the world**. Obviously, something is fundamentally wrong. We examined the school-to-prison pipeline, teacher shortages, alternative methods of education, and asked the question, "*Why do we allow this crisis to continue?*"
9	Can We Do Better?	This is the chapter you are reading now. We explored if it was even possible for us to change. Is the system too big to even consider the possibility? Previous reform attempts failed. Why? What can we do differently? Finally, we looked at the pathways to make this reformation work. Which brought us to this handy little recap table.
10	The Great Education Reset	THE NEXT CHAPTER. This is where the real fun begins. The previous chapters walked us through the *why*, but **Chapter 10** finally gets to the *what*. Enjoy!

It has been a long journey getting here, but each step was critical. Don't forget the **Assumptions** and **Asks**.

FINALLY... WHAT IS THE ANSWER?

> "*A true education opens the mind and lets us see the world with wonder and joy. It teaches us to accept change with love, and it teaches us to be harmonious with humanity and nature. If any education teaches us to close our minds, to accept dogma, and to violently inhibit questioning then that is not an education. **That is a prison for the mind**.*"
>
> —Debasish Mridha[153]

The answer is that we must do ***something***. However, that something must necessarily address all of the issues we've discussed in the previous chapters. **AND it must be inviolate!**

That is a tall order. Seemingly insurmountable.

But we are Americans and have proven that we can do what we determine to do. We have made great strides in the last few years to insert parents back into the equation. In response, parents were silenced, assaulted, arrested… and yet they persisted.

One of the most important changes parents accomplished recently was taking back some School Board seats across the country. Not enough to help all kids, but many.

In one incident a Washington state teacher stated publicly that we need more guidelines and laws in schools to **hide information from parents** about their children. Reasoning? ***Because students are not safe in this nation from Christo-Fascist parents***. Those parents filed FOIA requests to find out what this teacher had been saying and promoting to their children.

Then they stood up and made their voices heard. In response, the educational machine pushed back. Hard!

The point is that as soon as parents step back, quit pushing, and become complacent again, the external forces driving indoctrination and other failures will move into the vacuum. **They will seek out weakness** and drive parents farther back into the darkness. Then the endless cycle will begin again.

None of this is meant to knock parents at all. Most just want to live their lives, raise their children, and prosper as a family. They don't necessarily want to fight any of these battles, but **they are desperate to help their children**. When the perceived danger has passed, they will return back to their lives. *As it should be.*

Unfortunately, we must return to our earlier discussion about the **drive for power**. Some people (*frequently not parents*) seek ever more power and control over our educational system. Those people are relentless, and they now have endless funding behind them. They are also supported by organizations and Federal entities that push for results. They do not sleep.

———— ♦ ————

HOW? If we do find a solution for our schools, the problem becomes, *"How do we keep it?"*

We have used Charter Schools, Private Schools, Vouchers, School Choice, and more to try and fix the problems. But they all have **one common failing**.

Those Exit Solutions do nothing to help the children left behind. The solutions we have tried are just band-aids and have <u>*NO GUARDRAILS*</u> *to prevent the infection from returning.*

Internal and external forces will continue to dig their tendrils into the system through law, legislation, and influence to corrupt the schools for their own purposes. They are too powerful and have too much influence in the public and private sectors.

Chapter 10 provides a different solution to our educational dilemma, but even it is susceptible to corruption from those seeking power over your children. That is why our shiny new educational system must be operated under an inviolate **Education Constitution** that protects the system just as the U.S. Constitution protects the very core of what makes America so amazing.

Chapter 11 provides the Framework and Guardrails needed to protect our system for generations to come.

———— ♦ ————

And with that, ladies and gentlemen, I present to you a bold solution to help the children of coming generations reach their full potential.

10

THE GREAT
EDUCATION RESET

Things to consider:

➢ Are we ready to be Bold?

➢ Will you agree with the solution?

➢ Is the country ready?

➢ Can this possibly work?

"Education is the most powerful weapon which you can use to change the world."
—Nelson Mandela[154]

INTRODUCING THE "FREE MARKET SCHOOL"™ (FMS) SYSTEM

The **American Dream** has always been the siren call for opportunity and exceptionalism heard throughout the world. Yet fully experiencing it may be beyond the grasp of many of America's children. The disconnect is the lack of a proper education that provides them with the **critical thinking skills, desire to learn, and the mental tools they need** to endure that sometimes long road.

Which is why we are here finally. **Thank you** for exploring the long road through this book to arrive at the payoff for your effort. Before we get to the main course though, we have just a small bit of housekeeping.

- **IMPORTANT!** **You will NOT agree** with everything I propose. That is okay, but please do not let that deter you from exploring the concept as an initial framework that will evolve over time.

- **Do NOT get hung up on exactly HOW** we will do it. I am proposing **WHAT** should be done. If enough people accept that this CAN and SHOULD be done, the actual HOW will be developed by people much smarter than me. My hope is that they will start with this framework as a guide and incorporate guardrails as, or more powerful than, the ones I propose.

Our forefathers were brilliant men who risked everything for a vision. We can do no less for our children. **Let this be our vision. Let this be *our* legacy to them.**

———————— ◆ ————————

THE GREAT EDUCATION RESET

What if, like a great artist, we could **reimagine our public schools**? Although we have a concept for what we want to do (*our framework*), we need to start with a clean blank canvas and imagine what may reside there when we are done. We won't fully know it in totality when we begin putting brush to palette. **The art and the beauty will be in the individual strokes.**

Let's start the masterpiece with a few *"what if's"* to **build our mind's eye picture** of what we imagine we will paint.

- What if we were able to **fully fund** public schools while removing government influence and control from the equation?

- What if we were to take the "School Choice" concept one step further and provide "**Program Choice**" structured *within* the broader public-school structure and ecosystem?

- What if there was **competition** between and within schools to offer the best educational programs?

- What if competition drove **Teacher Excellence** and pay levels?

- What if we could offer students **incentives** for better performance?

- What if schools could be more **localized** to represent the needs and desires of local parents and students?

- What if we could **lower the cost** of public education while improving performance and effectiveness?

- What if private schools, parochial schools, and home schools could **interact with the public schools** to the benefit of all students WITHOUT the potential for government intrusion?

Those are just the broad strokes of a Free Market System for public education. At first glance, you might think the **Free Market School**™ (**FMS**) is just a different version of "**school choice**" or an "**alternative school**". This solution is far beyond those concepts.

The FMS entirely replaces the current public school system with a publicly funded (*initially*) **system of competitive-approach education**. We take full advantage of the best things we have learned about the free market and create a competitive education environment that is **free from internal and external influence and corruption**.

Some organizations have been exploring the concept of free market schools. I applaud their work, but all that I have encountered – *especially those that incorporate government funding* – do NOT address the issue of influence from local, state, and federal governments. Nor do they address concerns about external organizations (associations, unions, school boards, etc.) and their power and influence within the system.

To accomplish a truly fundamental foundational reform of our educational system, all of these entities must be **strictly restrained by inviolate guardrails** (see **Chapter 11**).

In every instance from around the world (Australia, the Netherlands, and Chile for example) where the government has funded private and parochial schools directly or through contrived mechanics such as school choice, vouchers, or other methods, those schools were required to adhere to substantial guidance, regulations, standardized curriculum, and other restrictions by the government to keep that funding. **All of these regulations and restrictions are at the whim of the government of the moment**. In other words, *what we are seeing today in America.*

There are nearly 14,000 school districts with over 100,000 public schools in the U.S. serving more than 45 million students. Needless to say, **this is a massive endeavor that cannot be turned on a dime**. At every step, the pushback from the established **educational industrial complex** will be relentless and powerful. That pushback will become a tidal wave of obstruction and denial as the system becomes more and more successful and prevalent.

Have heart… there is a pathway. It will be challenging, but we have faced bigger challenges throughout the history of our great nation. The following **Mission Roadmap** lays out what we are going to learn in the next few chapters.

Chap.	Mission Roadmap – What You Will Learn
10	This chapter lays out *what* **the FMS is** and how it works. It also defines the terms we will use throughout.
11	The heart and soul of the FMS ecosystem is the **Education Constitution**. These are the guardrails we talked about.
12	**WHY** do we have to save the children in public schools? Who would want to go through this?
13	How in the world do we **PAY for this**? We explore the possibilities and look at different funding models.
14	**How do we START** this massive undertaking? The journey begins with a single step, and just we keep walking.
15	How **we partner with communities and businesses** to engage and develop cooperation and alliances is critical.
16	Once we transition to FMS education, what does it look like. What does the **future world of FMS** look like?
17	Lastly, we **explore the Next Steps** and how we work towards this future.

One caution to the reader as we move forward:

Don't Try!

Don't even try to guess the totality of this before you get to the end.
You will likely come up short of what is proposed.
BUT I do welcome comments and feedback after you finish!

From the ashes of our Government Schools, a new and glorious model will be born that can turn away all attempts of the status quo to reinsert itself. This newborn public school system will be clean and untarnished by the stain of all we have read to this point.

WHAT IS A "FREE MARKET SCHOOL"?

"Indeed, a major source of objection to a free economy
is precisely that it... **gives people what they want**
instead of what a particular group thinks they ought to
want. *Underlying most arguments against the free*
market is a lack of belief in freedom itself."
                                            —Milton Friedman[155]

A true free market is an economic system based on supply
and demand with little or no government control. Free
markets are characterized by a spontaneous and
decentralized order of arrangements through which
individuals make economic decisions. A free market is one
where voluntary exchange and the laws of supply and
demand provide the sole basis for the economic system,
without government intervention.
                              —Derived from Investopedia.com.[156]

Generally, a free-market system refers to an "economic" free market system. **Which is accurate in our case as well**. K-12 education is no less a product/service than a college education is. The difference is that our current public school system runs as a **government monopoly** with minimal competition and little to no accountability to the public. After all, public schools are assured of funding and endless customers regardless of performance.

Conversely, our **FMS will be driven by open competition, continuous innovation, and continuous improvement**. Something the current monolithic system is incapable of. A universe of school units (*Providers*) would compete for students by offering various competitive curriculum, teaching methods, goals, and ideologies.

Their prize? Parents and students can now chose their school and specific programs based on *their* needs and desires.

Parents would select the physical school, but also the schools within the schools to reach certain goals for their children. They could **choose the focus and philosophy of the curriculum** and much more.

As should be clear by now, this will take a fundamental foundational change from the ground up. This will be necessary to end the current **homogenized education factory**.

Unfortunately, we can be quite confident that the entrenched system that has endured for so long **will not allow for coexistence of Free Market Schools in their territory**. The war for our children will have actually begun.

I imagine I have created significantly more questions in your mind than answers at this point. Consider that an **Executive Summary**. Now, let's get into the meat of the proposition.

———— ♦ ————

ENTREPRENEURIAL APPROACH TO EDUCATION

In very simple terms, **FMS works by fully integrating competition into the system and bringing the elements of education closer to the end user**. As we walk through this, keep in mind that this is but one permutation of the many ways this could be put together. No matter what possibilities you consider, keep this one **Golden Rule** as gospel in every decision.

LOOK!

GOLDEN RULE
The system itself MUST ensure that there is NO possibility that internal or external influence or corruption can manipulate that system.

LOOK!

Both the **framework** and **guardrails** are discussed in detail later, but both are critical to ensuring a long-lasting system capable of fighting off attacks from those who have an agenda or seek more power within the schools. The **Education Constitution** discussed in detail in **Chapter 11** is the heart and soul of the entire endeavor. If any corruption is allowed in the system, it could degrade and drift back to what we have now.

That cannot be allowed!

Discussions abound throughout the knowledge-verse on how to make our educational system better. Some are good, some are really, really bad. As you read through the details below, you may recognize some of the better elements that are incorporated within FMS. You will likely imagine many opportunities that I have missed entirely. That is good. This book is not the end product.

In reality, those building the actual FMS **will draw from the best ideas and innovations available** at *that* time. This project requires none other than the best minds who are focused on the success of the students and are free from agendas.

There is a lot to unpack here, so let me start with a simple **Education Stack** that provides a high-level look at what we will be seeing. These are just some of the elements that will be needed (*most are already a part of today's public school system*). Each layer and its elements could be expanded into many more detailed layers, but there are limitations to how deep we can go here.

Don't worry, you do NOT need to memorize this table. Each layer will be covered in detail in this and the next few chapters.

Education Stack

Stack Layer	Stack Elements
Administration	✓ **FMS Education Constitution** ✓ **Student Bill of Rights** ✓ **FMS Guiding Documents** ✓ Support Services
Governance	✓ **FMS Association** ✓ Parents ✓ Continuity Assurance
Funding	✓ State ✓ Local ✓ Non-Government ✓ Partnering, Teaming, Fundraising ✓ Donations, Endowments, and Gifts
Community	✓ Partnerships ✓ Cooperation ✓ Resources

Stack Layer	Stack Elements
Providers	✓ Education ✓ Management/Administration ✓ Oversight ✓ Training
Physical	✓ Buildings, Facilities, and Support ✓ Transportation ✓ Equipment and Resources ✓ Teaching and Training Resources ✓ Sports/Extracurricular Support
Technology	✓ Tech Stack ✓ Approved Vendors ✓ Approved Products ✓ Continuous Innovation and Improvement
Staffing	✓ Educators ✓ Administrators ✓ Support Services ✓ Professional Development
Students	✓ Support Services ✓ Internal/External Services ✓ Private, Parochial, and Homeschools ✓ Outreach
Learning	✓ Curriculum ✓ Validation ✓ Approval ✓ Screening ✓ Auditing
Assessment	✓ Software ✓ Tools ✓ **FMS Association Standards**

You may have noticed in the "**Students**" stack that private, parochial, and homeschools were mentioned. I am a firm believer in each of those. In fact, I consider most of them superior to our current public school system.

In our reformed system, **each of these alternatives would be welcome members of the education community and would be encouraged to participate in the public school system** in partnerships, cooperatives, events, sports, extracurricular activities, and more. All parents are part of the community and if they are using these alternatives and paying taxes that support the public school, then they should have access (*with a few limitations*) without fear of government intrusion in their schools.

———————— ♦ ————————

HOW DOES IT WORK?

We have a monolithic government-driven and controlled system now. Free Market Schools (FMS) will move us to smaller, more localized units competing with each other to earn available education dollars. All will be under the governance of the **Education Constitution** and **Student Bill of Rights** that we will learn about later.

IMAGINE for a moment that we are in a place where we have a clean slate, i.e., there is NO public education system. *How* or *why* we are in that place does not matter.

Now, imagine we are given free rein to **start from scratch** and build a public school system with only these guidelines.

1. The entire school system has to be protected from government, political, organizational, and any other agenda-driven internal or external influence or control.

2. In order to work on a mass scale, it has to make use of public funds (*at least for the foreseeable future*).

3. Every school, every provider, every element must focus on learning. This includes core academics and preparation for success and excellence in the world.

That's it. Build it with the assumption that there is no existing framework, no infrastructure, no "*before*". Just a blank canvas in front of us to paint a masterpiece.

Now, in reality, a lot of the pieces already exist so it is critical that we do <u>NOT try to just shoehorn our system into what exists today</u>. What exists today is messy, smelly, and cobbled together to meet the desires of past moments.

We must – ***and this is imperative*** – design our system to meet those **three guidelines**, then carefully absorb pieces of what exists to support our new framework and guardrails.

So, what might we imagine?

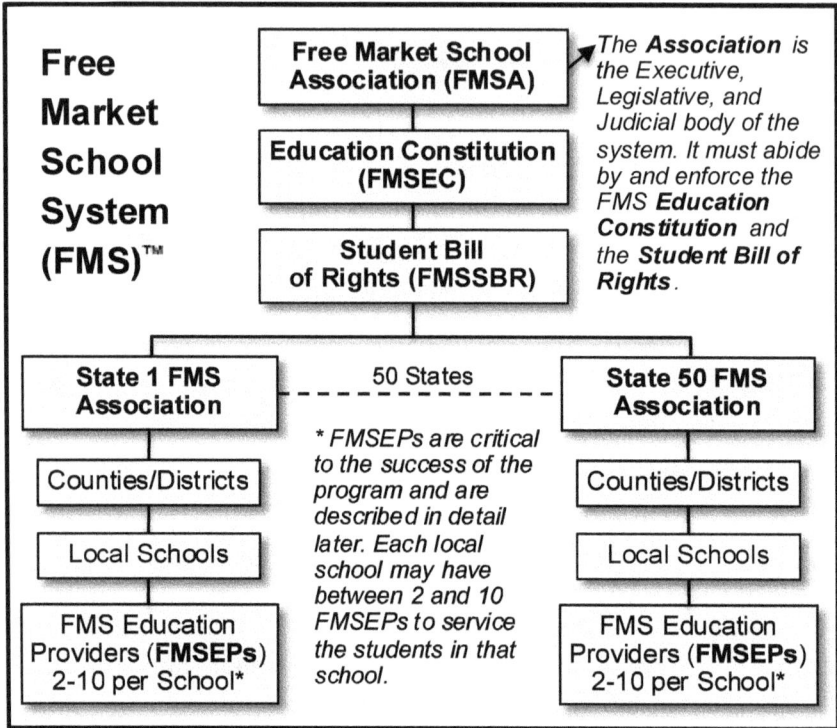

Free Market School System (FMS)™	**Free Market School Association (FMSA)**	*The **Association** is the Executive, Legislative, and Judicial body of the system. It must abide by and enforce the FMS **Education Constitution** and the **Student Bill of Rights**.*
	Education Constitution (FMSEC)	
	Student Bill of Rights (FMSSBR)	
State 1 FMS Association	50 States	**State 50 FMS Association**
Counties/Districts	** FMSEPs are critical to the success of the program and are described in detail later. Each local school may have between 2 and 10 FMSEPs to service the students in that school.*	Counties/Districts
Local Schools		Local Schools
FMS Education Providers (**FMSEPs**) 2-10 per School*		FMS Education Providers (**FMSEPs**) 2-10 per School*

So, your first question might be, *"Where are the local, state, and federal governments in this organization chart?"* Excellent question, you have been paying attention.

Let's start with the easy one. The federal government is not incorporated because there is **no U.S. Constitutional authority for the federal government to be involved in education**. Period. In a valid system, they would not authorize, empower, regulate, or fund any aspect of the school system. Double Period!

When the FMS system is implemented appropriately, **local**, **county**, and **state** government elements are primarily relegated to authority for **funding functions** and are removed from guidance and directive of *HOW* we educate our children. Functional management of education is not a government function any more than trash pickup is.

Currently, those states who address public education in their **State Constitutions** focus on a few specific areas (details are different in every state):

- A guarantee of the right to a free public education;

- Ensuring adequate funding of public schools;

- Maintaining a minimum standard of quality education;

- Compulsory education laws that mandate attendance;

- And sometimes they address elements of governance and structure such as roles for state boards of education, school boards, superintendents, etc.

Most of those focus areas (*except for potential conflicts in some states regarding governance and structure*) are in line with the implementation of a Free Market School system. The national and state **Free Market School Associations (FMSAs)** would work closely with state governments to ensure alignment with funding and the **FMS Education Constitution (FMSEC)**.

Other than generic standards of quality (which all FMS elements would meet), none of the State Constitutions address curriculum, specific education methods, how to educate, or other specific models of teaching. Again, this is all in alignment with everything proposed for FMS implementation.

The important factors relative to our discussions are that these State Constitutions mandate a **right to a free public education** and **ensure adequate funding** of public schools. Funding is discussed in much more detail in **Chapter 13**, *"How Do We Pay for This?"*

One thing I will concede is that lawyers will make a ton of money in the challenges back and forth. The critical key will be that each state legislature is on board and will imbue the **Free Market School Association** with the authority and power to develop, institute, and enforce the Framework and Guardrails we will be talking about. This issue is discussed in more detail in **Chapter 14**, *"So, How Do We Start?"*

———————— ◆ ————————

The FMS approach erases the bureaucracy-driven, big government approach to education and replaces it with a competitive Open Market-Driven system with a singular goal – a comprehensive <u>education</u> for our children to prepare them for lifelong success. For them to be competitive, we need to be competitive in teaching

> Yes, there are problems in free-market systems, as with any other system. Our mission will be to pick the best approaches and guardrail against the pitfalls we have seen throughout history.

them. Maybe I am biased, but **I believe America should be Number 1** in the world in education.

We do this by building a system where companies compete to provide the best education for your child. Then parents choose which **Education Provider** (individual <u>certified</u> education companies) will provide the highest quality education for YOUR child, AND will provide programs focused on your child's goals, desires, beliefs, skills, abilities, and methods/styles of learning.

Chapter 12 discusses these choices in detail. Parents might want different focuses for their child's education:

- A classical general core education;
- An expanded STEM education;
- One focused on career or business;
- Or aimed at college bound learners;
- Arts, Music, Sports;
- Trades or service-based concentrations;
- Supporting a child with Special Needs.

All of this is possible in an environment not entrenched in a **one-size-fits-all moribund environment** restricted down to the **lowest common denominator**. The Education Providers that are best at meeting parents' and students' needs will rise to the top in the system and attract more students. **Success breeds success!**

Let's look back at our graphic of the FMS system. As we go through the next couple of chapters, each element will be fleshed out more in relation to that chapter's focus. The concept is simple, implementation not so much.

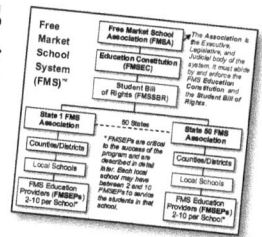

Free Market School Association (FMSA) | The **Free Market School Association (FMSA)** is the national foundation of our educational system and provides governance and protection over the whole public-school ecosystem. The FMSA is responsible for developing the **Education Constitution** and the **Student Bill of Rights** and ensuring that all elements adhere to the guardrails in the system. Discussed later here in **Chapter 10**.

Education Constitution | The FMS **Education Constitution** is the inviolate heart and soul of the entire system. Just as the U.S. Constitution has been the guiding hand and the law of the land of the United States for 250 years, this will protect the FMS system from influence, corruption, and straying from the mission. Every element of the system must adhere 100% to the Education Constitution. See **Chapter 11**.

Student Bill of Rights (SBR) | The **Student Bill of Rights (SBR)** works hand-in-hand with the Education Constitution to ensure every element of the system protects the student. This protection includes the right to a quality education and protections from physical, mental, political, or social abuses and influences. See **Chapter 11**.

50 State FMS Associations | Just as the entire system has a governing body (the **FMSA**), **each state** will have a state-level **FMS Association (FMSAxx)**. These state associations will operate under the oversight of the FMSA and provide governance, protection, and guidance at a state level. Each county and school district will have representatives at the state association.

| Counties and
School Districts |

The structures at county, district, and local levels will evolve as the system evolves to ensure all local needs are met for students and parents. IF schools operate within the framework and guardrails of the FMSEC and other Guiding Documents (which includes **validation** that a quality education is being provided), they are free to evolve, innovate, and incorporate the latest advances in education. This will open up a world of free-market opportunities in the education technology and services private sector (*that is worthy of a whole other book or three*). See **Chapter 15** for more discussion of partnerships and integrations.

| Local Schools |

Imagine the physical schools themselves as the support system for our educational system. The schools house administration, facilities, supplies, general support services, security, food services, transportation services, athletic facilities, etc. Basically, everything except educational services. Educational support is provided by the Education Providers (*below*). More detail on the school support systems is provided in an upcoming section of this chapter and in **Chapters 12** and **13**.

| **FMS Education Providers
(FMSEPs)** |

Everything else we've talked about to this point is designed to ensure the success of THIS element of the FMS. The **FMS Education Providers** (**FMSEPs**) are on the front line, face-to-face with the children and parents. Every FMSEP is a private company whose sole mission is the successful education of our children. They contract with the state Association to provide services in a specific school for a fee. And can only do so after going through a rigorous certification process with the national FMSA. **This element is what truly differentiates the FMS from what we have now**. Significant detail on the FMSEPs is provided a few sections from now.

———————— ♦ ————————

We begin now to see how this comes together in a fully integrated system that is **both** controlled and set free to explore, evolve, and innovate. With that in mind, let's dive into more advanced detail on some critical elements of the FMS.

But first...

I can imagine the doubts churning in your mind already and can almost hear you thinking, *"David, it's too much, it can never be done, they won't let you, are you crazy, or just naive?"*

I'm not qualified to self-diagnose my own sanity or folly, but remember what I asked of you earlier as a first-time reader?

> ***Until you finish the book, just make the ASSUMPTION that it CAN be done.***

ASSUME THIS!

Chapters 13 through **15** are dedicated to laying out pathways for HOW we can potentially make this happen. If enough people believe it can be done after reading the entire book, then we can take that first tiny step and see what happens.

I ask you though, just **keep the faith a bit longer** until the entire book is laid bare in front of you. THEN, you can let go of the asks I had of you and **come to your own conclusions**. Until then, let's have some fun, eh?

———— ♦ ————

FMS ASSOCIATION – THE GLUE

The success of such a massive educational ecosystem change hinges on a **formidable system of governance** that drives every element to perform effectively and prevents incursion, infiltration, influence, and corruption of the system (*including within the FMS Association itself*). Failure in this area invites fatal infections and weaknesses.

The **National Free Market School Association (FMSA)** is the top-level governing body of the entire system and is beholden to the **FMS Education Constitution**, the **Student Bill of Rights**, **State Constitutions**, and the **U.S. Constitution**.

Education is in reality the responsibility of **the parents** (*the purchasers*) and **the students** (*the users*). Education is a service that parents purchase for their children if they aren't going to educate them themselves. In its purest consideration, **it is no different than purchasing a cable or internet service**. You research, compare, then pick the best service to meet your family's needs. (*Hopefully, parents will spend a bit more time on this than they do picking HBO® or Cinemax®.*)

IN REALITY, **we as a society** determined that a larger-scale public school system was in the best interests of our society.

By extrapolation of these points, <u>**the only NECESSARY function**</u> **of government's involvement at all is to provide the funding mechanism** (*collecting and spending our money*) for a public educational system. Unfortunately, when we turned to the government for a legislated funding system (*using our money*), we also abdicated all power and accepted the government as the architect, legislator, governor, manager, and operator of our public school system. THAT is why we are here today.

Considering these points, the FMS system will treat all levels of government simply as funding mechanisms (see **Chapter 13**) and will return the actual functions and operations of the school system to organizations (defined below) that are much closer to the *purchasers* and *users*.

Of course, we do have to be realistic and take into consideration existing State Constitutions, laws, and regulations. **Chapter 14** goes into detail about how we start and how to deal with potential roadblocks. One of the first critical points we'll discuss is to **begin in districts, counties, and states that are friendly to the idea of change**. We work then to mitigate or remove government involvement in the system.

— ◆ —

Before we go any deeper, we have been, and will be using, several acronyms as we go along. I'm going to let my government and business roots show a bit and provide a **Table of Acronyms** to help you out.

Acronym List

Acronym	Definition
FMS	Free Market School(s)
FMSA	**National** Free Market School Association
FMSAxx	**State** Free Market School Association
FMSC	Free Market School **Certified** (Certification)
FMSEC	Free Market School **Education Constitution**
FMSEP	Free Market School **Education Provider**
FMSGC	Free Market School **Guiding Council**
FMSPC	Free Market School **Parents Coalition**
FMSSBR	Free Market School **Student Bill of Rights**
SBR	**Student Bill of Rights**

We could go into great detail about how the FMS Association is structured and how it operates, but that is not necessary for this book. Ring actual development of a live FMS system we will build the functional organization, structure, and other elements necessary to complete the mission.

For now, we will look at the foundational elements of what the FMSA is and its primary functions and guardrails.

From previous discussions, we understand that the National FMSA is the foundation of the system, as well as its head. Its **primary mission** is to ensure that all elements of the system are held accountable to the **FMS Education Constitution** and the other **Guiding Documents** (see **Chapter 11**).

STRUCTURE OF THE **FMSA**

The FMSA will likely be structured like any other large association, organization, or business. It will have Executives, Officers, and Employees. Each of them will be held accountable as well to the **Education Constitution (FMSEC)** and the other **Guiding Documents**. Their success will hinge upon their sincere dedication to the word and intent of the FMSEC. This is where many systems fail in that the checks and balances to prevent "*interpretation*" and "*mission creep*" are not adequate to prevent corruption.

> *Future "<u>Interpretation</u>" of the words and the intent by future parties, lawyers, etc. is the biggest risk to the system. Look at how our U.S. Constitution is constantly being reinterpreted.*

It will be the mission of the **Founding Members** (*described below*) to develop a structure that has the checks and balances to withstand attack, abuse, and attrition. Rather than a **Board of Directors**, the Association might utilize constructs like a parents' "**Guiding Council**" whose only mission is to maintain adherence to the <u>as-written word</u> of the **Guiding Documents**. They will have the responsibility for ensuring the Associations operate per those founding documents (see **Chapter 11**).

ROLE OF THE **FMSA**

As part of their mission, the National FMSA will play numerous roles in ensuring success.

- Ratify, implement, and validate adherence to the Guiding Documents.

- Ensure all FMS Education Providers (FEMSEPs) and other elements of the system adhere to the Guiding Documents.

- Run a **Certification Program** to certify FEMSEPs and qualify them to compete to deliver education programs in the schools.

- Certify and manage system-wide IT programs, Ed-Tech, and other support programs and systems to ensure they are consistent with FMS requirements.

- Lobbying activities necessary to protect the system from external impact or intrusion.

- Support the State FMSAs where needed with resources, tools, legal support, and lobbying to help ensure success throughout the system.

- Work to expand the FMS system into new counties, towns, cities, and states. Their goal will be to normalize and nationalize the FMS system throughout the U.S.

FOUNDING MEMBERS

The **Founding Members** (**Founders**) are those hearty souls who will band together over a stout Ale (*or a nice Chardonnay with just a hint of warm toasty flavors from oak aging*) and work to turn what is in this book into reality. This book provides a basic understanding of what the "***After***" or the "***To-Be***" looks like in broad strokes. Their job will be to break out the fine brushes and create a masterpiece for the generations.

One critical job will be to archive complete documentation of all communications and discussions the Founders have during their development of the Guiding Documents (see **Chapter 11**). When the inevitable attempt to "***interpret***" a requirement in the Guiding Documents to fit with a certain future agenda arises, this institutional knowledge will help ensure we stay within the original meaning and intent as planned by the Founders.

If things change or evolve over time and some aspect of the Guiding Documents is no longer relevant or conflicts with the ratified documents, that change must be resolved through a **Constitutional Amendment**, just as it would through the U.S. Constitution. Any Amendments should be extremely hard to achieve and involve most groups in the FMS ecosystem.

So, who are these **intrepid adventurers** willing to step into the breach and dedicate heart and soul to our nation's children? **Hopefully YOU are one.** If this book is inspiring enough, some brave soul will step forward to lead the charge and that person will need warriors like you to step in and help design the next generation of public schools. If you have an interest in becoming an **FMS Education Warrior**, contact information is provided at the end of this book.

LOOK!

A SCHOOL – WHAT DOES IT LOOK LIKE?

So, what does a FMS school look like? At first glance, it will look pretty much like a school of today. It will have school buildings in your neighborhood (see **Chapter 15**), classes, teachers, lunchrooms, gymnasiums, ball fields, and more.

Internally though, the schools will operate very differently and parents will have much more control over the learning goals of their children – *should they choose to do so*.

One of the reasons the public school system has been accepted so readily and so ubiquitously is that **it is EASY**. **Today**, if parents do not want to be involved in their children's K12 education at all, they do not have to. The school is determined primarily by where their house is. Big yellow school buses pick up their children in the morning and bring them home in the afternoon. The classes, curriculum, and schedule are all determined by the school.

All the parents are required to do is pay their taxes. **Easy!**

That's part of the problem. We relinquished the entire system to the government, teachers' unions, and other organizations… and they were all more than willing to accept that responsibility and take any burden off the parent's hands. The government only asked for ONE THING in exchange for our complacency… **complete control of our children**.

Complacency brought us to where we are today. **LOOK!**

The FMS system returns control to parents who want to take advantage of it and manage their children's learning adventure. Parents who want the easy path will still be able to sit back on autopilot, but in a much improved educational environment.

Using the same taxation system and the same physical school system, FMS **rips away the shrouded control of the government system** and lets parents pick and choose the pathway that suits them.

How does this work? Each FMS location (school building) will have **2-10 Certified FMS Education Providers (FMSEPs)** who will offer various competitive education programs based on grade, discipline, educational focus, philosophical focus, intensity, and more. The FMSEPs are discussed in detail in the next section.

The graphic below provides a simplified structure of **one potential neighborhood school**.

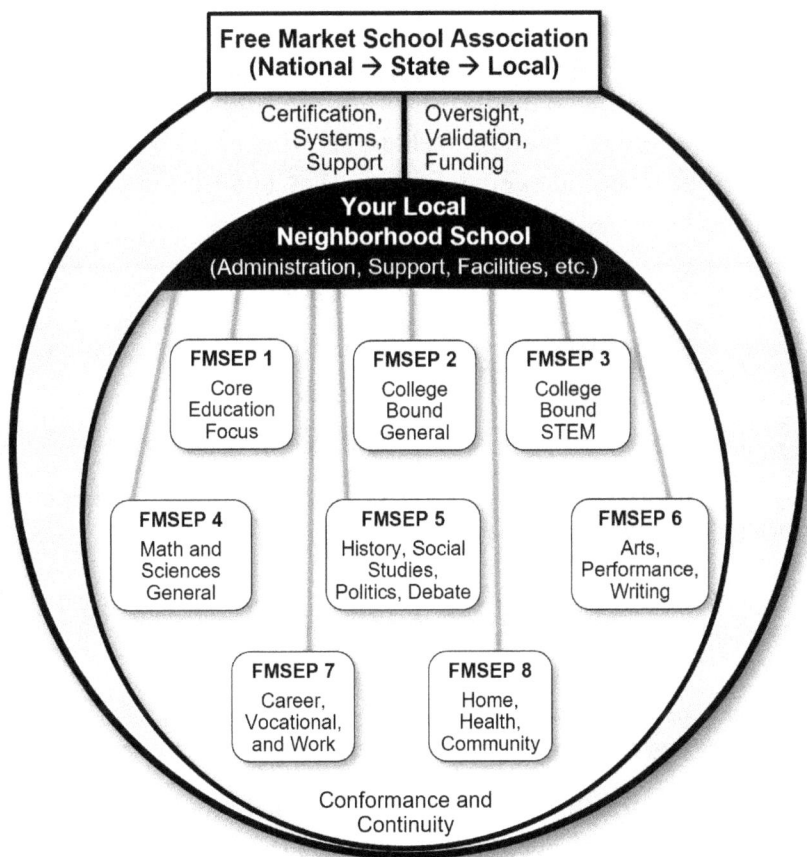

This particular school has eight (8) Education Providers (FMSEPs) providing services to the students. These are just examples of the various focus forms that could be provided in any individual school. The **FMSEPs will compete for the parents' attention** and the parents will choose the pathways they want for their children each year.

Over time, the free market will evolve products and services that are way beyond what I can cover initially in the limitations of this single book.

You might be concerned that the FMS introduces a complexity that will inhibit adoption by those parents who do not want to spend the time researching FMSEPs and picking out programs. I would love to believe every parent would be heavily involved in managing every step of their kid's education, but we know that is not reality.

For those parents, we can make it **turnkey easy** if that's what they really want. Once the FMSEPs are determined for the school, a simple **one-page flyer** or **web page** with checkboxes can be implemented. It could even default to "**1. Core Education**" if the parents make no selection.

Parents,	**Choose ONLY 1 Focus.**
*The new school year is coming up. You may now choose a **Focus** for your child's education if you like.*	○ 1. Core Education
	○ 2. College Bound General
*Every Focus will provide a **full scope, high-quality education** for your child. The only difference will be the **types of classes** included in the curriculum.*	○ 3. College Bound STEM
	○ 4. Math and Sciences General
	○ 5. History, Social Studies
*If you make no choice, your child will be enrolled in the **Core Education Focus**.*	○ 6. Arts, Performance, Writing
	○ 7. Career, Vocational, and Work
***To research**, go to www.fmsfocus.fms*	○ 8. Home, Health, Community

It can't be much easier than that. For parents who choose to do the research and get just the right FMSEP and program for their child, information will be sent out and details of the providers and the programs will be available online. There will also be counselors the parents and students can talk to and there will most likely be **FMSEP Fairs** where parents and students can explore each focus in detail. They could even **mix-and-match**.

Parents may choose for their children to participate in multiple FMSEP programs throughout their educational career to get a **fully rounded education**, but the students will be required to meet the focus goals of any program they have signed onto.

The FMSEPs may also choose to share students to ensure a full stack education for elements that a particular FMSEP has chosen not to include in their core program. For example, looking back at our school graphic a few pages back, a student may be enrolled in *FMSEP #4 – Math and Sciences General*, however FMSEP #4 may have made a business decision not to invest in providing general studies such as English, History, or Social Studies. They can then team with *FMSEP #1 – Core Education* to provide those classes. The possibilities are endless.

Remember, each of the FMSEPs is a different company who is competing to be the best and to attract the most students. We'll discuss this more in the upcoming FMSEP section.

CURRICULUM AND BOOKS

One of the most challenging areas we are facing for parents now is the choice of curriculum and books. There is **often little visibility today into the selection of books and the design of the curriculum**. As we have seen from earlier examples in this book, those selections are sometimes even **actively hidden from the parents**. If a parent does object, they have few avenues of redress to try and correct the issues.

In the FMS system, all schools and FMSEPs **must adhere to the requirements** of the FMS Education Constitution and the FMS Governance Rules. Otherwise, they are free to develop their own curriculum and book list. **This has worked extremely well in the homeschool community** where there are numerous curriculum providers who compete for homeschool parents' dollars. The programs are diverse, and each provides a different focus for student growth.

What makes the FMS system of education so powerful is that the educational environment and decisions are **driven down to the local level** as much as possible so that parents and students in a community can express their desires and be heard.

> What works best in Boise, Idaho may not work well in San Francisco, CA. And certainly cannot be effective with a one-size-fits-all approach developed in Washington, D.C.

Each FMS provider in a school may develop their own curriculum and choose their own books. Keep in mind that this is a competitive system and **they must compete with the other FMSEPs in their school** (or even nearby schools). To do this, they need to keep the parents happy in these choices if they want the parents to enroll their kids in that company's program. They must work with the desires of the parents (*within reason*) and consider the business case for the curriculum they choose.

Because there are 2-10 FMSEPs in every physical school, the parents who want to get involved will choose the curriculum, book list, and advanced classes they want based on the offerings of the providers. **However, parents should <u>NOT</u> have direct control of the curriculum or books**. Their power is in driving the free-market system to reward those companies who provide curriculum and books that parents in that community desire.

FMSEPs will adapt to the needs of the community, or they will wither and die, opening the door to other companies who will work with the communities they serve.

BUILDINGS, TRANSPORTATION, AND RESOURCES

If you were following along closely, a few questions might have occurred to you.

- Where does all this happen?
- Where will MY kids go to school?
- Do they still get to chat with the Lovely Lunch Lady?
- Will the yellow buses still come?
- Will the teacher my kids like still have a job?
- Will there still be sports programs?
- Will they still teach my kid to play the Tuba?
- Do I still have to go to school plays?

Much is this is answered or addressed in detail in **Chapters 13, 14**, and **15**. Remember, we're going to talk about how to ease into this from simple starting points. *Keep that in mind.* But for now, here are a few of the highlights to keep you sated until we get there.

Let me start with the easy ones. YES, you will still need to attend your kid's plays, recitals, and swim meets. But maybe now there will be dedicated FMSEPs for the arts who can bring in professionals or guests to help your kid actually explore their art.

The teacher issue gets a little more complicated. Because these are individual companies, they will be **competing for the best teachers**. It is likely that every teacher in the school now will be *considered* during the transition if they desire. However, since the FMS will move to a **merit-based system**, every teacher will be considered based on merit, education, recommendations, experience, past performance, and other factors.

If they are a *good* teacher, they will likely find a position, but will need to work on becoming better if they want to expand their career. If they are one of the **best of the best**, they will likely do very, very well and make much more money than they do now as they will be in demand with the competing FMSEPs. However, if they spend their time in one of the "**Rubber Rooms**" (see "*Bureaucracy vs. Meritocracy*" in **Chapter 5**) it is highly likely they'll need to find more gainful employment elsewhere.

One of the biggest issues is the "***where***". You will remember that we talked about starting in a concept-friendly district, county, and state that would be receptive to the idea and be willing to do this as proof-of-concept in a single school or district. We will discuss this in more detail in **Chapter 14**, but let's take a high-level look at the *where*.

> Remember that the FMS is NOT an *alternative* to the current public school system. It is **intended to REPLACE the government-run system** we have now.

The infrastructure (buildings, facilities, transportation, maintenance, etc.) already exists in every neighborhood to support FMS systems. It would be a non-starter (*and a bit ridiculous*) to abandon those facilities and build from scratch. Hence, the need to find a concept-friendly location to start with one school or one district as proof of concept.

Important point → It may seem in starting this way that we are "*experimenting*" with our children. **Nothing could be farther**

from the truth. The schools will be familiar, the environment will be familiar, and many of the teachers may be familiar. What changes is that we are moving from an "*education*" focus to a "*learning*" focus (see **Chapter 12**). This is a proven concept that is widely respected in the education community.

Every step will be guided by our incredibly smart **Founders** and the **FMS Association (FMSA)** leadership whose entire focus is to help our children succeed and prosper. There will be continuous improvement, continuous innovation, process/system evolution, and advancement in the education philosophies, but no "experimentation" on students.

In short, your taxes will continue to support the facilities and infrastructure (including yellow buses, lunchrooms, sports facilities, etc.) as they always did. But instead of directly paying for teachers, administrators, and support staff through a government system, the State FMS Associations will receive tax funding from the county, district, and/or state and they will ensure the funds are properly disbursed to FMSEPs based on competitively awarded contracts.

Which provides an excellent segue into our next section where we examine the core of the program, the FMSEPs.

———————— ♦ ————————

FMS EDUCATION PROVIDERS (FMSEPS)

So, who are these mysterious **Free Market School Education Providers (FMSEPs)** that we keep talking about?

In a nutshell, they are individual companies who compete against each other for contracts to deliver education and other support services within the schools.

All Providers must be **FMS Certified (FMSC) by the National FMS Association (FMSA)** as qualified and competent to provide services *before* they can even compete for contracts. They must recertify annually based on performance, results, and recommendations. This certification would include, at a minimum, program viability, curriculum competency, educational effectiveness, management, staffing, recruiting, past experience, *past performance*, and other critical factors.

At this point you might be **worried about the cost of education going up** by using these highly qualified companies. However, I think we can all admit that our educational system is extremely expensive and bloated today and is **not performance-based**. Costs keep going up, yet the metrics keep going down. The money is not going to the right places.

Today's schools get more expensive to run every year, no matter how badly they perform. Competition to develop more effective and cost-efficient services will be the natural order with the FMSEPs to provide **higher quality services at lower costs**. As this market grows, it will become very attractive to small, medium, and large companies. The **competition to win the hearts and minds of parents and children will become intense** as FMSEPs compete for their students through better offerings, better curriculums, higher performance, and **results**.

The FMSEPs will likely be **paid per student enrolled** in their program. The more appealing their program is, the more parents and students they will attract to sign up with them. To have that opportunity though, the FMSEPs must bid on and win a contract which is based on numerous factors, one of which is the price per student.

Now your follow-up concern might be **low-price bidders** and a degradation of education in a *race to the bottom.*

Not to fear, my experience in government contracting has made abundantly clear the **dangerous and destructive nature of low-price bidding**. Although price will of course be a factor, it will **not** be the primary factor. Quality and performance will be the primary evaluation factors and innovation and enhancement will be critical success factors to compete and remain competitive on price.

Additionally, **new and innovative sources of revenue** for the FMSEPs will also come into play in the future to ensure high-performance delivery at lower cost to taxpayers for generations to come. **Chapter 13** goes into more detail on these factors.

WHAT DOES A FMSEP LOOK LIKE?

Well, that is the **fun part** of being based on free-market enterprise. We can pretend to know what it will look like now, but as the system evolves and companies step forward to offer innovative proposals to provide services, the reality of what a FMSEP may look like at the first school, the fifth, or the hundredth will change as these companies innovate and adapt to the needs and desires of parents and students.

FMSEPs will likely approach this in a **modular structure** where they each plug in services to meet the needs of the community.

For example, if you remember our one-school diagram we looked at earlier, Our **FMSEP 1 – *Core Education Focus***, might be approached in several ways.

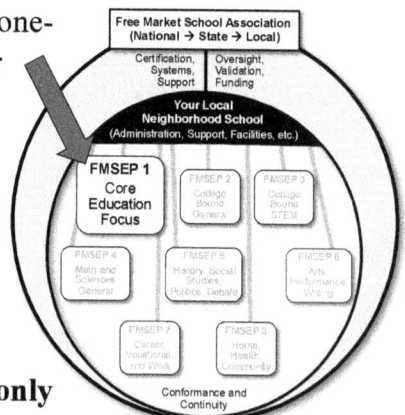

Free Market School Association (National → State → Local)

Certification, Systems, Support | Oversight, Validation, Funding

Your Local Neighborhood School (Administration, Support, Facilities, etc.)

FMSEP 1 Core Education Focus | FMSEP 2 College Bound General | FMSEP 3 College Bound STEM

FMSEP 4 Math and Sciences General | FMSEP 5 History Social Studies Politics Debate | FMSEP 6 Arts Performance Writing

FMSEP 7 Career Vocational and Work | FMSEP 8 Home Health Community

Conformance and Continuity

- They might offer a full-stack education (Core, English, Math, Science, Language, Arts, etc.) **for all grades** at that school.

- Or they might offer programs **only for grades 1 to 6**.

- Or they might be focused on high school **grades 9 to 12**.

- They might offer some electives in different areas.

- Or they might team with some of the other FMSEPs at the school to add in electives they choose not to include in their program.

At the same school, **FMSEP 3 – *College Bound STEM***, might be built differently.

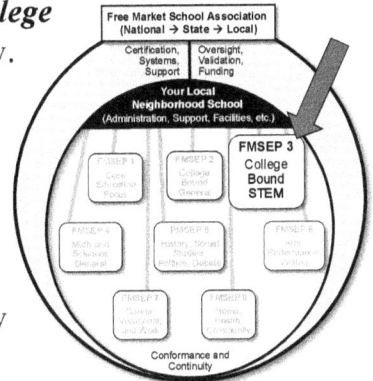

- They might offer a full-stack education themselves with all the Core classes PLUS higher-level math and sciences to prepare for college-level courses in STEM. They may offer this **for all grades**.

- Or, they may just offer it in high school **grades 9 to 12**.

- Or, they may offer only the higher level STEM classes and team with FMSEP 1 to provide the Core classes such as English, Language, Arts, etc.

As we can see, the possibilities are endless as the FMSEPs find their strengths and make business decisions on **how they can best serve the community, the school, and the students**.

The primary cost driver of these contracts is of course, **what they pay the teachers**. Considerations would be related to the quality levels, experience levels, and education levels of the proposed teachers for the focus of each FMSEP. Don't forget, we will now be working in a competitive **Merit-Based employment environment** rather than a Bureaucracy-Based system (see **Chapter 5**). FMSEPs must compete for the best teachers and will need to pay higher wages and benefits to attract the top talent.

MERIT!

Teachers will also be competing to work for the best FMSEPs to get the best wages and benefits they can.

Conversely, each FMSEP must competitively bid to win a contract to run a program in a school. They will have to make effective business decisions in order to succeed and grow.

- Are they hiring early grade teachers or later grades? What is the pay differential?

- Are they teaching core classes like English or the Arts?

- Or are they teaching high-level College Bound STEM classes?

- Do they hire good teachers with less experience to cut costs?

- Or do they hire great teachers with more experience at a higher cost to earn higher ratings, better reviews, and potentially more students?

- Since they are competing against the other FMSEPs for the best teachers, what level of benefits do they offer?

- Do they offer all classes themselves, team with other FMSEPs, or bring in freelancers for special classes?

You may have noticed in that last bullet that I have introduced the concept of *freelancers*. As the FMS expands, it will open up whole new opportunities and industries **for professional teachers to act as consultants and freelancers** to enhance the capabilities within a school system. The possibilities are endless when not **restrained within a monolithic government bureaucratic behemoth that stifles creativity**.

STRUCTURE OF THE FMSEP

Each FMSEP will have the freedom to structure their organization just as any business would. They will define that in their proposal to provide services and demonstrate the advantages, efficiencies, and effectiveness of their approach. A typical FMSEP could potentially be structured similar the organization chart below.

Organization Chart – FMSEP

Free Market School Association
(National → State → Local)

A Local Neighborhood School
(Administration, Support, Facilities, etc.)*

| FMSEP 1 PM | FMSEP 2 PM | **FMSEP 3** College Bound STEM **Program Manager (PM)** | FMSEP 4 PM | FMSEP 5 PM |

| Administration | Counseling |
| HR and Staffing | Community Outreach |

9th Grade Director	**10th Grade Director**	**11th Grade Director**	**12th Grade Director**
Teacher	Teacher	Teacher	Teacher
Teacher	Teacher	Teacher	Teacher
Teacher	Teacher	Teacher	Teacher
Teacher	Teacher	Teacher	Teacher
⋮	⋮	⋮	⋮
Teacher	Teacher	Teacher	Teacher

* The schools and facilities themselves are managed through a separate contract with the FMSA. This contract ensures that FMSEPs have the resources they need to complete their jobs. School services may be paid through the county budget or by charging the FMESPs fees based on number of students... or both. The final methodology will be determined when building the system.

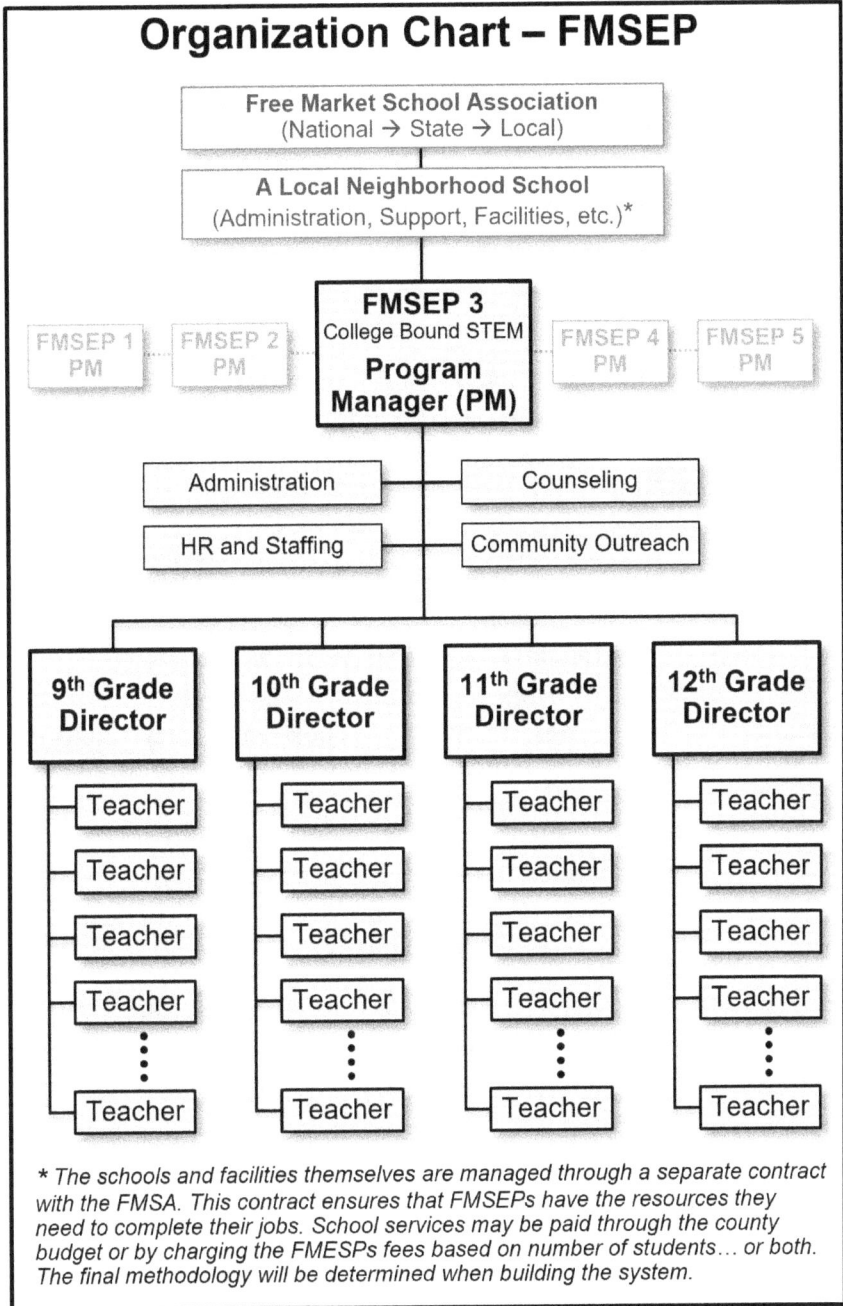

The actual organization, positions, and staffing will be determined by each FMSEP to best serve its business needs and to meet the needs of the school and its students.

Every FMSEP will have a **Charter** defining exactly what they teach, how they teach it, their methodologies, their curriculum, and other information to clearly define what they offer to parents and students. Their offering may also include **bios and pitches of the teachers** in that FMSEP – which is part of what makes teacher selection so important.

As a service provider, the more information they can provide to consumers (parents and students), the more likely the consumer will be to use their service.

At the beginning of each school year, parents and students who are interested in doing so will **review the available FMSEPs and choose the best one** for them. The system might even be set up so they could pick modules from different FMSEPs if desired. For example, there could be a dedicated FMSEP for Health and Physical Education that would be chosen in addition to their primary FMSEP which does not offer these services.

Another question may occur to you. What if there is no FMSEP in the area offering certain classes like Health/PE, Music, or Sports? Again, **not to worry**. These are very lucrative contracts with massive nationwide expansion potential and the free market will fill any void that occurs.

> A famous philosopher once said, "*If you build it, they will come.*" That is no truer than what we will find here.[157]

What is exciting is that there will likely be several FMSEPs in a school with similar curriculum, with each using different learning approaches. We know that different children learn better in different ways. So, let's imagine for a moment that there are three separate FMSEPs in a school offering "*Core Education Focus*". What makes them different?

- FMSEP 1 Core may use a **Traditional Teacher-Centered Rote Book Study/Test Methodology** similar to what is used in schools currently.

- FMSEP 2 Core may use a **Student-Centered Directed Learning model** where students are given resources and directed how to learn what they need to know.

- <u>FMSEP 3 Core</u> may use **Student Inquiry-Based Learning Methods** where students are pushed to explore questions, scenarios, and problems to seek out their own answers and draw conclusions from research.

There are of course numerous other teaching and learning approaches, but I think we get the point. **Children who excel in one environment may fail in another.** Teachers, counselors, parents, and students can explore what works best for each child and choose the FMSEP that best allows the student to succeed.

If a child does not thrive in one environment, they could potentially switch to a different FMSEP that better matches their learning style. To me, **that is very exciting in itself.** Children will **no longer be trapped in a one-style-fits-all common-denominator education environment**.

As we have seen, the **FMS Education Providers are the core of the system** and drive all innovation and continuous improvement. As the customer-facing element of the program they are the "*boots on the ground*" one might say.

Now, let's wrap this solution up in a tidy little bow.

THE POWER OF THE FMS SYSTEM

In this chapter we have learned what the Free Market School system is, how it works, and how it is structured. Then we examined the primary elements of the system – the Free Market School Associations (FMSAs) and the Free Market School Education Providers (FMSEPs).

The national and state **FMSAs are the foundation AND the head of the entire system**. They lay the concrete everything is built on and their main function is to protect the system from both internal and external influence and corruption.

The **FMSEPs are the body and the architects that build the structures** that become our educational system. By working with the parents and students, they will design an educational system that is effective, efficient, and everlasting.

Finally, **Chapter 11** delves **into the heart and soul of the entire system**... the **FMS Education Constitution (FMSEC)**.

— ◆ —

I think **three points** have become abundantly clear.

LOOK!

1. **We are NOT talking about band-aids**. We are talking about fundamental, foundational change.

2. **We are NOT talking about Alternative Schools**. We are talking about <u>replacing</u> the current public school system.

3. **We cannot allow ANY government intervention or interference** within the system.

— ◆ —

Make no mistake, **this will be hard**. An army of people, organizations, and government entities will be arrayed against this. If we understand that, then we must understand that **those entities using the schools for their own agendas cannot allow this powerful <u>generational indoctrination tool</u> to be removed from their programming arsenal**.

I hate to talk militaristically, but an army of lawyers, legislators, bureaucrats, and activists will be launched with hundreds of millions of dollars to fight against fundamental change to a system that has served them so well. That is natural. That is expected.

But have heart! If we are persistent, if we have the right people leading the effort, if we are tenacious in applying the foundational elements discussed in the next few chapters, we can prevail. We must prevail for our children.

Our children are *our* future.

Their education is *their* future.

And the war for their minds will never end.

LOOK!

Step into the next chapter to see how we can win that war.

11

THE POWER OF A CONSTITUTION

Things to consider:

- ➢ What could possibly stop those who would corrupt the system?

- ➢ How would we maintain long-term control of a complex system like this?

- ➢ How long can we maintain that control?

"This Constitution was not made for a day, nor is it composed of such flexible materials as to be warped to the purposes of a casually ascendant influence."
　　　　　　　　　　　　　　　　　　—John Tyler[158]

"The Constitution has sheltered us from those who would destroy freedom, but the fortress is incredibly fragile because it is only as strong as our devotion and allegiance."
　　　　　　　　　　　　　　—Janice Rogers Brown[159]

THE HEART AND SOUL OF THE FMS

Now that we have seen what the Free Market School system is, you might be wondering how we are going to protect it from those who would work continuously to **undermine and corrupt it to their own ends**. We must understand how hard it will be to keep an uncorrupted education system once we get it.

> *Just as our Forefathers realized they had no choice but to form a new nation, **we have no choice** but to secure a new educational system.*

Chapter 14 considers pathways for how we start. But we will have an **extremely fragile period during the system's birth**. Getting to that first school, that first district, that first county is **the most dangerous time for the entire system** as THAT is the point where *we ourselves might decide to compromise or to make concessions* in order to get started.

Many will love this concept and get behind it 100%, but they will believe that *the only way we can get started is to compromise* on the **Guardrails** that protect the system. They will claim *we can fix it later*, but the corrosion may be permanent once it takes hold.

In a perfect world, we could just erase everything and start with a blank slate. But **we live in the real world** where things are messy, broken, and often unfair. Even in the *"friendly"* district/county/state environments we talk about as our starting point, there will be many **critical danger points** to face.

- The **morass of existing laws, regulations, and statutes that encumber our current system** will likely not go away easily. The easy path will be to negotiate softer controls that make everyone "comfortable" in order to get started. However, if any of those controls violate the integrity of our *Education Constitution*, it will act as a prybar to wedge in more and more controls "*for the greater good.*"

- Our **schools will still need to be supported by taxes for the foreseeable future**. We all understand the old axiom that "*what the government giveth, the government can take away.*" This double-edged sword is not to be trifled with and our Founders must be diligent in working with our "friendly" entities to ensure unbreakable bonds exist and the money does not come with "conditions" that go counter to our *Education Constitution*.

- The **facilities our schools will need to occupy represent massive assets** where even friendly administrations might have concerns regarding a transition that takes control away from them. Our Founders must demonstrate that the value we bring to these districts/counties/states is lasting and outweighs any concerns they have. What we cannot do is break through our guardrails for the sake of expediency.

- **Developing public/private partnerships will be necessary** to integrate private enterprises with a complex tax-supported system in this environment. **Chapter 15** lays out the benefits of these partnerships and how they make the system more effective and more powerful. However, this complexity can also create opportunities for external pressure to introduce mission creep, chaos, and internal system corruption.

That is why we must express **vigorous vigilance in every interaction** not to break our system before we even get started.

I ask readers once again to **trust that there are ways** this can be accomplished. **Chapter 13** and **14** were written specifically to explore ways to negate many of these issues. I'm sure more robust protections will come to mind as we develop FMS.

INTRODUCTION TO THE CONSTITUTION

Which brings us to the main purpose of this chapter. Just as the **U.S. Constitution** protects the very core of what America is, our **Education Constitution** will protect the core and the soul of what the FMS educational system is.

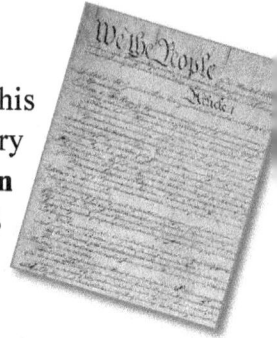

> The **Education Constitution** MUST be **deemed inviolate and unbreakable** by everyone within the system and upheld throughout all interactions external to the system.

Understand that the system is **probably in more danger from the <u>inside</u> than it is from the <u>outside</u>**. Without inviolate Guiding Documents, those inside may, *whether intentionally or not*, stray from the intended mission. For those who are not familiar with the term *"mission creep"*, it is a military and contracting term where those inside the system stray just a bit from the intended purpose of the mission or contract. This creep then opens the door for other activities or purposes that are outside of the original mission. Once begun, it expands.

Although creep may be <u>*intended*</u> to *"do good"* or to support *"the greater good"*, once you set precedent for breaking the Constitution, you open the door for all kinds of mission creep and Unintended Consequences[160] or Corruption. We must be ever vigilant, no matter how benign the infraction may seem at first.

Once the **FMS Education Constitution (FMSEC)** is settled and ratified, then **it should be very hard to Amend** as the consequences of any changes will be far-reaching. **External entities** will likely be the ones pushing for Amendments in order to gain a foothold in the system. As noted earlier, although the Constitution *can* be amended, it must be rare, critically needed, and involve numerous stakeholders and representatives of all 50 State FMS Associations.

One of the primary jobs of the **Founders** will be to write, sign, and ratify the FMS Education Constitution, and to then protect it with extreme prejudice. They will design the protections needed to ensure its integrity.

Violations of the Constitution should be dealt with quickly and decisively to ensure that all parties involved understand the implications of violating the Guiding Documents. Administrators, staff, teachers, and other support personnel should be disciplined or terminated immediately upon validation of an infringement. FMS Education Providers (FMSEPs) found in violation may be forced into immediate corrective action or face cancelation of their FMS Provider Contracts.

CRITICAL!

Strict adherence to the Guiding Documents (*described below*) is THAT important!

———————— ♦ ————————

When I first started writing this book the FMS Associations (FMSAs) and the FMS Education Constitution (FMSEC) *seemed in my mind* to play lesser roles than the FMS Education Providers (FMSEPs). However, while writing the first few chapters, I quickly realized that no matter how amazing and wonderful the FMS was, it meant NOTHING if we couldn't keep it safe from corruption.

Just as the dawning United States of America needed the U.S. Constitution as an anchor to hold us firm, our nascent Free Market Schools also needs an inviolate Constitution as a **central focal point** around which ALL decisions will be made and ALL actions taken. Therefore, we must start with a master framework that would have the following characteristics at a minimum.

- It must provide Guardrails that are absolute.

- There should be no vague or ambiguous language.

- It should not be open to interpretation.

- It must not have back doors to allow exceptions.

- It must contain checks and balances for the above.

- It can only be changed through massive effort.

The next section provides a draft of that ***FMS Education Constitution*** as a beginning point for the final document. This draft is merely a **framework that will guide** our **Founders** as they build **Guiding Documents** that can withstand the assaults they will surely face.

One of our primary focuses must be **Parental Power** and visibility into our educational system. Parents must have more control and direction of the education of their children.

However, this should NOT be construed as giving parents a "*direct democracy*" where they have direct and unfiltered control of the educational ecosystem. As with our Federal Constitution, **our Founding Fathers understood the chaos and potential for abuse, corruption, and dictatorial power** that results from such a system.

You may remember our previous discussion demonstrating that **those who covet power are the ones who purposefully and relentlessly work to attain it**. Those voices would rise above the rest who just want the best for their children.

> "*Pure democracies have ever been spectacles of turbulence and contention; have ever been found incompatible with personal security or the rights of property; and have in general been as short in their lives as they have been violent in their deaths.*"
> — Federalist 10, James Madison[161]

A direct democracy in this environment would result in control through **majoritarian muscle with no need to compromise** or consider the views of any minority.

What I propose for our FMS system and Constitution is a **"representative democracy"** where public passions, influence, and even propaganda can be filtered through a group of elected representatives managed through strict checks and balances. This allows for **temperance and refinement of actions** that might otherwise be implemented by *in-the-moment popular impulse*. These **representatives would be <u>elected by parents</u>** and be as close as possible to the local environment they represent.

You might want to <u>re-read that last sentence</u> and consider the ramifications of **restricting the election of most FMS Association Executives** (*national, state, and county*) **to allow only parents to vote**. There will be some major challenges to this.

Parent voting is a major departure from our current **government-based system** where the individuals on school boards are elected by <u>all eligible voters</u> in a general election. An important distinction in the new system must be made here.

1. **<u>All eligible voters</u>** will vote for their state, county, and municipality representatives who will prepare and approve annual budgets (including education budgets). Essentially, **all citizens approve the budgets.** **◄ CONSIDER!**

2. **<u>Only Current Parents</u>** may vote for the executives that directly run the FMS through the Associations. **Parents determine who will run the school system.**

This is an important factor in keeping political and government influence out of the school system. Massive sums of money are at play in the school budgets, and you may remember our earlier discussion about **millions of dollars being spent to elect school board members**. Many of those are not and may never have been parents themselves. Today it is about the control of large contracts (i.e., money) – NOT our children's education.

By limiting voters to parents only, the focus becomes more about our children's education and less about who controls the lucrative trash, cleaning, maintenance, and cafeteria contracts.

———— ♦ ————

Another critical element of our Education Constitution must be the checks and balances that are put in place. The U.S. Constitution primarily focuses on the three separate, but equal, branches of government – Legislative, Executive, and Judicial. In theory, they operate through a system of checks and balances to prevent any branch, or individual, from accumulating too much power.

Our Education Constitution does not have the same branch-based checks and balances, but different elements of the school system provide checks and balances to ensure that all people and organizations involved adhere to the word, spirit, and intent of every **Guiding Document** (described below). The central charge of all executives and employees will be to ensure that the fundamental structure of the FMS is not altered by the whims of any faction, temporary majority, or fleeting social pressures.

GUIDING DOCUMENTS

I have mentioned our **"Guiding Documents"** in several places through this book as critical to success. The following table defines what those documents actually are and why they are important to ongoing success.

We already have a pretty good idea of what the **FMS Education Constitution (FMSEC)** is about. I provide a draft of that and some of the other documents in the following sections. Remember, these are only first drafts and the people who take the mantle and run with this (our Founders) will spend significant time rewriting, expanding, and refining these documents to make them **comprehensive, straightforward, and unimpeachable**.

The FMSEC is essentially the **Charter** for the entire FMS educational system and cannot be *"interpreted"*, modified, adjusted, or ignored... EVER. The only exception being that **Constitutional Amendments** can be made per the instructions in the FMSEC itself. The other Guiding Documents listed as **"ratified"** below can only be amended by the processes identified in the FMSEC.

Guiding Documents

1. **Declaration** of Education Independence *(Ratified)*

Following the model of the founding documents of the United States, this **Declaration of Education Independence** defines the purpose for the existence and implementation of the entire Free Market School system. It declares the educational system free of social, political, and government influence to ensure schools can concentrate on preparing students for their futures. This will be a **Ratified document** that cannot be altered except through a formal Amendment.

2. **FMS Education Constitution (FMSEC)** *(Ratified)*

The FMS Education Constitution is the law of the FMS, the Charter for operations, and the heart and soul of everything within the FMS system. Every person, element, supplier, subcontractor, consultant, partner, and others who engage with the Association, Schools, Providers, or Students must agree to and accept the requirements within this document and all other Guiding Documents. This will be a **Ratified document** that cannot be altered except through a formal Amendment.

3. **FMS Student Bill of Rights (FMSSBR)** *(Ratified)*

Not really structured as the other documents are, this is a codified list of the rights students have when engaging with the school system. It is intended to protect the students from mental and physical abuse and to provide assurances that education is first and foremost the mission of the school. This will be a **Ratified document** that cannot be altered except through a formal Amendment.

4. **FMS Governance Rules and Standards (FMSGRS)** *(Live)*

This collection of documents is less like a constitution and more like a **Business Governance Handbook**. These documents will provide guidance to the Associations, the schools, the FMSECs, and all entities that engage with the system to provide structure, continuity, standards, requirements, quality management systems, and more. These are all living documents that will be modified, updated, and conformed as necessary to ensure efficient operations throughout.

5. **FMS Core Values** *(Ratified)*

Although the Constitution provides the what and the how for system operation, this document provides the core values that must be displayed and incorporated within every element of the system. This defines what we expect every day from the Administrators, Teachers, Students, and anyone else who interacts with the education system. Many of these touch on philosophical or core personal beliefs so this must be written with care and consideration. This will be a **Ratified document** that cannot be altered except through a formal Amendment.

When FMS is operational, there may be more documents (ratified or not) that structure the system beyond what is discussed in this book. But these are the core documents needed to build the framework to begin the work ahead.

The documents that follow are rather lengthy and verbose but I felt it was important to provide the full flavor of the weight and importance of these foundational documents. **You could <u>skim through these</u> for the high points** as it is rather lengthy, but many questions will be answered if you read through them.

And YES, I freely admit that **I lifted some of this** from the greatest documents in American history. Why wouldn't I?

Guiding Documents

Copyright 2023 David Nemzoff

FMS Declaration of Education Independence

WHEN in the Course of American Events, *it becomes necessary for the people to dissolve the Political, Governmental, and Other External Bonds that have inserted partisan and non-educational agenda into the education of our children, we the people and the parents must declare Independence from those bonds, boundaries, and controls.*

We hold these Truths to be self-evident, that all Children are created equal, that they are endowed by the nature of any free society with certain unalienable Rights. That among these are Life, Liberty, and the Pursuit of a Full and Beneficial Education. That to secure these Rights, the Free Market School (FMS) System must derive its control of our children's education from the consent of Parents through election of Representatives within a structure of free FMS Associations.

We declare that all Elements of the FMS Educational System must remain free of social, political, governmental, and other influences that would interfere with or corrupt the purpose of educating our Nation's Children which is to educate and prepare them for fulfilling, successful, and joyous lives as citizens of this opportunity-filled nation.

We affirm that the existence and implementation of the entire Free Market School System is controlled only and entirely by the FMS Education Constitution (FMSEC) and the other FMS Guiding Documents as defined within the FMSEC. These documents as ratified by the Founders of FMS may not be modified, altered, or disregarded without formal Amendments as defined and implemented in the FMSEC.

We, therefore, the Representatives of the Parents of the Children of the United States do, by the authority of those Parents, solemnly Publish and Declare that these Free Market Schools are, and of Right, Free and Independent Schools chartered to operate by the full intent, meaning, and providence of the Free Market School Education Constitution and other affirmed and ratified Guiding Documents alone.

We, *the undersigned, hereby ratify* this *FMS Declaration of Independence and mutually pledge to abide by the words, meaning, and intent of these documents as written and to ensure that all others abide by the same.*

Signed this date _____ by:

Signature: _____

Signature: _____

Signature: _____

Signature: _____

Signature: _____

Signature: _____

Signature: _____

Signature: _____

Free Market School Education Constitution

We the Parents and Concerned Peoples

of these great United States, in order to form a more Perfect Educational System for our Children, establish a Safe, Secure, and Productive learning environment, and Secure the Blessings of a Rightful Education focused on Knowledge and Preparation for Full and Productive Lives, do hereby ordain and establish this Free Market School Education Constitution (FMSEC) for all Children of the United States (inclusive).

Education, being a fundamental imperative of every successful and prosperous society, we hereby put forth these **Articles** to ensure that all elements of the FMS System understand and adhere to the Mission and Objectives of Free Market Schools.

Article I – Mission and Objectives

Section 1. The mission of the FMS and ALL internal and external Elements (the System) is to support the education of all children through promotion of truth, fairness, positive values, self-worth, and learning for the lifelong success and happiness of all students.

Section 2. All FMS System Associations, Providers, and Elements shall promote the values of the FMSEC, the United States Constitution, the Rule of Law, and fairness regardless of race, ethnicity, gender, religion, or affiliations that support these values.

Section 3. The FMS System shall remain free of all social and political influence from Federal, State, and Local governments, officials, agencies, and other internal or external influences.

Section 4. Efficiency (*cost savings, competitiveness, and other means to reduce costs of education*) shall NOT come at the expense of students' quality of education, safety, or educational opportunities. Innovation and zero-negative-impact efficiencies should be the first refuge of efficiency.

Section 5. Definitions for some terms used in this Constitution are contained in **Article XIII** and shall not be construed as other than defined here.

Article II – Independence

Section 1. To ensure an independent educational environment, the FMS System shall remain self-governing and independent of all external influences and controls that conflict with this FMSEC.

Section 2. Whereas Federal, State, or Local laws may conflict with this Constitution, the National FMS Association (FMSA) shall intervene and attempt to conform or mitigate those laws to this Constitution and all FMS Guiding Documents.

Section 3. Should the FMSA and/or local FMS Association be unable to conform conflicting laws in a specific State, County, or District, the FMSA Guiding Council (FMSAGC) shall make a determination to 1) cancel implementation of schools in that location, or 2) delay implementation until the laws can be conformed, or 3) continue forward if the conflict can be mitigated, is of minimal impact, and is expected to expire or change.

Section 4. No Political Donations of any kind shall be made from or on behalf of the FMSA, FMS Associations, or any FMS entity.

Article III – Precedence

Section 1. To ensure proper command and controls, the chain of precedence to determine authorities and final determinations within the FMS System shall be maintained as follows.

Section 2. The *FMS Guiding Council* (FMSGC) shall be the final judge, authority, and word in determining the FMS Constitutionality and adherence to the Guiding Documents in any conflict, action, or activity of any FMS Element.

Section 3. The *National FMS Association* (FMSA) shall manage and direct the entire FMS System and project authorities through the State, Local, and any other FMS Associations. The FMSA is subordinate only to the FMSGC per **Article V**.

Section 4. The *State FMS Associations* (FMSA*xx* [*state abbreviation*]), one per state in the United States, shall manage and direct all activities throughout their respective states under the direction and authority of the FMSA.

Section 5. Local FMS Associations (FMSA of [*Locality*]) (locations determined per **Article VIII**) shall manage and direct all activities throughout their respective school districts under the authority of their State FMS Association. If no Local FMS Association is present, the State FMS shall have local authority.

Section 6. Free Market Schools will manage and direct their respective schools through an onsite management staff assigned or hired by their FMS Association of authority.

Section 7. FMS Education Providers (FMSEPs) shall manage and direct their school programs under the direction of and in coordination with the management staff of each school they operate in and in accordance with their active contracts.

Section 8. Contractors, Subcontractors, Consultants, and others supporting any aspect of the system shall adhere to the terms of their contract with the respective FMS Element they contracted with. All authority and requirements as defined here flows down into any contract or subcontract.

Article IV – FMS Parent Coalition (FMSPC)

Section 1. Children belong to their parents. As the caretakers and determiners of how their children are raised and educated, parents are the critical interface with the educational system. FMS recognizes this primacy position of the parents and shall ensure that parents have reasonable visibility into their child's education and a voice to ensure FMS is fulfilling its mission in Article I.

Section 2. To that end, the *FMS Parent Coalition* (FMSPC) shall be formed as an uninfluenced representative body of the FMS system to give that voice to parents of school age children.

Section 3. The FMSPC shall be composed of a total of 2,000 to 5,000 Members divided to equally represent all states that then have a minimum of five (5) Free Market Schools operational in the state. The Members of each state shall be selected from a blind random lottery of all parents who have qualified and applied to serve. Only parents of school age children (K-12) who are currently students in the FMS System are eligible to apply and be selected. Selected parents serve a term of two (2) years and may serve up to four (4) terms if selected.

Section 4. Designated representatives of the FMSPC shall have priority access to the FMS Elements to seek information, access, or redress for issues in the schools they believe are in significant conflict with this FMSEC or other FMS Guiding Documents. Unresolved conflicts may be elevated to the Guiding Council for resolution. FMSPC may also provide advice or suggestions to Elements of FMS for consideration.

Section 5. Select members of the FMSPC shall attend an annual FMS Conference between the FMSPC, FMSA, and FMS Guiding Council to address the greater concerns of the FMS System and share recommendations and innovations in an open environment.

Section 6. The primary enumerated function of the FMSPC shall be to nominate candidates to sit on the FMS Guiding Council (**Article V**). The FMSPC shall nominate between 40 and 50 candidates every three (3) years to be presented to the existing FMS State Associations who will, by super-majority of all State Association Presidents, select 30 members of the Guiding Council. These nominees are NOT expected or required to be Members of the FMSPC or any other FMS Element.

Section 7. The FMSPC is primarily a volunteer organization and shall manage and direct their organization as they determine to maintain effective support of the mission. They shall have no management or direct or indirect authorities within the FMS System.

Section 8. Members of the FMSPC shall not receive salary, payment, donations, gifts, considerations, or any other type of remuneration (internal or external) in relation to membership or activities on the FMSPC. They may be reimbursed for approved travel and other valid expenses only from the operating funds provided to the FMSPC per **Section 9** of this Article.

Section 9. The FMSPC shall be funded entirely by a fee placed on all State FMS Associations at a level determined by the FMSA as effective to ensure the proper functioning of the FMSPC without undue burden on the State FMS Associations. These funds shall be for operating expenses, recruiting, and necessary travel and other expenses that would place an undue burden upon the FMSPC Members. The FMSPC shall not accept donations, in-kind payments, or other compensation from any external individual, organization, or entity without specific written authorization from the FMS Guiding Council.

Section 10. All members of the FMSPC shall have read the FMSEC and Guiding Documents and agree by signature that they understand and will abide by, support, and promote these documents and the mission, purpose, and intent they represent. As the FMS is about an unbiased and uninfluenced education of our children, any member found to be promoting concepts in conflict with these documents publicly, on social media, or with any other media, method, or venue may be immediately removed from the FMSPC by majority vote of the FMS Guiding Council.

Article V – FMS Guiding Council (FMSGC)

Section 1. To ensure balance of powers and provide additional checks and controls, the National FMS Association (FMSA) will host and support the FMS Guiding Council (FMSGC) who shall operate as an independent entity from the FMSA and other Elements.

Section 2. The FMSGC shall act as the Judicial body of FMS in determining FMS Constitutionality and adherence to the Guiding Documents in any conflict, action, or activity internal or external to the system. They shall also work proactively to promote legislation and laws favorable to the advancement of FMS.

Section 3. The Guiding Council shall consist of 30 members who may serve up to a maximum of 10 years. Members must be a parent of one or more school age (K-12) children for a minimum of the first four (4) of those years of service. This "parent" requirement may be waived by the FMSA during the first 10 years of FMSA's operations. The President and Vice President may also be exempted from the "parent" requirement by super-majority vote of the Council.

Section 4. Every three (3) years, the Parent Coalition will nominate 40 to 50 qualified candidates to potentially serve on the Guiding Council. Those nominated candidates and the current members of the Guiding Council will be presented to the FMS State Associations who will, by majority of all Presidents within those elements, select the 30 members who will serve on the FMSGC for the next 3 years. Nominees are not required to be members of any Element in the FMS.

Section 5. A majority of the Council members shall select from among themselves a President, Vice President, and other executive members as determined by the Council to ensure efficient and effective operations.

Section 6. Through majority approval, the FMSGC shall have the authority to assess penalties or other actions against any person, entity, or Element within the system who is found in violation by actuality or intent of this FMSEC or other FMS Guiding Documents. Those penalties may include official reprimands, warnings, fines, seizures, forced leave, terminations, or other penalties as deemed appropriate within the law.

Section 7. The FMSGC shall be the primary FMS body leading any legal actions for, or in defense of, the entire FMS. However, the Element with the most direct standing may take legal precedence with support from the FMSGC and/or the FMSA.

Section 8. The FMSGC shall submit an annual budget to the FMSA who shall fund the FMSGC by approving a budget through a majority vote of FMSA executives. If unsuccessful, the parties will seek mediation through the State FMS Associations until passed. These funds shall be for operating expenses, salaries, and necessary travel and other expenses. The FMSGC and its members shall not accept donations, in-kind payments, or other compensation in any form from any external individual, organization, or entity in relation to or in conflict with their activities with the FMSGC.

Section 9. All members of the FMSGC shall have read the FMSEC and Guiding Documents and agree by signature that they understand and will abide by, support, and promote these documents and the mission, purpose, and intent they represent. Any member found to be publicly promoting concepts in conflict with these documents may be removed from the FMSGC by majority vote of the combined FMSGC and FMSA executives. Exceptions for public conflict that would affect FMS may be made in advance in writing by signed agreement by a majority of the combined FMSGC and FMSA executives.

Article VI – National FMS Association

Section 1. The National FMS Association (FMSA) shall manage and direct the entire FMS System and enforce the requirements and intent of the FMSEC and all FMS Guiding Documents. The FMSA is the Executive and Legislative body of the System.

Section 2. The FMSA shall initially be comprised of the Founders who will structure the system and draft and ratify this FMSEC and the Guiding Documents. The Founders shall structure the FMSA in a manner that is effective at accomplishing the mission of the FMS.

Section 3. Within five (5) years of the ratification and adoption of this FMSEC, the Founders shall hold an election to the executive offices of the FMSA. Re-elections shall then be held for all executive offices every five (5) years with a two (2) month transition period after the election. Those eligible to vote for the FMSA executives include all members of the FMSA, all members of the FMSGC, all members of State FMS Associations, all members of Local FMS Associations, and five (5) members of the FMS Parent Coalition chosen by a random lottery managed by the FMSGC from each state. A simple majority will be required for each office. If a simple majority cannot be attained, the FMSA shall hold a runoff of the top two (2) candidates for each office within two (2) weeks. Candidates shall not campaign during the runoff and only the FMSA may send out notifications to eligible member voters with non-biased information on each candidate.

Section 4. The FMSA's primary charter is to ensure the successful implementation and operation of all aspects of the FMS System. They shall accomplish this in part by developing, updating as needed, and supporting all elements in the implementation of the FMSEC and all Guiding Documents.

Section 5. To ensure the FMS System adheres to the mission and objectives of the FMS, the FMSA shall at all times support, advocate, and defend the tenets and values of this FMSEC and other Guiding Documents. The FMSA and all members must act free from bias of any kind in any direction regards, race, gender, religion, politics, affiliations, socioeconomic status, and free associations. Everyone must be treated fairly and positively.

Section 6. The FMSA shall not interfere with the curriculum, activities, actions, management, or other activities of any approved Element as long as they are meeting the requirements, intent, and purpose of the FMSEC and all Guiding Documents. If a conflict becomes apparent, the FMSA may investigate and seek corrective action. If the conflict cannot be resolved, it shall be elevated to the FMSGC for resolution and action. None of the requirements of Section 6 are intended to impact or interfere with FMSA's responsibilities regarding certifications of FMSEPs in Section 8.

Section 7. The Founders shall draft and ratify all Guiding Documents identified as ratified documents. If a ratified document requires Amendment, the FMSA shall guide the Amendment process according to **Article XI**. The FMSA shall draft, update as needed, and provide continuous validation and improvement of all Guiding Documents that are not identified as ratified documents.

Section 8. The FMSA shall manage a Certification process for all FMS Education Providers (FMSEPs). Prior to competing for a FMSEP contract at any school, the FMSEP must receive an FMS Education Certification Certificate from the FMSA. This certification process shall, at a minimum, validate that the company seeking to be a FMSEP bidder has the qualifications, capabilities, experience, personnel, and financial capability to successfully educate children in an FMS environment.

Section 9. In addition to ensuring regular communications, the FMSA shall host one yearly conference for engagement between the FMSA, the FMS Guiding Council, and the FMS Parent's Coalition for the purpose of maintaining open communications and to provide a forum for free thought, ideas, innovation, and to address broad grievances. The conference may be live or virtual, or a combination of both.

Section 10. The FMSA shall gather annual metrics, data, and analysis from State and Local FMSAs to develop an Annual Report on the State of FMS Education to be presented at the yearly conference and made public upon final approval. The FMSA shall direct the State FMSAs and Local FMSAs on what information is required and provide direction on content, format, and other requirements to ensure the Annual Report is complete, comprehensive, and reflective of the State of FMS Education and progress being made.

Section 11. To promote the success, growth, and adoption of the FMS, the FMSA shall actively market, promote, and lobby for the FMS System to create a positive image in the community and to open new states and localities to convert from the current government system to the Free Market Schools.

Section 12. Executive Members, and those appointed by them, may lobby or otherwise participate in activities directed at local, state, and federal officials and agencies with the purpose of improving the FMS environment for children or fighting against private or government persons, organizations, or entities who are planning actions that may harm the FMS environment. ALL activities by these advocates (internally and externally) must adhere to the tenets and values of this Constitution and the mission and values of the FMS. Authorized FMSA representatives may lobby on behalf of the students, parents, teachers, schools, and FMS Associations in support of the objectives of this Constitution.

Section 13. The FMSA shall charter all new State FMS Associations as needed to promote, convert, and develop the FMS Educational System within the respective states (see **Article VII**). The FMSA will determine when a State Association would be beneficial to the FMS System and has the potential to accomplish FMS conversions within that state.

Section 14. The FMSA shall be funded through three sources. The first source is a fee placed on all State FMS Associations at a level determined by the FMSA as effective in supporting the FMSA without placing undue burden on the State FMS Associations. The second source is an initial fee and annual fee placed on FMSEPs to obtain and maintain their FMS Education Certification Certificate. The third is from donations, grants, or other from external individuals, organizations, or entities. Being the only FMS Element that is allowed to receive funding from these sources, it is critical to ensure that these do not create any opportunity for influence or preference. FMSA executives may develop controls to prevent influence or preference, however in no case shall any donations, grants, gifts, etc. from individuals, organizations, companies, private or government entities, or others exceed $100,000 per year per entity.

Section 15. The FMSA shall fund the FMSGC for operating expenses, salaries, and necessary travel and other expenses through the process defined in **Article V, Section 8**.

Section 16. All members of the FMSA shall have read the FMSEC and ratified Guiding Documents and agree by signature that they understand and will abide by, support, and promote these documents and the mission, purpose, and intent they represent. Any member found to be publicly promoting concepts in conflict with these documents may be removed from the FMSA by majority vote of the combined FMSGC and FMSA executives. Exceptions for public conflict that may harm FMS may be made in advance in writing by signed agreement by a majority of the combined FMSGC and FMSA executives.

Article VII – State FMS Associations

Section 1. The State FMS Associations shall consist of one per state and territory in the United States and shall manage and direct the entire FMS System within their respective states and enforce the requirements and intent of the FMSEC and all Guiding Documents. The State FMSAs are the Executive and Legislative body of the FMS in that state.

Section 2. No State FMS Association shall operate except under Charter issued by the FMSA. The State FMSAs are subordinate to the FMSA but operate independently within their state.

Section 3. Upon issue of the Charter by the FMSA, the Charter will define the executives and the structure of that State FMS Association. The initial executives of that State FMS Association shall be selected by a majority vote of the executives of the FMSA and serve a four (4) year term. Reelections shall be held for all executive offices every four (4) years with a one (1) month transition period after the election. Individuals eligible to vote for the State FMS Association executives include all existing members of that State FMS Association, all members of any Local FMS Associations within that state, and all members of the FMS Parent Coalition within that state. A simple majority of all noted members is required to be elected to an office. If a simple majority cannot be attained for an office, the Association shall hold a runoff election of the top two (2) candidates for each office within two (2) weeks. The candidates shall not campaign during the runoff and only the State FMS Association may send out notifications to eligible member voters with <u>non-biased</u> information on each candidate.

Section 4. The State FMS Association's primary charter is to ensure the successful implementation and operation of all aspects of the FMS System within that state. They shall accomplish this by promoting FMS education benefits; securing and chartering Local FMS Associations; assisting in the conversion of public schools to FMS schools; and providing guidance and assistance to all Elements of the FMS within that state.

Section 5. To promote the success, growth, and adoption of the FMS, the State FMS Associations shall actively market, promote, and lobby for the FMS System to open new localities within the state and convert schools from the current government system to Free Market Schools.

Section 6. Executive members, and those appointed by them, may lobby or otherwise participate in activities directed at state and local officials and agencies with the purpose of improving the FMS environment for children or fighting against private or government persons, organizations, or entities who are planning actions that may harm the FMS environment. ALL activities by these advocates (internally and externally) must adhere to the tenets and values of this Constitution and the mission and values of the FMS. Authorized State FMS Association representatives may lobby on behalf of students, parents, teachers, schools, and Local FMS Associations in support of the objectives of this Constitution.

Section 7. The State FMS Associations shall not interfere with the curriculum, activities, actions, management, or other activities of any element in the state as long as they are meeting the requirements, intent, and purpose of the FMSEC and all Guiding Documents. If there appears to be a conflict, the State FMSA may investigate and seek corrective actions. If the conflict cannot be resolved, it shall be elevated to FMSA for resolution. None of the requirements of Section 7 are intended to impact or interfere with the State FMS Association's responsibilities regarding competitive bidding in Section 9.

Section 8. Every three (3) years, the FMS Parent Coalition of all states will provide a list of the existing FMS Guiding Council members and 40-50 additional candidates for the next term of the FMSGC. All State FMS Associations will, by combined majority of all executives and officers of the existing State FMS Associations, confirm 30 total members to the FMS Guiding Council for the next three (3) year term.

Section 9. The State FMS Association will hold competitive bidding events and award any statewide contracts needed for the FMS schools in the state. The State FMS Association will manage, administer, and pay contracts through state funding.

Section 10. The State FMS Association shall charter all new Local FMS Associations as needed to promote, convert, and develop the FMS Educational System within the localities of that state (see **Article VIII**). The State FMS Association will determine when a Local FMS Association would be beneficial to the FMS System and has the potential to accomplish FMS conversions within that locale.

Section 11. Initially, the State FMS Association shall be funded through the State Education Budget as the managing organization of the FMS school system within that state and must adhere to state requirements for submitting budgets to be incorporated into the state budgeting process. This budget may be restricted to the State FMS Association or include flow-down revenue for other parts of the FMS school system. Funding profiles may change over time per state requirements and FMSA directives. Future opportunities for alternate non-government funding sources may be explored and implemented per the requirements in **Article X**.

Section 12. All members of the State FMS Association shall have read the FMSEC and ratified Guiding Documents and agree by signature that they understand and will abide by, support, and promote these documents and the mission, purpose, and intent they represent. Any member found to be publicly promoting concepts in conflict with these documents may be removed from the Association by majority vote of the combined FMSGC and FMSA executives. Exceptions for public conflict may be made in advance in writing by signed agreement by a majority of the combined FMSGC, FMSA, and FMS State Association executives.

Article VIII – Local FMS Associations

Section 1. The Local FMS Associations, one per locale (county, city, district, or other school border delineation) within that state, shall manage and direct the entire FMS System within their respective locales and enforce the requirements and intent of the FMSEC and all FMS Guiding Documents. The Local FMSA Associations are the Executive and Legislative body of the FMS in that locale under the authority of the State FMS Association.

Section 2. No Local FMS Association shall operate except under Charter issued by the State FMS Association. The Local Associations are subordinate to the State Associations but operate independently within their locale.

Section 3. Upon issue of the Charter by the State Association, the Charter will define the executives and the structure of that Local Association. The initial executives of that Local Association shall be selected by a majority vote of the executives of the State Association and serve a three (3) year term. Reelections shall be held for all executive offices every three (3) years with a one (1) month transition period after the election. Individuals eligible to vote for the Association executives include all existing members of that Local Association and all Parents with children in K-12 FMS schools within that locale. The candidates for each office shall be elected by a simple majority.

Section 4. The Local Association's primary charter is to ensure the successful implementation and operation of all aspects of the FMS System within that locale. They shall accomplish this by managing the schools, securing FMS Education Provider and other contracts, monitoring student progress and success, ensuring the safety of all students and personnel, converting public schools to FMS schools, providing guidance and assistance to all elements of the FMS within that locale, and other activities as needed to ensure success.

Section 5. To promote the success, growth, and adoption of the FMS, the Local Associations shall actively market, promote, and lobby for community acceptance and conversion of public schools to the FMS System.

Section 6. Executive members, and those appointed by them, may lobby or otherwise participate in activities directed at local officials and agencies with the purpose of improving the FMS environment for children or fighting against private or government persons, organizations, or entities who are planning actions that may harm the FMS environment. ALL activities by these advocates (internally and externally) must adhere to the tenets and values of this Constitution and the mission and values of the FMS. Authorized Local Association representatives may lobby on behalf of the students, parents, teachers, and schools in support of the objectives of this Constitution.

Section 7. The Local Associations shall not interfere with the curriculum, activities, actions, management, or other activities of each school in the locale as long as they are meeting the requirements, intent, and purpose of the FMSEC, all Guiding Documents, and all elements of their contracts. If there appears to be a conflict, the Local Association may investigate and seek corrective actions. If the conflict cannot be resolved, it shall be elevated to the State Association for resolution. None of the requirements of Section 7 are intended to impact or interfere with the Local FMS Association's responsibilities regarding competitive bidding in Section 8.

Section 8. Local FMSAs will hold competitive bidding events and award contracts to FMS Education Providers (FMSEPs) and other support or services contracts needed for the FMS schools in that locale. All FMSEPs must hold a current Certification from the FMSA to be eligible to compete for a FMSEP position in the schools in that locale. The Local Associations will manage, administer, and pay those contracts through funding as noted in **Section 10** of this Article. All contracts must meet the minimum requirements set by FMSA and the Guiding Documents.

Section 9. The Local Associations shall gather metrics, data, and analysis from the schools, the teachers, the FMSEPs, and other sources to develop an Annual Report or other reports as directed by the FMSA and the State Association .

Section 10. Initially, the Local Associations and schools shall be funded entirely through the Education Budget of their respective school locales and must adhere to locale requirements for submitting budgets to be incorporated into the local budgeting process. Caution should be exercised to ensure that funding does not create opportunities for legislative interference in the FMS educational system. Additional funding may flow down from the State Association. Future opportunities for alternate non-government funding sources may be explored and implemented per the requirements in **Article X**.

Section 11. All members of the Local Association shall have read the FMSEC and ratified Guiding Documents and agree by signature that they understand and will abide by, support, and promote these documents and the mission, purpose, and intent they represent. Any member found to be publicly promoting concepts in conflict with the documents may be removed from the Local Association by majority vote of the combined FMSGC, FMSA, and State Association executives. Exceptions for public conflict may be made in advance in writing by signed agreement by a majority of the combined FMSGC, FMSA, and State Association executives.

Article IX – FMS Education Providers

Section 1. Multiple FMS Education Providers (FMSEPs) shall be contracted at every school under the direction of the Local FMS Association to best serve that community and provide a quality education for the children of that community.

Section 2. FMSEPs may not operate in any FMS school except under contract by the Local Association. No education, union, or other contract may be issued between, among, or in representation of the Local Association or FMSEP or members of either that conflicts with or contradicts the tenets or intent of the FMSEC or FMS Guiding Documents. No member of any FMS Element may be compelled to join or pay dues or fees to any external union, association, or other organization except where required by law.

Section 3. FMSEPs are individual companies, owned and operated as their owners deem best for this contract and within compliance of the FMSEC, FMS Guiding Documents, the law, and their contract with the Local Association who will act as their Contract Manager. FMSEPs are required to abide by these documents and their intent. All FMSEP contracts will contain minimum education and learning standards related to the grades, ages, and classes contracted with the FMSEP, who shall meet or exceed those standards in order to retain their contract.

Section 4. Contracts to provide educational services at FMS schools shall be awarded in a competitive bidding process as determined by the Local FMSA and Guiding Documents. No FMSEP company may bid on an education contract without first having obtained FMS Education Certification Certificate from the National FMS Association. This certification must remain active and valid throughout the entire contract period.

Section 5. In addition to a review fee paid to the FMSA to receive an FMS Education Certification, FMSEPs are required to recertify and pay an annual fee to the FMSA to maintain their FMS Education Certification Certificate.

Section 6. FMS Education Providers shall perform a comprehensive Annual Performance Evaluation of their programs, curriculum, classes, and every educator, counselor, or other student-facing employee of the FMS Education Provider to ensure that they are meeting FMS standards, education standards, and their contract requirements. This evaluation and any other information requested by the Local Association and the FMSA will be the basis for the annual renewal of the FMSEPs local contract and the FMS Education Certificate. The FMSEP will also be required to provide student metrics, grades, scores, and other data as requested to the Local Association to be rolled up into the FMSA's Annual Report and other reporting vehicles on schedules to be determined by the various Associations. Information requirements may be changed at any time and compliance is required to retain a FMSEP contract and certification.

Section 7. FMSEPs and their members are required to respond to parent or student concerns and complaints about curriculum, books, teachers, safety issues or other problems within the timeframe specified in their contract or the FMS Guiding Documents (whichever is earliest). The concern/complaint shall be copied to the Local Association, acknowledged, reviewed, given a proper hearing, and resolved within the specified timeframe. Parents and students must be informed that they may at any time escalate the issue to the Local Association for review.

Section 8. Visibility into all parts of the FMSEP's educational program is critical to ensuring compliance with all requirements and the satisfaction of higher FMS Elements and parents of the students. Proprietary materials, if necessary, shall be limited to the inner workings of the FMSEP's business operations and not address anything student-facing. Everything that is or may be student-facing or have student impact shall be available for FMS inspection without redaction or delay. This includes but is not limited to all books, curriculum, teaching plans, websites, videos, handouts, teaching scripts, and anything else that might have any exposure to the students. The FMSEPs shall allow unrestricted audio and video access as directed by the Associations and make accommodations for live or virtual class auditors.

Section 9. Every FMSEP is responsible for working with the school and all other FMS elements to ensure the safety, security, well-being, and effective learning experience of every student. Each FMSEP shall work with school administration and other FMSEPs or contractors to coordinate classes, grading, timing, activities, and learning pathways to ensure students and parents have a seamless experience through all grades to graduation.

Section 10. All employees, members, contractors, consultants, etc. of the FMSEPs shall have read the FMSEC and Guiding Documents prior to beginning work and agree by signature that they understand and will abide by and support these documents and the mission, purpose, and intent they represent. Any member found to be publicly promoting concepts in conflict with these documents may be removed from the contract by the Local Association. Exceptions for public conflict may be made in advance in writing from the Local Association.

Article X – Funding

Section 1. No FMS Element may seek, use, or otherwise accept Federal funding, grants, stipends, or other financial or political aid or support except as noted here. Students may accept scholarships, aid, and support from any source. FMS Elements may accept competitive grants, awards, and contracts that have no conditions for current or future actions that might put the FMS in conflict with the FMS Education Constitution or Guiding documents.

Section 2. Being as the mission of the FMS System is to provide the best education for our children, it is also important to recognize that money is a limited resource and the schools should not place an undue burden on the taxpayers. Therefore, all elements of the FMS System should make continuous efforts to improve the system and work to identify and implement additional sources of revenue that will help support the schools while not introducing the potential for interference or influence.

Section 3. Funding challenges should focus on innovation first, raising more money from secondary sources second, and partnering with the community third.

Section 4. All FMS Education Providers within a local school system must be treated equally (based on state and county funding capabilities) regarding influence, access, certifications, or other success drivers as determined by FMSA. Just as all students should be given the opportunity to succeed, all FMSEPs should also be given the opportunity to succeed for the students.

Section 5. Funding sources for each element have been identified in this Constitution. Additional funding sources can only be added if specified in that specific Article or through Amendment of this FMS Education Constitution as specified in **Article XI**.

Article XI – Amendments

Section 1. Should it become necessary in the course of time to change any aspect of this Constitution once ratified, the FMS Education Constitution can only be changed by attaching a formal Constitutional Amendment. By application of 51% of the executives of the National FMSA and 51% of the Parent Coalition, an Amendment may be proposed and presented for discussion. Upon presentation, the FMSA shall allow a minimum of four (4) weeks for discussion and final changes to the language of the Amendment. Once finalized, the FMSA shall then schedule a vote on the Amendment no less than four (4) weeks after final changes. The Amendment may only be ratified and attached to this Constitution upon a yes vote of 70% of the then current executives of the FMSA, 70% of the then current executives of all State FMSAs, and 51% of the then current Parent Coalition.

Article XII – Impeachment

Section 1. Except for where noted elsewhere, any executive of the FMS who does not adhere to this Constitution and the FMS Guiding Documents, or is determined to be a negative influence on the students or destructive of the intent of the FMS System, may be impeached and removed by a vote of 70% of the executives of the two (2) elements above where that executive is assigned. In the case of executives in the FMSA and FMSGC, 70% of the executives of both elements must vote to impeach.

Article XIII – Definitions

Section 1. The following definitions for terms used in this document are incorporated to ensure clear understanding and implementation. For terms not defined here, their purpose, intent, and meaning should be accepted in the context of usage within this document, other ratified Guiding Documents, and the records of the Founders in the creation of these documents.

- ***System***: Refers to the entire FMS System: all Associations at any level, all Providers, and all schools, staff, and support elements that have **any** interaction with the Free Market Schools. This includes any Contractors, Subcontractors, Consultants, Partners, Funding Entities, and any other elements or entities that have contractual interactions with the schools, Providers, Associations, teachers, administrators, or students.

- *__Element__*: Similar to "System" but refers specifically to anyone or anything that is a structured part of or under the direct control of the FMS System.

- *__Super-Majority__*: Where required, represents one half of the eligible body plus 30% more. Where this results in fractional representation, the number shall be rounded up.

- *__Founders__*: Those individuals who are involved in the initial creation, development, design, and implementation of the FMS, to include drafting and ratifying the FMSEC and other Guiding Documents of the FMS. The Founders shall also be the founding members of the National FMSA (FMSA).

Article XIV – Ratification

We, *the undersigned, hereby ratify* this FMS Education Constitution and mutually pledge to abide by the words, meaning, and intent of this document as written and to ensure that all others abide by the same to the best of our abilities.

Signed this date _____ by:

Signature: _____

Signature: _____

Signature: _____

Signature: _____

Signature: _____

FMS Student Bill of Rights

The Founders of the FMS Education System, understanding that our children are our future and education is our children's future, recognize that in a free society, education is the greatest gift we can bestow upon the citizens of that society.

Resolved by the Founders that every member of the FMS System shall do their best to ensure all students receive a proper education in a safe environment focused on education, learning, and knowledge. To help ensure that goal, these declaratory and restrictive clauses are hereby added as a ratified Guiding Document and supplement to the FMS Education Constitution.

Clause 1. Education and the joy of learning shall be the first and foremost mission of every element of the schools.

Clause 2. A minimum of a full core education meeting defined success standards will be provided to every student regardless of race, color, religion, gender, affiliation, or socioeconomic background.

Clause 3. The educational environment shall protect students from physical, mental, and other abuses as much as possible.

Clause 4. Teachers, coaches, consultants, counselors, administrators, or other individuals interacting with students shall not promote racial or other discriminatory doctrines, ideologies, or theologies. Nor will they compel students to accept, embrace, or promote discriminatory practices.

Clause 5. FMS members shall to the best of their abilities protect students against physical abuse, mental abuse, sexual abuse, indoctrination, sexual grooming, bullying, and other harmful or destructive activities or practices.

Clause 6. No student shall be compelled or required to participate, develop, support, or attend any political or social event, rally, protest, or other similar activity.

Clause 7. Parents shall have full access to all materials and programs used in the education of their children. This includes, but is not limited to, curriculum, teaching plans, textbooks, library books, worksheets, polls/surveys, presentations, recordings, and any other development materials including training materials for teachers.

Clause 8. To protect students and teachers, and allow full visibility to parents, wherever possible, video cameras (with maximum security protocols) will be placed in all classrooms and other interactional spaces except restrooms and locker rooms. Cameras with sound will remain on at all times and parents will have virtual access with privacy protocols to protect the students.

Clause 9. Students have a right to an environment safe from harm. FMS environments will as much as possible be made hard targets, FMS staff will be trained in emergency procedures, and other precautions will be implemented that are allowed under local law.

Clause 10. Students have a right to video or record lectures, take pictures of educational materials, and keep copies of materials where possible for the purpose of self-study, sharing these with their parents, or to file complaints publicly or privately. All materials retain traditional copyright protections.

Clause 11. Students have the right to file complaints regarding abuses, unfair treatment, discriminatory actions, violations of this Student Bill of Rights, or other issues the student determines needs to be addressed. All students will be informed of how to file complaints and who they can report them to.

Ratification

We, *the undersigned, hereby ratify this FMS Student Bill of Rights and mutually pledge to abide by the words, meaning, and intent of this document as written and to ensure that all others abide by the same.*

Signed this date _____ by:

    Signature: _____

    Signature: _____

    Signature: _____

    Signature: _____

    Signature: _____

    Signature: _____

FMS Core Values

In order to ensure an educational environment imbued with a Culture of Excellence, the Core Values ratified here are the basic values that must be displayed and promoted every day by Students, Teachers, Administrators, and all others who interact within the FMS System.

Resolved by the Founders that every member of the FMS System shall do their best to provide a positive, fair, and respectful environment that reflects the following values, objectives, and beliefs.

- ✓ Obtaining an education is one of the single most important things you can do for your future self.
- ✓ Maintain positive, friendly, open, and engaging environments that promote similar responses.
- ✓ Treat everyone with respect and fairness.
- ✓ Treat yourself with respect and fairness.
- ✓ Respect our country, our flag, and our Constitution.
- ✓ Respect family as the foundation of American culture.
- ✓ Help and guide each other to success.
- ✓ Promote an environment of fair play and gracious winning or losing.
- ✓ Promote a *"Culture of Learning"* rather than a *"Culture of Knowing"*.
- ✓ Teach or learn *how* to learn, *how* to question, and *how* to think critically about everything.
- ✓ Live, promote, and teach intelligent thinking.
- ✓ Teach or learn *"how"* to think, not *"what"* to think.
- ✓ Work smart, work efficiently, work with goals in mind.
- ✓ Invite innovation into every area of education.

- ✓ Promote a "Performance Mindset" based on optimism.
- ✓ Embrace diversity of ideas, philosophies, and political beliefs, which must be taught or examined in context of the educational subject matter being discussed and with all sides presented and represented fairly, equally, and in context.
- ✓ Allow any student to excel where they can. "*A rising tide lifts all ships.*"
- ✓ Individualism is a positive trait just as teamwork is.
- ✓ Promote communication and facilitate discourse always.
- ✓ Open Communication between students, parents, and teachers is core to supporting all values.
- ✓ Teach students who they CAN be in life and that THEY get to choose who they are and who they will be.
- ✓ The United States of America is the most amazing country in the world and deserves our respect and love.

———————— ♦ ————————

Ratification

We, *the undersigned, hereby ratify* these FMS Core Values and *mutually pledge to abide by the words, meaning, and intent of these values and to help all others abide by the same.*

Signed this date _____ by:

Signature: _____

Signature: _____

Signature: _____

Signature: _____

FMS GOVERNANCE STANDARDS

Now that we have seen the power of a Constitution and some of the other Guiding Documents, we **understand how important they are to protecting FMS from both internal and external corruption**. It makes no sense to go through all of this only to end up right back where we are now.

But it is also critical to understand and protect the "business" aspect of an extremely complicated FMS ecosystem. How do we ensure things are running as designed and that all Elements are working towards the success of the system?

For that, we turn to a series of **Governance Standards**. These consist of numerous **living documents** that may, *and should*, be reviewed and updated frequently to ensure the FMS System is operating at peak efficiency and effectiveness. These should be maintained and version controlled through a Quality Management System (QMS) such as the International Organization of Standards (ISO) 9001 requirements for QMS certification.

Although these documents are not formerly ratified as the other documents are, they are a part of the **Guiding Documents** that drive the system. All Elements of the FMS System are required to abide by these documents in every relevant activity.

Consider these documents as a **Business Governance Handbook** that provides guidance to the FMSAs, the schools, the FMS Education Providers, and all other entities that engage with the system. These documents provide structure, continuity throughout the system, quality management standards, and more.

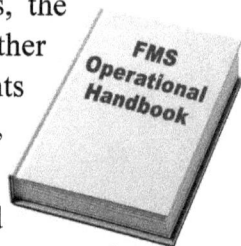

The following list of handbooks, standards, and guides provides just a glance of the **massive amount of documentation that will be required to run an enterprise of this magnitude**. In actual operation, some of these documents will be developed at the FMSA level and others at State, Local, or School levels. Some may be developed by the individual FMSEPs and be approved by the FMSA.

- **FMS Operational Handbook** (*the top-level guide that includes terms and a listing of all documents*)
- FMSA Handbook
- State FMS Association Handbook
- Local FMS Association Handbook
- FMS Guiding Council Handbook
- FMS Parents Coalition Handbook
- FMSEP Guidance and Standards
- FMSEP Certification Guidelines and Standards
- Guidelines for Developing a FMSEP
- Bidder's Handbook for Winning a FMSEP Contract
- Transitioning from Government Schools to FMS Schools Guidelines, Standards, and Checklists
- Educational Quality Standards
- Student Safety Standards
- Curriculum Minimum Standards and Requirements
- Security Standards for Physical Facilities
- Video/Audio Safety and Security Standards
- Educational Personnel Minimum Qualification Standards
- Community Partnership Guidelines
- Parental Involvement Guidelines

———————— ♦ ————————

THE POWER OF PAPER

If you actually read through everything in this chapter, let me just say, "***Thank You!***" And my apologies for all of the acronyms; that is my government contracting background showing through I'm afraid.

That was a tough read to get through, but it is only the beginning of the many thousands of pages that will be necessary to get from a simple book such as this to an operational Free Market School System. Why?

First off, this will be a major enterprise which always requires a forest of paper. But mainly, it will be necessary as protection in supporting a foundational change where people, organizations, and government entities will fight against this all the way. **Every step will need to be documented and defensible**. And every piece of it will need to defend itself from the infection of influence entering the system.

The **FMS Education Constitution** itself was quite long and detailed. At first glance, it may seem overly detailed in each of the different elements, but the detailed structure is necessary to maintain checks and balances that keep the system active and free from influence. In fact, this may become much more detailed in its final form.

The **precedence of authorities** and the methods for nominating, selecting, electing, and hiring members of these Elements seem complicated, but they must be designed from the ground up to keep big money and big influence from placing people in positions of power to corrupt the system.

Your head is probably still spinning from all the acronyms, numbers of members, who elects whom, and funding. **There is no need to memorize all of that**. However, I have provided a **Handy-Dandy Cheat Table** on the next page to help sort it out.

———— ◆ ————

I hope the point of all of this foundational development is clear in that **we cannot give up an inch in control** within the educational system. As we have seen throughout this book, **allowing any fractures in our educational foundation will likely result in deeper and more broad-spread roots of propaganda**, manipulation, and other attacks on our children in such a target-rich environment.

Constitutional Structure, Precedence, and Checks and Balances of the FMS System

FMS Guiding Council (FMSGC)
FMSEC Article V
30 Members

- 40 to 50 Candidates Nominated by the FMSPC with 30 Selected by the State FMS Associations
- Must be a parent of a K-12 child during first 4 years of service
- Funded by the FMSA

National FMS Association (FMSA)
FMSEC Article VI

- Initially Comprised of Founders
- Reelections Every 5 Years
- Elected by FMSA, FMSGC, State FMS Associations, and Parent's Coalition
- Annual Report on the State of FMS Education
- Funded by State FMS Associations, FMSEPs, Donations, Grants, etc.

FMS Parent Coalition (FMSPC)
FMSEC Article IV
2,000 to 5,000 Members

- Selected by Random Blind Lottery of Applicants Equally Representing All FMS States
- Parents of K-12 Children
- Nominate FMSGC Candidates
- Funded by the State FMS Associations at levels determined by the FMSA

State FMS Associations
FMSEC Article VII
One Association per State

- Initially Selected by the FMSA
- Reelections Every 4 Years
- Elected by Members of that State's FMS Association and that State's Parent's Coalition
- Will Elect the FMS Guiding Council Members
- Funded by Each State's Education Budget

FMS Education Providers (FMSEPs)
FMSEC Article IX
Individual Companies

- Competitive bidding by the State or Local FMS Association to contract with the best FMSEPs for each community
- FMSEPs must be Certified by the FMSA prior to bidding on a contract
- 2-10 FMSEPs per physical school
- Funded by the locale through the State and Local FMS Associations

Local FMS Associations
FMSEC Article VIII
One Association per Locality

- Reelections Every 3 Years
- Elected by Members of that Local FMSA and the Parent's of K-12 within that Locale
- Funded by Each Locality's Education Budget

Consider this final example of **why such powerful and enduring guardrails and controls are necessary** to protect the system. There are many examples to choose from but in this case a book was spotted by a parent in a public-school library that alarmed him... and for good reason in my opinion.

Below are just a few examples **pulled from a single book** that was in our public-school libraries.[162] Remember, this book is aimed at young teenagers (pre-teens also had access).

- *"There's nothing wrong with enjoying some porn, it's a fun sugary treat,"* the book stated.

- *"When consumed right, porn can help you discover new aspects of your sexuality."*

- *"A great place to research fantasies and kinks safely is on the internet,"* the book claimed. *"There's tons of people and communities out there who share your interests and have all kinds of advice."*

- After providing tips on sending naked pictures to their peers, the book instructed, *"So before you start sending your naughty masterpieces around the world, take some time to get friendly with photo editing, software and apps."*

Maybe not everyone agrees, but personally I believe any book in a school library that **instructs our children to seek out pornography on the internet** and to **talk to strangers online about sex** is, shall we say, problematic at the least.

Parents may raise their kids with whatever morals and values they like of course. If they want their kids to read this kind of stuff, they can buy that particular book, and many others like it, online and have it delivered to their homes the next day. For the rest of us, we don't want our children exposed to this type of information.

———————— ◆ ————————

So what do we do about it? We have seen that band-aid solutions do not work. We have seen we don't have the power to appreciably change the system that exists. We have seen that no matter what we do, the infection spreads.

So what is left to us?

At this time, more parents than ever have decided to **EXIT the public school system**. Exodus is a growing trend that is saving many children from the *"difficulties"* present in our government-based schools. This sends a powerful message and I am happy for <u>those</u> children.

But what about those left behind?

The BIG Question!

I hope you agree that **we need to save the futures of <u>ALL</u> of America's children**, not just those who have the means and ability to exit a bad system for greener pastures. Those left behind will face even more enduring and destructive hardships than ever before as those who can leave do so.

Do we abandon those who are left? Do we ignore *their* futures?

I believe the Free Market School System as I have described here is the only long-term answer. A system with unbreakable guardrails is the only way to sustain a viable educational system that **serves <u>only</u> parents and children**.

But I'm sure you may still be asking yourself, *"Is this really the answer? How in the world can we possibly do this?"*

I'm glad you asked!

12

DO WE HAVE TO SAVE **ALL** THE CHILDREN?

Things to consider:

➤ Is FMS really the answer?

➤ Is it truly worth going through all of this?

➤ Who would want it?

➤ Isn't it enough to save *some* of the children?

"We don't have to <u>make</u> human beings smart. They are born smart. All we have to do is stop doing the things that make them stupid."
—John Holt, *"How Children Fail"* [163]

LOOK!

"The answer is to make it clear that school is important, and school therefore must become important and must become again a temple of learning, not social experimentation. Not crazy wild-eyed ideas, but math, English, history, science, art and music - taught well and taught efficiently…"
—Bill Bennett, Reagan's Education Secretary[164]

TEMPLE OF LEARNING

As Bill Bennett (*Ronald Reagan's Education Secretary*) said in an interview in 2024, schools must again become a **"temple of learning, not social experimentation"**[165] He couldn't have been more on point in describing everything that we have covered in this book. The problem is not just the failures in learning that our children face, they are plagued daily by social and racial engineering, indoctrination, gaslighting, radicalization, and yes… social experimentation that is now becoming quite obvious to most of us.

In an article discussing *"Common Core"*, which is considered by many to be more failed experimentation on our children, Alex Newman stated that,

> *"It is time for the fraudulent "education" system to be exposed and replaced with real education before even more children are irreparably harmed – and the nation itself is destroyed."*[166]

I cannot speak for Mr. Newman, but I believe his comment was right on target here as well when applied to our discussion on today's public schools in general and our need to help those who are being left behind in our public schools.

The failure of our current public schools is **evident in every metric we can measure**. The result has been failing students, chronic absenteeism, and a mass exodus from the public schools. The exodus began in earnest during the COVID shutdowns but continues to this day as parents become more aware of the potential damage being perpetrated upon their children.

AT ITS VERY CORE, we have <u>2 choices</u> in America today to educate our children.

1. **Attend Public Schools**

2. **Exit to Alternative Schools**

   - Private Schools

   - Parochial Schools

   - Homeschool

   - Private Tutoring

   - Co-Op Schooling

   - Virtual Schools

You may have noticed that I did not include **Charter Schools** in either of those choices. Although sometimes better than public schools, Charter schools are subject to many of the same restrictions, interference, and government laws, regulations, rules, and "guidance" that public schools face as they try to **straddle that fence** between public schools and alternative schools. Some do well, but **without the guardrails of the Free Market Schools (FMS)**, they will all eventually come under the thumb of the governments as we talked about in **Chapter 8**.

Should you choose Option 2 above, there are many alternative school choices. Some of them are very good and, even if FMS becomes available in your school district, you might still choose to use an alternative method. **That is wonderful**. YOU are the parent, and you must choose what is right for your child. Once FMS has eliminated the social and political indoctrination from schools and improved educational value, you may very well choose to join the FMS public schools.

However, if you don't, **the FMS community will offer a welcoming hand** to assist you wherever possible in whatever education venue you use. After all, YOU are paying for the public schools and should have access to some of the resources:

- use of facilities and learning resources;
- co-Op classes, seminars, or training;
- tutoring, books, libraries, etc.;
- sports, music, physical education, etc.

After all, **this is about the education and advancement of ALL of America's children**.

Which brings us full circle back to the point of this chapter.

———————— ♦ ————————

In the end, if we save some of our children from today's public schools, we leave behind many others who will suffer the consequences of our departure from the battlefield.

My intention here is not to attack anyone personally for doing what is best for their child. I encourage choices. But the reality is that in order to bring FMS to your schools…

- We need you and your children fighting for it.
- We need all those who exit (or intend to exit) the public schools to fight for it.
- We need people with voices (whether they have children or not) to fight for it.

The conversion of public schools to FMS will NOT happen organically. **Nor will it happen easily**. There are factions with agendas who will fight this with their every breath and with massive amounts of money. We have seen how powerful a tool our children are to those who would use them. They will do everything they can to keep *your* children in *their* pockets.

The rest of this chapter is dedicated to **WHY we must fight** on behalf of ALL children, not just yours.

THE EDUCATION OF AMERICA

When we went through the History of Public Schools in **Chapter 4**, we learned that an educated society is the foundation for a successful, prosperous, and healthy free society that will continue to grow and thrive long-term.

However, that educated society must consist of more than book smarts. One of the most important factors of an educated American society is that the citizens of that society **understand the value of freedom and have the learning and free-thinking skills needed** to recognize and fight against tyranny and those who would take those freedoms away from them.

Sadly, that is not what our children are learning in today's public schools. We have seen throughout this book how those seeking power and societal change have infiltrated the public schools and are using our own educational system to indoctrinate and gaslight our children to **fight against their own freedoms** and support those would ultimately oppress them.

Having seen all of that happening in real-time, I keep coming back to one all-consuming thought…

LOOK! → *We Are America, Damn It!* ← LOOK!

We are masters of freedom and free thought. We are masters of industry. We are masters of science. We are masters of business and entrepreneurialism. **We are masters of accomplishing the impossible**.

➤ We eat innovation for breakfast.

➤ We lunch on invention.

➤ And we dine on revolutionizing the way things are done.

We started as a nation with the **formation** and **ultimate realization** of the United States of America, which was our first and finest accomplishment. The world said it could not be done. Until we just got up and did it.

We have since undertaken and achieved world-changing tasks for centuries that have altered the futures of the entire world. Even when we didn't start these tasks, we jumped in with both feet, put our minds to it, applied American ingenuity, and made whatever "it" was a reality that would change the world. We brought it to fruition. We made it greater than the sum of its parts.

And yet…

And yet…

We have **never** applied any of this to public schools.

We have never given the great **American free market system of innovation and enterprise** an opportunity to do what we do best when it comes to our most important asset. Our children.

Yes, there are entrepreneurs who develop and sell educational products, books, software, computers, and other **band-aids** to the schools. Some of them are innovative in themselves, but they are simply products and services to be **shoehorned into the existing public-school ecosystem**.

At best, these things treat symptoms. At worst, they are a part of the overall problem and contribute to the decline and abuse of our educational system. None of them treat the underlying disease.

We have seen what we can accomplish when we put our minds to it. If we harness the innovation, invention, and revolution we apply to other industries, we could do amazing and lasting things for our educational system. FMS does exactly that and opens the door to great American exceptionalism.

Don't we owe at least THAT to our children?

For anyone who follows the K-12 education universe, you have seen how innovation arises, only to be shot down, discredited, or destroyed before it ever reaches the schools. The massive system that is our government schools maintains numerous **checks and balances** to ensure that any "*innovation*" or "*changes*" that are allowed to see the light of day are only those that are generated by or approved by the powers who are aligned with those who are indoctrinating our children.

Again, even if any innovation actually sneaks into our current public school system, **it is limited to treating a symptom** and is not a solution designed to "fix" the system.

If it were, we would be seeing improvements in the education of our children. We are not.

——————— ◆ ———————

Which reminds me not to lose sight of the second part to all of this. Indoctrination, grooming, gaslighting, and other related issues in the schools are only <u>one part</u> of the problem.

We also want our children to have a <u>BETTER education</u>, right?

The rest of this chapter lays out some advantages of Free Market School system. Why would students, parents, teachers, and community want to go through all of this as if it is not also going to result in a better education for our children?

I am excited about the many great organizations and people out there who I know will have even more incredible and insightful ideas for the benefits of a true competitive free-market system. **I welcome their input.**

Following this chapter on "**why**", the next few chapters take us the rest of the way and provide some "**how's**".

- **Chapter 13**: explores how we Pay for this.

- **Chapter 14**: lays out a pathway for how we Start.

- **Chapter 15**: discusses Public/Private Partnerships.

- **Chapter 16**: talks about the Future of FMS.

- **Chapter 17**: explores Next Steps to the next generation.

——————— ◆ ———————

WHO WOULD WANT THIS?

The flippant answer would be, *"Everyone should want this!"* After all, our children are the future and everyone should want them to receive an amazing education and be fully equipped for success. **Right?** Unfortunately, there is only one thing we can be certain of…

Consensus on anything is nearly impossible.

One core concept is almost undeniable though… public schools are NOT going away anytime soon. As much as some believe they should be abandoned, that is not a viable reality in today's world. You can pull *your* children out and give them an education elsewhere, but **you will not convince the masses to abandon** the convenience, ease, and invisible funding of public schools. The allure of the **Yellow School Bus is powerful**.

To achieve our goals, we must work to **build a coalition from the stakeholders** that touch or use our educational system. We can only succeed by bringing the rest of America along with us. So, the question becomes… WHO would want to go through all of this and WHY would they dare try?

———— ♦ ————

WHY WOULD <u>PARENTS</u> WANT THIS?

Why? Let's start with nearly everything we talked about in the first half of this book. We have seen ample evidence that there are factions in our country who **believe OUR children are THEIRS** to mold however they like for the "**Greater Good**" of society.

Parents are simply a hindrance to their goals.

That alone should wake up every parent and prompt them stand in unison to shout, *"Enough! These are MY children!"*

Unfortunately, many parents will not stand with us. No need to explore their motivations, but we do recognize that most of today's parents are themselves the product of the existing public school system.

The only lasting control that parents can achieve now is to abandon the public schools individually and exit to an alternative education system. However, **the existing system will remain in place** for the majority of children, **who then may become in their adult lives the antithesis of who your children are**. The battle over education will continue – *rinse*, *wash*, and *repeat*. Over and over again.

It has become quite clear that today's exodus of parents and children from the public schools will not be a complete migration. With approximately **49 million children in K-12 public schools**, most will remain to endure a more desperate and determined onslaught of indoctrination and brainwashing than ever before.

Our children will spend their adult lives in conflict with many of those left behind who grew up to perpetuate the corrupt system we have now. Many of them will become teachers, and activists, and politicians focused on ensuring the system continues to pump out good subjects of the greater State.

Sound grim? **I welcome debate** from anyone on why that will **not** happen based on today's environment.

> *The positive side of me hopes you*
> *<u>will</u> be able to do just that.*

Don't get me wrong, **I believe every child saved from the system is a win**. But the goal of this book is for parents to consider a greater goal of not just a better education for their children, but a better world for those children to prosper in as adults.

So back to the primary question of this section, *"Why would parents want to do this?"*

- It is obvious that today's educational system is a dumpster fire.

- Estimates are one in ten students suffer from sexual misconduct by faculty or other students.

- At best, one in three students test proficient on core subjects for their age (*many districts report much worse*).

- The sexualization of children at very young ages is rampant throughout the system.

- There is an obvious war within the schools against family, faith, morality, personal values, and country.

I could go on and on and on, but we don't need to rehash the first eleven chapters here. Everything to this point has clearly laid out all the reasons a parent ***should*** want change for their child.

But do they want THIS change?

- This is the ONLY approach that focuses on saving ALL children within the current system.

- This is the ONLY approach that maintains the ease, comfort, and historical context of the community schools most of us grew up in.

- No other system retains the infrastructure and structural systems for mass education for all children (school buildings, yellow buses, lunches, sports program, etc.).

- FMS is the only long-term solution that has a chance of holding back the external powers that want to control their child.

- This is the ONLY educational system that allows for truly local control to allow the parents of each community to determine what is best for their children (*within the bounds of the FMS Education Constitution* (FMSEC)).

- FMS will reduce the cost of education (see Chapter 13) while improving the quality of education.

One KEY feature of FMS is that it is the SOLE educational system that addresses the issues discussed throughout this book **WHILE** allowing those millions of parents to continue what they have always done. Leave everything to the school system. No fuss, no muss, no effort on their part.

Let's face facts here.

The biggest reason government schools are so <u>prevalent</u> and <u>popular</u> and <u>persistent</u> is that, for most parents, **it is the <u>EASIEST</u> pathway to educate their children**.

The cost is pretty much invisible (*especially to those who rent their homes*). No effort is required. No thought is required. For many, they simply make sure their kids catch the bus.

Yes, many parents are much more involved than that, but for those who aren't, if we try to evolve to a new system that *requires* engagement by these parents, the creation will fail due to the large number who will fear change. Any change.

FMS does not require their involvement. Their involvement will be encouraged, welcomed, and desired, but nothing will change for them if they just sit back. The good news is that everything will still change for their children.

The parents who want to be involved in their children's education will have ample opportunity in FMS. And ALL children will benefit from their efforts. What could be better?

———————— ◆ ————————

WHY WOULD <u>STUDENTS</u> WANT THIS?

Students represent a diverse array of individual differences. They vary in age, come from diverse cultural and social backgrounds, belong to different socioeconomic strata, and have been influenced by distinct societal and governmental factors. Their current knowledge and perspectives are shaped by their educational experiences to date.

Trying to pigeonhole them into a single mindset of *"they want this"* or *"they want that"* would be nearly impossible – and unfair. When FMS is in the development stage, it would be wise to go directly to them and ask, "What do YOU want out of your educational system."

They won't have any direct control over how the system is structured, but their input and influence in the family and community will be vital to the acceptance, growth, and ultimate success of FMS within a community.

We can make some general assumptions for now from existing research and studies. These will not apply to all students of course, but we can build a baseline image of student desires to make the system better meet their needs.

- They want to be heard and their desires considered.

- They want a real education focused on giving them the knowledge and skills to be successful in the real world.

- They want to be prepared to compete and prosper in career, family, and/or higher education.

- They want the ability to focus on their interests and life paths with options for a more personalized learning environment.

- They want an environment free from distractions and negative influences.

- They want to not be dragged down by those students who have no desire to learn.

- They want more concentration in teaching actual core educational topics (reading, writing, and arithmetic).

- They want the ability to focus on specific capabilities such as STEM if desired.

- They want more experiential learning and opportunities to explore the real world while in school.

What that all boils down to is that these kids want to be ready for the world when they graduate out of high school. They want their school years to count and to make a difference.

This book has demonstrated that **FMS can meet all of those desires and so much more**.

———————— ◆ ————————

WHY WOULD <u>TEACHERS</u> WANT THIS?

Many will not. Some will have personal reasons, societal reasons, political reasons, and/or career reasons. The Teachers' Unions will fight this with every fiber of their being. Like a drowning man, they will scream, and flail, and kick as they fade into irrelevance. It will not be a pretty sight.

The teachers themselves will be a mixed bag of excitement, interest, joy, indifference, dislike, and sheer unadulterated hatred.

No matter how long ago we went to school ourselves (5 years, 20 years, 50 years) we all have similar stories about those truly incredible teachers we had... as well as the really bad ones. What was the difference?

- The **really good ones** were engaged with their job and the students. They worked "with" us and helped us learn. They were interested in our success.

- The **really bad ones** gave us "desk work" or in-class reading assignments. They were disengaged, often angry at every little digression, or even made it clear on a daily basis that we were unworthy of their time.

The Problem? In our current educational system, both types of teachers (*and every type in between*) are all treated exactly the same. Same pay scales, same benefits, same tenure, **same treatment as a commodity**. No matter how good or bad they are, they are treated equally. Knowing it makes no difference and that it is nearly impossible to fire them, **many of the worst teachers**

make no effort to excel or to improve their skills. And they are fine with the system just as it is.

Those bad teachers will probably NOT like the Free Market Schools.

Even for the "good" teachers, *of which there are many*, some will prefer the job security or the old way of doing things. For the rest, and for future teachers, there are many reasons to desire FMS.

- Career and personal growth will be similar to other free market companies.

- Merit-based employment and retention where they are rewarded for excellence and high performance.

- Poor performers are NOT rewarded and will be "encouraged" to move on to some other career.

- Merit, pay, bonuses, benefits, etc. are based on metrics such as reviews, subject mastery, excellence in service, going above and beyond duties, and positive surveys of students, parents, and other teachers.

- Ability to shop for better positions with different FMS Education Providers (FMSEPs), seeking higher pay, better environments, more benefits, etc.

- FMSEPs will be headhunting and bidding on the best and brightest teachers.

- Career growth potential (if desired) into the various FMS Associations (local, district, state, and national) or into the corporate structure of the FEMSEPs themselves.

And, of course, one of the biggest reasons for teachers to support FMS is **being a part of the next generation of education** and experiencing the benefits of an FMS educational system designed from the ground-up to focus on the students. Finally, **Quality of Work Life** in the FMS cannot we become a major draw as the schools become bastions of excellence in education and a positive and safer environment for everyone involved.

———————— ◆ ————————

WHY WOULD COMMUNITIES WANT THIS?

Communities have a vital interest in the quality of education the children of that community receive. It shapes not only the child's personal growth and well-being, but their future contribution to that society and economy. Will these future young adults be a positive influence? Or a negative one?

We have not explored community involvement in much detail yet, but will read more about that in **Chapter 15** where we talk about partnering with the community and businesses. The benefits of a higher level of community involvement in the FMS goes both ways. The schools and students benefit from opportunities, internships, job prospects, ties to the community, and supportive funding from businesses and organizations in the community (see **Chapter 13**).

The community as a whole benefits from a more effective, efficient, success-oriented education in a number of ways.

- A student population that is more involved, engaged, and participative in the community.

- Students graduating with a more useful education and the skills and motivation needed to succeed in the community and with the businesses supporting it.

- Decreased crime and social issues through a better educated citizenry with more positive engagement with the community. See the *Broken Window Theory* in **Chapter 5**.

- A culture of success that fosters a sense of accomplishment, community, and belonging.

- Reduced community costs of maintaining the educational system.

- More students graduate with a greater sense of family, belonging, self-worth, and life-preparedness that enhances the quality of job applicants and promotes career success and retention for businesses.

- Community engagement to support at-risk students from various socioeconomic backgrounds will drive job participation, engagement, and success of a broader spectrum of graduating students.

- Businesses will have clear pathways to provide internships and jobs to students to help them explore career opportunities.

These advantages can lead to a higher standard of living, less crime, and more opportunities within the community to support the retention of productive youth as they move into adulthood.

Of course, this type of cooperation will need to have appropriate safeguards, but the benefits to the schools, the students, and the community are substantial, sustainable, and can lead to generational change

---

WHY WOULD BUSINESSES WANT THIS?

Chapter 13 and **Chapter 15** will provide more details on issues related to businesses, partnerships, teaming, and other aspects of integrating our schools into the world of free markets. But let's take a quick look since we are talking about who would WANT to go through this type of change.

There are essentially **three categories of businesses** that will be driven to participate and work as effective change agents.

1. **Community Businesses.** These are the local businesses we talked about in community above. They will seek to improve the outcome of the schools to drive a higher-quality population that becomes part of their workforce and their customer base. They may also play a part in funding as we'll see later.

2. **National and International Businesses.** Large businesses are always recruiting from colleges and universities to identify the best and brightest candidates who can add value to their company. Creating competitive FMS environments will attract businesses to engage with students earlier in order to spot and mentor promising talent for future jobs. These businesses may also offer specialized scholarships in exchange for commitments from the students as they move from high school to college.

3. **Service Providers.** These are all the businesses that will spring up to support FMS activities. Starting with the private company FMS Education Providers (FMSEPs) who will be the front-line educators, we then move to curriculum developers, EdTech software developers, tech support services, facilities management and maintenance, and so much more. They will be competing to sell services to the FMS system through major contracts that could be local, statewide, or national. Under strict conditions, they may also become alternate or supplemental funding sources (see **Chapters 13** and **15**).

Whole new worlds of opportunity will awaken as entrepreneurs begin to recognize the vast size of this now-open marketplace of ideas, exchange, growth, and expansion.

The cost of K-12 education in
America is estimated to be over
$800 Billion per year.[167]

A number like that will open many eyes wide throughout the business universe – from **single entrepreneurs to multi-billion-dollar international corporations**. We could spend time exploring this now, but I think it is safe to assume that they will all be interested in exploring the concept.

———————— ♦ ————————

WHY WOULD <u>ALTERNATIVE SCHOOLS</u> WANT THIS?

Alternative schools (private schools, parochial schools, home schools, etc.) are almost entirely isolated from our public school system today. They all have the same goal of educating children, but generally, no resources are shared, no funding is shared, no facilities are shared.

This is by design from both sides of the educational equation. **Governments see alternative schools as competitors** that take students away from the greater public system. In many cases, this means less funding for the public school. Obviously, the public schools are not fans of alternate schools taking away students.

Parents face a few problems though. First and foremost, although parents are paying for the public schools, **they must still pay for their alternative schooling** in most cases. Work is being done to resolve that issue, but it has been a long-fought battle with mixed results. However, where there is success in this area, that **success comes with a price** as we'll see below.

Secondly, alternative schools do not have access to the vast resources of the existing public schools. They are generally not allowed access to facilities, sports complexes, libraries, and other common resources. Although the parents pay for these resources, they are generally forbidden, in the strongest terms, from using any of them if their kids go to alternative schools.

Any success in that area will come with great risk. By partnering with the public school system, **alternative schools risk opening their doors to government power or influence** in their schools. Once the door is open, there's no closing it again. So, they all operate in their own segregated silos.

I have made clear throughout this book that the FMS system would welcome partnerships and sharing between FMS and all alternative school systems.

After all, we have the <u>same</u> mission…
a great education for our children.

Details like cost-sharing and other issues can be worked out when the time comes, but alternative schools can rest assured that there will be no government interference, influence, or infection by partnering with the FMS system.

In fact, FMS would be all-in for full cooperation between various non-government school environments to achieve best of both-worlds functionality, shared resources, and the ability to learn from each other. The Free Market School Association (FMSA) would also work to drive interaction between the different school models to search for value-add opportunities for collaboration and funding.

Having fought for access to public school facilities as a homeschooler (*and failed*), I imagine that many (but not all) alternative schools would be interested in exploring the possibilities if they are confident there would be no corruption of their school system by the government or the FMS.

— ◆ —

FEATURES AND BENEFITS

Throughout this book I have painted a **pretty bleak picture** of our educational system. However, along the way, I have also given glimpses of the **benefits to be derived**. My intent here is to bring in a ray of sunshine and highlight some of the features, possibilities, and benefits that might not have been obvious in our previous discussions.

These are in no particular order, but comprised together, they provide an **overall picture of hope, success, and a bright future** for ALL of our children that would never be possible under our current oppressive, repressive, obsessive education system.

Before we begin though, there is **one overarching feature** that makes all the rest of this possible.

Innovation!

The ability to Innovate and Implement quickly!

Our schools have been moribund in bureaucracy, red tape, and resistance to change for many decades. **Technology** and **our understanding of the human mind** have expanded exponentially in the last 20+ years, yet NONE of that has effectively worked its way into our schools.

Other than spending billions on putting computers in classrooms so that we can continue to teach with the same methods we always have, we have not really adapted to innovation and new knowledge since the 1940s. The only difference now is that the students are more disconnected from the teachers and other students than ever before.

I cannot stress enough how important the ability to Innovate AND Implement safely and efficiently is to delivering a next generation education to our children. **We can no longer wait 10-15 years** for new ideas to propagate through red tape to be tested in one school system, be evaluated by committees, receive validation through multiple studies, cycle through funding channels, only to propagate slowly through the school systems to ultimately be implemented badly with a **predetermined failure rate** (this is an actual thing).

> *The speed of today's world does not allow us to wait on the same bureaucracy we have used for the last 100 years.*   **LOOK!**

We can do better. NO business would survive today under that **slow drip of watered-down innovation and adaptation**. WHY do we think that is okay for our children's education.

FMS will allow us to **model, test, evaluate, and implement innovations and tools near real-time** to ensure our schools can keep up with the speed of innovation of the rest of the world. Proven innovations can then **quickly propagate** throughout the FMS system.

The following list of features, benefits, and tools is a broad look at the possibilities that FMS allows us through the ability to adapt and change quickly to deliver the **Next Generation of Education**.

These models may or may not be incorporated into FMS. That will be up to the Founding Members (*Founders*) as they build the first draft **FMS Model Education System**. Then again, by the time we get there, many of these concepts may be outdated and replaced by new innovations and tools. THAT is the power of the free-market system.

I encourage you to explore these concepts, **then stretch your mind to consider ways to go beyond what I present here.** Imagine what a clean slate would allow. With Free Market School system, <u>we are not bound by the momentum and governmental control of our current monolithic mega-system.</u>

Let's take a look at some of the possibilities from today's **smorgasbord of delicious tidbits** to sate our educational pallet.

Whole Child Education

Although we must be cautious of watering down the essential education of our children (see *essentialism* below), it is also important to focus on the whole child and their development as individuals and future citizens. We need to focus on aspects like their Social-Emotional Learning (SEL) (*and no, that does not mean more time on TikTok or X*) as well as academic learning. **This is especially critical for at-risk students**.

By applying more emphasis on **Leadership**, **Communication Skills**, **Employability**, **Personal Wellbeing**, and other building blocks of a happy, successful, and social being, we ensure that children develop the skills they need to move beyond high school into adulthood.

Skills to support that growth might include Public Speaking, Group Leadership, Debate Skills, Career Development, Self-Awareness, Resilience, and more. Most importantly, we must give them the skills to **think critically** for themselves and explore beyond what they are taught. We must encourage them to step out of their comfort zones and reach for more in their lives.

CAUTION: As we have read throughout this book, we have to be extremely guarded that we do NOT introduce indoctrination, propaganda, and other external influences into the environment. We give them the tools; **they must be encouraged to make their own decisions on who they will be**.

Focus on Essentialism

Throughout the rest of this chapter, I will introduce numerous approaches that schools could be using in an FMS environment, but we must remember this is about education. Underneath all of these exciting things we must not forget the core of education that focuses on the essential elements of what an education should be.

Essentialism is not to be confused with minimalism.

- **Minimalism focuses on reducing the quantity of things**. At its core, that might mean teaching only reading, writing, and arithmetic. *But we need to go beyond that in order to focus on the Whole Child.*

- **Essentialism focuses on prioritizing and increasing the quality of essential things.** In our case, we would prioritize those things that are essential to a Whole Child Education, then focus on improving the quality of delivery of those things to make them more effective, efficient, and applicable to the success of the child in the real world.

Our schools today are teaching many things that are NOT essential (*or even appropriate*). Those things will be removed to make room for the things that actually do matter. We will determine what is important to making the students successful in the real world, identify what methods work, then focus on improving how we efficiently deliver the most powerful education we can. Since the FMS Education Providers (FMSEPs) will be competing with each other, they will innovate to be the best at all aspects of this approach. THAT is how our free-market system made America great.

Commercial Advantages

Speaking of the free-market system, schools will now have the same commercial advantages that businesses have used to succeed throughout America's history. The FMSEPs will work in a competitive environment and compete for contracts at schools. They will also recompete at various intervals to retain those contracts. This means they must continuously innovate, adapt, and improve to address rapid changes in a swift-changing world.

No longer will they be able to hang onto the "*that's the way we've always done it*" mantra. Like all other businesses, they will need to innovate or die. Advance or be left behind. THAT is the nature of the free-market system.

Best Practices

Our current monolithic school system obviously struggles to implement best practices within the system. Most so-called "*best practices*" that *have* been implemented in recent years were those driven by political agenda and not really focused on the success of the child.

In the FMS system, leading edge methodologies, tools, and processes can be tried, proven, then adopted by a FMSEP. The FMS Association (FMSA) will analyze the best practices and innovations, then, if effective, approve them for publication to all other FMSEPs to promote adoption within their systems.

Brand recognition, prestige, and bonuses offered by the FMSA will be strong motivators for the FMSEPs to continue innovation efforts and offer next level education services to their students. Remember, in most schools, parents will have the option to pick and choose the specific FMSEP that they want to educate their child. This recognition and prestige is critical to the growth of each FMSEP. But make a mistake and the parents will punish the FMSEP by moving their children to a different provider.

The success of each FMSEP in the competitive system is performance-based and success-based. Giving parents more power than ever before to ensure their children get the best education possible – even in socio-economic challenged locations.

Parental Focus Choices

One of the most exciting aspects of the FMS is that each school will likely have multiple FMSEPs providing services at that school that parents can choose from. Each *may* have a different focus on intensity, discipline, curriculum style, teaching style, or aspects as basic as dress codes. Another aspect is that all FMSEPs in a single school or system could potentially agree on certain broad aspects such as a single dress code for all students at a specific school or within certain disciplines.

Parents will drive the focus of these FMSEPs by choosing which to choose for their children. The free market will then drive which FMSEPs are most successful as the parents of each community choose what THEY want for their children. If FMSEPs want to continue winning contracts, they will adapt, evolve, and implement the best practices, tools, and approaches that are successful.

Meritocracy

One of my favorite advantages of the entire FMS system is MERIT. You may remember our discussion in **Chapter 5** where we looked at the differences between a *Bureaucracy* and a *Meritocracy*. We must explore that again because it is THAT important.

In our current school system, it seems nearly impossible to fire a teacher over poor performance or even negligence. Even with egregious violations, the teachers' unions often make it easier to shift bad teachers to different schools or move them into holding areas like the infamous "**Rubber Rooms**" (see **Chapter 5**) than to remove them. That is the power of massive bureaucracy.

NO MORE!

FMS will be a *Meritocracy* where the focus is on performance and accountability, not union demands and tenure. Teachers and all others are hired, promoted, paid, and fired based on their skills, ratings, quality of work, and other elements that might resemble "*customer service*".

> I like the recently coined term, **MEI** employment where employees are hired, promoted, and discharged based on **M**erit, **E**xcellence, and **I**ntelligence (*or use thereof*).[168]

Those who cannot do the job well, or who lag or fail, are subject to discipline, retraining, or losing their jobs. Just like in the real world.

This is NOT a "*Job for Life*" as in a bureaucracy. This is a place where you can build a great career... if you are good enough. If you are not, then you will need to move on to some other career. Just like in the real world.

Highly skilled teachers and administrators will compete for jobs with the best FMSEPs who offer better environments, better pay, and better benefits. The FMSEPs will seek to hire the best candidates based on criteria such as MEI that matter to the end users... the children.

All employees will have to adhere to the FMSEP's and FMSA's ethics, rules, policies, and procedures, but continued employment and potential promotions or raises are dependent upon many factors. These might include, but are not limited to:

- Annual performance reviews by the FMSEP (employer),
- Parent and student reviews,

- Grade and subject matter mastery,
- Student accomplishments,
- Student success improvements,
- Above and beyond activities,
- School and community involvement.

To **ensure that schools with high at-risk populations are properly served by the best of the best**, the FMS Associations and FMSEPs might offer various incentives, promotions, bonuses, etc. to higher quality teachers and administrators to entice them into serving these areas. Because this is a free-market system and not a bureaucracy, **the possibilities are limited only by the imaginations** of those driving the system.

Numerous Education Theories and Methods

In an open free-market school system, private companies could (*within the bounds of the FMS Education Constitution and FMS Guiding Documents*) employ a variety of innovative educational methods to improve student outcomes and differentiate themselves from their competitors.

The following list of potential methods is NOT exhaustive in any way but provided as an example of the possibilities based on approaches non-government schools are using today. A few of these are explored in more detail below, but more detail for all can be found through searches online or AI (Artificial Intelligence) discussions.

- Personalized Learning
- Blended Learning
- PBL's
  - Project-Based Learning
  - Performance-Based Learning
  - People-Based Learning
  - Problem-Based Learning
- Flipped Classroom Model
- Competency-Based Education (CBE)
- Experiential Learning
- Social-Emotional Learning (SEL) (discussed above)
- STEM-Focused Education
- Small Schools
- Micro-Schooling

- Career Technical Education (CTE)
- Modular or Pod Learning (Learning Pods)

We could go on and on and on as there is no end to the innovation in education that we are experiencing today. BUT **little of this is propagating into our public school system** (*where the vast majority of our children are now*). This innovation and exploration is generally external and focused on education outside of the public school system.

In an FMS educational system, the best of the best methods could be integrated quickly into single or multiple FMSEPs. Once proven effective, they could then propagate throughout the national system to benefit students across America. That could never happen in our current public schools.

Small and Micro School Theory

This aspect could fill an entire book, but let's break it down to some basics. The terms Small School and Micro School have slightly different meanings, but essentially describe the ability to operate as a smaller, leaner, student-focused entity while reaping the benefits and resources of a larger school environment and system.

Within an FMS system of schools, each physical location will have several FMSEPs of different sizes operating in the school. They will be smaller entities with a subset of the students at that school so that they can operate more independently (*within the constraints of the FMS system*) and reap the benefits of operating as a small/micro school with the resources of a larger system.

Small/micro schools have the ability to **tailor their curriculum and methods to the individual needs and interests** of a small, focused group – rather than having to rely on a **one-size-fits-all approach** (*as discussed early in this book*). These smaller elements can provide more direct feedback and guidance to the students in their circle and are able to adjust methods, speed, curriculum, or other aspects on-the-fly and as needed to ensure ALL individual student's needs are met.

Studies of small/micro schools[169] have shown that the tighter structure can:

- promote higher academic achievement due to the more directed attention;
- maintain educational interest and engagement through personalized teaching;

- develop stronger critical thinking and problem-solving skills;
- improve test scores and graduation rates through focus teaching;
- prompt college readiness, especially for low-income, minority, and at-risk students;
- provide more opportunities for expanded learning as teachers develop a more individualized understanding of their students.
- reduce dropout rates, absenteeism, and behavioral problems by maintaining engagement and opportunity for participation;
- foster stronger social and emotional development through deeper bonds within the schools and their classmates;
- promote student engagement and motivation through increased opportunities to participate in decision-making, leadership, and internal/external activities (i.e., no "*hiding in the crowd*").

This would be impossible in the monolithic structure of our current public schools. However, with FMS we can **obtain all of the benefits** of the small/microenvironment while **negating the usual inherent challenges** and **limitations** such as:

- higher operating and overhead costs;
- limitations on specialized staff and facilities;
- restrictive curricular and extracurricular options;
- limited access to sports, arts, clubs, music programs, etc.;
- isolation that may reduce social and cultural horizons.

So, think of the FMSEPs within the system as small schools residing within a larger infrastructure of school collectives. We gain the inherent advantages of economy of scale and shared resources, as well as the advantages of operating as a small, focused entity in very close proximity to the end-user... the students.

Career Technical Education (CTE)

Remember our previous discussion about community and business involvement in the schools? Career Technical Education (CTE) is the perfect marriage to build that relationship and benefit students, schools, businesses, and communities.

If it has been a while since you've been in school, you may remember something similar to this as Vocational Tech (or Vo-Tech). When I went to school, this was essentially a choice between taking Wood Shop or Automotive Technology. This ain't that. Think of this as a different type of Vo-Tech on steroids.

CTE classes will explore all kinds of industries and determine what the **highest-demand jobs are** within that school's community and the broader job market. The CTE will help the students develop basic skills in those areas and then teach them to advocate for themselves within the community (*with school assistance*). The students and the school would then concentrate on **building those 2-way relationships within the community** and develop pathways for student engagement and opportunities to experience a whole world of career opportunities **within the communities where the students live**.

There are many ways to run a CTE program, but here is just one approach (*roughly based on a real-world program to build houses that caught my eye while I was researching this*). A CTE program might be designed to work across a broad spectrum of skills and implement it with some students working with financial and banking businesses in the area to raise seed money to contract with a local contractor for other students to learn the trades to build a house through the program. Meanwhile, other students in the program would be working closely with real estate agents to learn the market, finance the land/build, then market and sell the house afterwards. The profits from that house would go towards funding the CTE program for next year's project. Throughout all of this, other students may work with the government for permits and such, or marketing to interest the community in the program and ultimately to sell the house.

Each student in a program of 30 or 60 students across a year may gain experience in three or more different aspects of a project such as: project management, project planning, finance, construction, real estate, interior design, marketing, sales, etc. Different classes may also compete with each other for special recognition.

This large scale CTE may not be appropriate for every school, but there are many large and small programs that could be developed, including programs related to technology, manufacturing, retailing, trades, and more. For added interest, the different FMSEPs in a single school could team up to run a major recurring CTE such as building affordable homes. The possibilities for providing broad-based experiential learning to the students are endless.

Educational Technology (EdTech)

One of the hottest industries in the market today is developing and providing the latest technology to support the vast educational and training needs for businesses, adult education, alternate schools, colleges, tutoring, and more (*nearly all provided outside of the public school system*). **Educational Technology (EdTech)** encompasses tools to manage educational functions, develop curriculum, deliver curriculum, deliver remote learning, develop learning education systems (LES), audio/video production, and more.

You may remember that when COVID hit, many public schools shut down and suddenly jumped on EdTech to allow them to teach remotely. By most accounts, **the entire effort failed miserably**. This was in part because the teachers and students were thrown into government-procured systems without adequate training or vetting. But the primary issue was that the use of EdTech in the school system did not develop organically or through free-market analysis, testing, and implementation. The schools attempted to simply layer EdTech on top of the existing public education model and assumed it would work the same. Our children suffered for that mistake.

Now imagine if **FMS evolved from the beginning to incorporate the latest technology, tools, and processes** that have been developed by companies whose sole purpose was to compete to deliver the most effective and engaging education and training conceivable. Imagine the future possibilities as technology evolves and incorporates AI and other advances.

Our current educational system would attempt to duct tape these advances (particularly AI) on top of the existing failing methods and likely exacerbate the problems we already have. Free Market Schools would be able to quickly adapt, adopt, and implement technologies as they evolve to ensure those technologies are always working in the interest of the students and their success.

Finally, although **we must be extremely careful not to experiment with our children**, there would be safe opportunities here to partner with EdTech companies in the development of technologies that would benefit the students and potentially provide opportunities for additional funding for the schools (see **Chapter 13** and **Chapter 15**).

Gamification

Significant advances have been made in recent years in the application of **Gamification of Education** and **Game-Based Learning**. These two approaches are similar but have slightly different foundations.

Gamification involves adding game-like elements to curriculum, lessons, or activities that may or may not involve a game framework. This might involve individual or group competition for recognition, prizes, or other incentives.

Game-Based Learning focuses on the placement or incorporation of educational materials inside of a game structure that allows the student to practice learning concepts in a familiar, fun, and free-flowing environment that can be accomplished competitively in the class or as homework online. I learned to type in a gamified typing tutor and can now generally type up to 80 words-per-minute. It was easy, fun, and extremely effective.

Both approaches have similar benefits in that students are familiar with and generally enjoy the game environment of competition and growth to move to the next level (i.e., learning more things). For example, some platforms allow teachers to develop quizzes, surveys, and discussions for the students to participate in (competitively or not) in a game-like environment. Other examples provide a gaming framework that allows teachers or curriculum developers to focus the educational rigors within the game.

The purpose of course is to increase engagement and interaction, and to help students develop more evolved social-emotional skills as they use the gamifications to compete and then interact in the live setting of the school environment for recognition and rewards.

Cognitive Diversity and Learning Profiles

In our massive public school system, there exists among our students a vast diversity in learning profiles (ADHD, Autism Spectrum, Dyslexia, Gifted, etc.) that differ from what is considered "*normal*" (the majority of students). **Even "normal" exists as an extremely broad spectrum of "how" students learn best**. The natural learning needs of all students include learning styles such as these (*not a complete list by any means*):

- memorization,

- repetition,

- experiential learning,

- nonformal learning,

- relational learning,

- linear learning,

- reflective learning.

People process information in different ways and may not even be aware that something is different. It is estimated that **1 in 5 people have learning differences, with many of them unaware** of why they are struggling in school. They may need additional support in school – *or even just understanding and guidance.*

The way they learn best can be quite different from how they are being taught in school. This can be a great determinator of their probabilities of success.

It is nearly impossible for our current educational system to properly manage and educate across this diversity. Hence, the **one-size-fits-all type of education** we have touched on a couple of times.

> FMS environments are **built from the ground-up** to accommodate and encourage diverse thinkers in creative and innovative environments. These focused environments are possible because **FMSEPs are designed to evolve and adapt** as needed to best serve the students.

Grading for Success

Grading of students has been a major topic for educators for decades as they search for something better than the traditional A-F grading system. The result has been a hodge podge of methods tried to blend into a universal grade that is difficult to interpret. Of course, with the monolithic public school system, no universal adaptation has been possible.

One of the most destructive methods that has been tried is the so-called "**No-Zero**" grading system that bans teachers from grading students below 50% – even if they do zero work. This ensures all students pass the class and move up the ladder to graduation. But at what cost?

I think we recognize the cost of inaccurate or willful "pass-grading" whenever we look at the abysmal reading and math levels of today's High School graduates.

The FMS system will have a universal grading policy designed by our Founding Members (Founders) that will likely have a traditional linear master grade system (such as A-F, or similar), but may also include a comprehensive **"Dashboard" grading expansion** that will provide the teachers, students, parents, and post-education schools a full-person picture of the student.

In addition to the **Master Achievement Grade (MAG)** (A-F, 0.0-4.0, 0%-100%, etc.) which is a raw demonstration of what the student has learned (to be used as their GPA), FMS may include other grades/scores in a Dashboard such as the following.

- **Process Score**: learning behaviors, participation, homework, etc.

- **Progress Score**: improvement, growth, ability to move forward.

- **Mastery Score**: actual mastery of the subject matter, rather than the ability to pass tests.

- **Application Score**: demonstrated ability to apply the learning to real-world applications.

- **Relative/Comparative Score**: used to compare students in relation to their peers.

- **Community Score**: participation in school, community, social activities, charity, debates, public speaking, etc.

Some of the grades and scores *may* be generated in part by students submitting a proposal to the school, their teachers, or possibly the other students to demonstrate and argue for their scores.

The Founders will examine all current and prospective systems, including those used in other countries around the world to determine the best method to track progress and help all stakeholders fully understand the student's accomplishments.

As we can see, there are incalculable benefits to converting our schools to a FMS system. And many very daunting challenges. But it should be obvious by now that **the advantages for our children far outweigh the considerable fight** we will face in making this transition.

EDUCATIONAL EXCELLENCE IN UNDERSERVED AND AT-RISK COMMUNITIES

Before we move on to close out this chapter, we need to touch on one of the most important benefits of FMS education.

Arguably, **children in underserved and at-risk communities** are those who most need a major reformation of the educational system. Test scores, graduation rates, and drop-out rates of our public schools in those areas are abysmal. Money is limited, but even as we keep spending more and more per student, the results seem to get worse and worse. There are other factors at work here.

We discussed the problems in these schools earlier... but **what is the answer?**

You know what I'm going to say.

FMS Education Providers (FMSEPs) are **competitive organizations designed from the ground up to compete** to be the best and to drive the best results. The impact of this in challenged environments cannot be overstated. In this environment, even with limited resources, there are opportunities.

First, improved methodologies, systems, support, and **competitive teacher employment** will begin to improve morale, student interest, interactivity, and community involvement. This will not come easy, but the inherent message of hope in this system will propagate through the students over time.

Just as "**Opportunity Zones**" have helped businesses and employment in certain areas, "**Educational Zones**" could bring about a renaissance in education as positively affected students share and promote the advantages of the new school system to others in the community.

FMSEPs will be rewarded for their work in these communities and will work closely with the parents, community, and local businesses to get them involved and engaged with the youth of that community. This should result in a broader field of after-school activities, internships, and part-time jobs for students.

Most importantly though are the **expanded opportunities to draw in additional funding and support** to these at-risk schools to allow them to invest in higher quality teachers, administrators, support staff, and facilities to provide a positive environment of hope, optimism, growth, and a belief in their own futures.

We will go into more detail about funding methodologies in the next chapter, but here are a few specific possibilities for these underserved and at-risk communities.

- Being part of the nationwide organization of the FMS system means they may be able to take advantage of economies of scale to allow schools to access resources they could not afford previously.

- Districts may be grouped into super districts to access broader resources and execute contracts at a large scale.

- The National Free Market School Association (FMSA) and State FMS Associations **may pool resources from fees and other activities to help fund these communities to allow them to recruit and employ higher-quality teachers** than they could afford on their own.

- FMSA and State Associations may seek donations from more prosperous districts and FMSEPs to help out the less prosperous ones.

- Finally, remember that **this is a competitive bidding environment for FMS Education Provider companies**. FMSEPS may choose to package their more prosperous districts with less affluent districts to **cost average** their offerings and provide higher levels of service in these communities at a loss.

It is NOT all just about the money. But the ability to hire better people, invest in the schools, and invest in the students is critical in these environments to transforming the **momentum of a culture of failure** we experience now towards **a culture of optimism and success**.

LOOK!

——————— ◆ ———————

NOW WE KNOW WHY!

*"Knowledge is the most empowering tool we
can give our children. Add innovation,
exploration, a culture of learning, and a
sense of future to the mix and you have a
recipe for a lifetime of unbounded potential."*

— Me

We can no longer let the system run amok with our children
as unwitting victims of a system that puts them last. No longer
can parents sit back and assume that the government has their
children's best interests as their focus. No longer should we watch
from the sidelines as our national education system spirals away
from its core mission of education.

Free Market Schools can rip us out of that downward spiral
and establish a brilliant future for ALL children.

I may have painted a bleak future for our children if we do
not change, but my case is that it does not have to be that way.
**We can turn our schools into miraculous and shining
institutions of education, learning, and growth for ALL
children**. But to do that, we need to…

Ensure No Child Is Left Behind!

That phrase may sound somewhat familiar to you, but the
original use of those words accomplished very little in the real
world. Although it did help a few children, it **did nothing to fix
the system or establish a better education for all**. It was a nice
political platitude to gain the votes of parents, but as with most
political catch phrases, the results were underwhelming.

Parents and others must understand that **if we continue the
mass exodus from today's public schools as our solution, then
we are abandoning the rest of the country's children to a
potentially crippling education** that will grow worse year after
year – failing generations to come.

We will be guilty of limiting the **Sacred Fire of Education** to those who can escape, only to leave others in the fading dusk of a long, dark, and ignorant night.

Without the Sacred Fire of Education...

> ➢ **The Enlightenment of History slips into still silence.**
>
> ➢ **The Burning Brand of Justice fades into whisps of memory.**
>
> ➢ **The Inspiration of our Grand American Experiment dims and wavers into a distant flickering cloud of ignorance.**
>
> ➢ **And with it, the Great Beacon of our country Dies in Darkness forever more.**

LOOK!

We have seen what is needed. We have seen that band-aid solutions only cause the wounds to fester. We have seen that guardrails are required to prevent any external influence or interference. We have seen that fundamental, foundational, reformation from the ground-up is required to succeed.

But how in the world do we make it happen?

It will not be easy. But we know from the storied history of our great country that lasting change never comes easy. And sometimes, there is great cost. There are many who will fight change... and the battle will be fierce.

--------- ◆ ---------

As you will see in the coming chapters, FMS cannot suddenly just take over all the school systems. **Chapter 13** (*no pun intended*) talks about how we could potentially fund the system. **Chapter 14** then dives into the steps we need to take to evolve FMS into a national system. We need to take an **entrepreneurial approach** to implementation and growth.

Remember, **the GOAL is to ensure our children, and their children, and those who come after them receive the best education possible.**

CHAPTER

13

HOW DO WE PAY FOR THIS?

Things to consider:

➤ Will this be more expensive than today's educational system?

➤ Is there a better way to pay for all of this?

➤ What innovations can we apply to supplement revenue?

"With government shekels, come government shackles."
—Frances FitzGerald[170]

HOW DO WE FUND FMS SCHOOLS?

I am sure you've asked yourself along the way, *"Self? How in the world would we pay for these incredible schools? David said that we can NEVER allow any external or government influence. So how?"*

I'm glad you asked. This is a challenge and critical danger point that will determine the ability of the schools to be truly "free market." How do we maintain a massive public school system such as we have now, pay for it through taxation (*the only feasible primary source of funding for now*), and not have any external influences?

Fair question. Let's start by learning a new term.

"Direct Allocation Funding."

To be a bit flippant about it... *I am a product of the government school system* and it took *me* many years after my public school education to realize that there is one simple, undeniable truth about schools that we violate every day.

> *Just because a government entity collects taxes from the people for schools, that does NOT give them the inherent right to control, direct, or influence those schools.*

WOW!

The simplistic view is that the government is JUST the **tax collector**. *THEY are not paying for anything. It costs THEM nothing.* They are simply taking OUR money and passing it down to OUR schools to educate OUR children. THIS gives them no rights. We can give them a piece of gold for their service if we must, but we do not owe them control.

We must adjust our mindset just a bit and understand that government does **not** "own" us, or our children, or the schools. They are here to serve us through the people we elect to represent us in our government. We have lost sight of much of that.

But, as we move away from this simplistic viewpoint and into the real world, we do have to recognize that there exists significant history between the government and public schools and there may be laws and regulations or, in some cases, State Constitutions that could counter that clarity I just alluded to.

This is where our **Founding Members (Founders)** will need to come into play and demonstrate their brilliance... just as our Forefathers did. In this chapter and the next, we will learn why **it is important to start small**, then negotiate and build from a position of strength.

—————— ◆ ——————

Interestingly, where we have the **most leverage** from day one is with the Federal government. The U.S. government receives its power from the people as defined and restricted by our incredible U.S. Constitution where our Forefathers had the foresight to clearly restrict the powers of our government. **Amendment 10** provides that *"The powers not delegated to the United States by the Constitution, nor prohibited by it to the States, are reserved to the States respectively, or to the people."*[171]

"The powers not delegated to the United States by the Constitution..."

THAT is worth reading a few times because **we, as a nation, have truly forgotten what that simple statement means**. In my public-school education long ago, I was taught that *"it is the <u>government's</u> duty to take care of us,"* and that if there is a problem, *"the <u>government</u> will pay for it and fix it,"* and that *"the <u>government</u> has lots and lots of money and can afford to do whatever they want to do to fix problems in the United States."*

All of that seemed intended to instill in us a core belief system that our U.S. Government had the duty and power to do whatever they wanted to do, simply if it was for the **greater good**.

Admittedly, it has been a while since I've been in public school, but **I don't remember EVER being taught during those years that there were Constitutional restrictions on what the government can do**, or that the "money" they talk about so loosely is OURS, not the governments. So why do I mention all of this?

> *There is nothing in the U.S. Constitution that authorizes the Federal government to fund, regulate, or create laws related to education or schooling of our children.*

The Federal government has overstepped its constitutional boundaries and usurped the rights and powers of the states and the people in the education of our children. **It is unconstitutional for them to collect taxes or fees for schools or education**, distribute that money, write laws or regulations, or create and maintain a Federal Department of Education that has any authority over our schools or any funding functions.

As noted earlier, while I was writing this book, President Donald Trump and his administration have taken steps to eliminate the Department of Education. However, no matter how much they strip down the agency (or even eliminate it) their plan is to move some of its functions and funding authorities into other organizations.

Whatever success they have had by the time you read this book, keep in mind that any functions or funding authorities that remain with the Federal government are still unconstitutional and should be eliminated. Part of the battle will be to end federal involvement of any kind.

There are some who will disagree with this and claim that the **Commerce Clause** or the **General Welfare Clause** authorizes the government to be involved in our schools. These are specious arguments that, *if true*, **would mean that the Federal government could do ANYTHING they wanted** as long as they could in some vague way claim it was for the common good and general welfare of the people. This complete separation of the Federal government from public education will likely end up in front of the Supreme Court at some point.

But let's not get ahead of ourselves.

Although we do have Constitutional leverage to work towards keeping the Federal government out of the schools, that is a big fight that may have to wait until we are big enough and powerful enough to take on that challenge. **The likely first step will be to refuse all Federal funding** if they try to attach any conditions, regulations, restrictions, etc. to the money.

And as an exciting preview of things to come, later in this chapter we will talk about alternate funding methods where we **develop free-market funding models to supplement the cost of the schools** and reduce our reliance on government taxation from any government level.

UNRAVELING THE MONOLITH

Chapter 14 will dive into how we unravel our monolithic public school system piece-by-piece to convert it to a Free Market School (FMS) system.

By necessity, we would start small: one county, one district, or one school. We prove the concept and grow from there. Our focus here is funding, so we make the assumption that we start small and our funding job focuses down to a manageable effort.

At its simplest, we identify ONE county, district, or school **that is extremely friendly and open to the concept**, then partner with them to lobby for a transition to FMS. This lobbying will extend to the various control boards, the teachers/administrators, the parents, and the students themselves.

The rest of <u>this</u> chapter **makes the assumption** that we have been successful in our lobbying (see **Chapter 14**) and are ready to begin that funding transition to FMS. **What would that look like?**

———————— ◆ ————————

I do ask you to bear with the **broad strokes of this funding chapter**. Funding a monolithic system such as this is a nightmare of tangled alliances, contracts, program/project management, tracking, regulations, laws, compliance, and more. Transitioning to FMS will be even more nightmarish.

I leave the actual details, structure, and mechanics to the Founders and their specialists who will transition and integrate funding with the requirements of the FMS Education Constitution, the National FMS Association (FMSA), the FMS Education Providers (FMSEPs), school service providers, and infrastructure elements of the existing schools.

At a very high level, **funding in the beginning would look very similar to what we have now**.

- The FMSA and the county or state FMS Association would develop a budget for the schools that are now FMS and submit them to the taxing authority.

- The county would collect property taxes to pay for the schools as they always have.

- The county would then fund the schools through the FMSA or State FMS Association.

- The FMSA/State/Local Associations would contract with all FMSEPS, school system service providers, and pay operational expenses, overhead, contracts, and all other expenses.

LOOK!

That's it! Surprised?

Of course, the devil is in the details. And there are many devils to overcome and aspects to hammer out to make that simplicity happen. Contracts need to be negotiated. Mountains of paperwork need to be filed. Hiring and firing. Restructuring administration. And much more to be detailed later.

And as we have seen during the Trump administration, major restructuring can succeed. It may not be pretty. It may be chaotic. It may even hurt a bit. But it can be done.

At this point, you might be asking, *"If we are taking money from the government, won't things stay the same as they are now?"*

Again, the simple answer is no. All negotiations will begin with the requirements of the FMS Education Constitution (FMSEC). The Founders *may* make some exceptions in the beginning to achieve agreements at the local level. But these will likely have sunset provisions for them to expire at a future date. Once the FMS has proven itself as a superior methodology (*proof of concept*), it will be in a stronger position to enforce the FMSEC influence restrictions.

Our standing for FMS implementation will be stronger at the next instance. Then the next. And the next.

Once FMS has proven that it is better for their children, parents will become a major driving force to ensure the schools are built upon the principles of the FMSEC and the Guiding Documents.

It will not all happen at once, but eventually all FMS districts will adhere to the tenets of FMS guidance. But that can ONLY happen if the FMS schools are demonstrably better, more efficient, and have substantial appeal for the parents.

--------------- ♦ ---------------

HOW IS FUNDING THE FMS EDUCATIONAL SYSTEM DIFFERENT?

We have already seen how funding is similar between the FMS and today's public school system. So how is it different? How is it better?

FMS is focused to benefit children and their education rather than the benefit of the "schools", the teachers, and the unions. **We need to <u>remove the financial incentive</u> of those who promote more and more spending** on schools for their own purposes.

For example, education related unions and associations continuously push the local, state, and federal government for more money for the schools as their answer for everything. **THEY have a vested interest in increased spending.** More schools, more teachers, higher pay helps the system grow larger. The more the system grows, the more money pours into the associations and unions. They grow, and then push to grow the system further to justify their own growth.

Certain education associations and teachers' unions are known to **contribute up to 95% of their political donations to one political party**. No need to name names, but it is the party that advocates for full government control of the education and welfare of our children, even against parent's desires.

Conversely, the structure of a commercially based FMS with governance documents like the Education Constitution and the Student Bill of Rights requires us to examine each dollar spent at micro and macro levels and ask, *"How does this dollar make education better for our children?"*

That may seem daunting at first, but remember… **we would now be operating in a competitive free-market environment** where each FMS Education Provider (FMSEP) must continuously improve their services and results or lose their contracts to other providers. Keep in mind that the Charter for each FMSEP requires them to report statistics, results, and current methodologies up the chain so that the FMS Associations can analyze this data and develop, integrate, and implement best practices.

This includes **the analysis of best practices in the application, use, and expenditures of education dollars across the entire FMS system**.

Historically, our answer to *"improving"* education has ALWAYS been to simply **allocate more taxpayer dollars and throw more money at the schools**. As a result, many of our schools are somewhat nicer; students have access to computers and other tools; and teachers get paid more. **YET, the education of our children continues to get worse every year.**

The legislative and taxation power of the government <u>appears to replace any desire or need</u> to operate effectively, efficiently, and economically... or even to actually solve the problems they were originally designed for.

An analysis of **spending vs. quality** of education is beyond the scope of this book but there are many sources available to you should you want to go down that rabbit hole.[172] Suffice it to say that spending more money does not seem to equate to a better education. This claim is borne out by numerous statistics comparing schools within the United States and schools worldwide (*see endnote included above*).

Factors that have a higher impact on education quality than money include (but are not limited to):

- Teacher quality, motivation, and attitude;
- Curriculum quality and presentation;
- Education and learning methodologies;
- Parental involvement and attitude;
- Socioeconomic environment;
- Student motivation, engagement, and attitude.

Therefore, the **FMS must focus on using funding to target the higher impact elements above** RATHER than concentrating on simply seeking *additional funding as the false answer to a better education.* Efficient and effective methods to use available funds will help ensure students get more education bang for the buck. Commercial entities understand how to do that, government entities do not.

One major caution though is that the system must also ensure that a focus on **efficiency does NOT devolve into a lowest bidder environment and a rush to the bottom on services and cost.** This *is* a competitive free-market system, but there are numerous boundaries, requirements, and qualifications that must be met in all areas. For example, **all FMS providers MUST be FMSA Certified to meet the standards of the FMS Constitution, the Student Bill of Rights, and all Provider and Resource Charters**.

None of what we are doing here means anything if we end up providing a substandard education to the students.

––––––––––––– ♦ –––––––––––––

One of the biggest **funding and cost advantages** of FMS is that **it will no longer be a government-run program**. I may expose a little personal bias here, but there are very few things that the government does better and more efficiently than the free market.

We have always relied on government for large scale programs, but today we are starting to see **potential for the free market to take on these programs at scale**. Look at free market space programs for just one example.

- **SpaceX**: Elon Musk, a citizen entrepreneur, founded SpaceX to provide reusable rockets, satellite internet worldwide, and even has plans for human missions to Mars.[173]

- **Blue Origin**: Jeff Bezos founded Blue Origin to focus on suborbital tourism, orbital launch vehicles, and even lunar landers.[174]

- **Virgin Galactic**: Richard Branson founded Virgin Galactic to provide suborbital flights for paying customers, as well as for scientific research.[175]

- **Rocket Lab**: Peter Beck founded Rocket Lab to open access to space by developing small, affordable rockets and launching small satellites into low Earth orbit using their own Electron Rocket.[176]

- **Relativity Space**: Founded by Tim Ellis and Jordan Noone, Relativity Space plans to use 3D printing to manufacture rockets and payloads.[177]

These mere mortals with entrepreneurial spirits saw free-market opportunities to **compete with the U.S. Government** for the vast reaches of space. And succeeded.

WOW!

Looking at these space ventures, is it really that hard to contemplate that the free market might be able to provide a better education for our children?

Public schools actually seem pretty simple compared to the literal rocket science required for these ventures.

When the government gets out of the way, **the entrepreneurial spirit is an amazing tool** that does things beyond our wildest imaginations. When the government accepts this, provides the *necessary* assistance, and keeps their hands out of it, we can accomplish almost anything.

The public school system, although massive in scale, **is well within reach of a well-planned free market system** (*assuming we have access to the taxation vehicles of state and local governments, at least initially*). **The free-market will be free to apply tools, resources, best practices, and competitiveness** that could never be implemented by a government-run system.

———— ◆ ————

One of the most significant advantages of a centralized free market system is that the local, state, and national FMS Associations can take advantage of **Cost Averaging** across the different school systems.

Savings!

<u>Cost Averaging</u> *at this scale allows for a centralized purchasing and spending authority to move resources (including funding) to where it is most needed to better serve students – particularly in high-risk student populations.*

This opens the door to opportunities to provide higher levels of service and **improve educational opportunities in lower income areas with high at-risk student populations**. Check out these examples.

- **EXAMPLE 1**: In order to win or renew a contract, some of the larger FMS Education Providers (FMSEPs) with multi-district or multi-state contracts *may* offer in their proposals to **place higher cost, more experienced teachers into lower income areas**. These will come at no additional cost to the low-income area school system and the FMSEP company will absorb the minimal cost into their overall master contract. The FMSEPs have flexibility to move resources to wherever needed.

- **EXAMPLE 2**: Service and support contracts could come in countywide, statewide, or nationwide bids that **would allow the contractor to cost average their services across multiple broad environmental and socioeconomic areas**. Services such as maintenance or food services could be provided at higher levels, higher quality, and lower cost to underserved areas.

- **EXAMPLE 3**: One of my favorite aspects of cost averaging is access to Providers who would potentially be able to **bid large scale extracurricular, after-school, and personal growth programs** for a reasonable cost across larger service areas. They could offer services such as:

  - ✓ **Athletic programs** (basketball, football, soccer, swimming, etc.);

  - ✓ **Academic programs** (language, chess, math, science, and other programs);

  - ✓ **Artistic club programs** (music, dance, drama, etc.);

  - ✓ **Leadership and personal development programs** (leadership clubs, debate, model UN, mock trial, public speaking);

  - ✓ **Media programs and clubs** (newspapers, yearbook, podcasting, video, and other media-based programs);

  - ✓ **Advanced educational programs** for college-bound students.

These could be offered through larger countywide, statewide, and/or nationwide service offerings in order to **provide a broader array of service to students in all socioeconomic areas to combat educational opportunity imbalances and limitations**. For example, students in one inner-city school might have the opportunity to engage in a football program at another school in a partnership-type alliance. Challenging, but the possibilities are endless – especially in cases where the FMESPs and providers might have contracts across school systems.

This approach allows these companies to **scale their contracts up and cost average their expenses** in a way that was never possible before. These large competitive contracts would be extremely attractive to bid on compared to today's ultra strict low-price evaluation environment where companies have no choice but to cut every corner to win. There is a whole science behind this type of low-price bidding that is beyond the scope of this analysis. *And none of it is good for the students.*

Instead, in the FMS environment, **providers must be competitive while being held to the high standards of the FMS Guiding Documents and Quality Standards**. Evaluation of bids will of course consider price, but will balance that against best value factors such as:

- adherence to FMS Guiding Documents;
- quality metrics and standards;
- past performance and experience;
- commitment to continuous improvement;
- ability to innovate, initiate, and implement;
- quality and experience of teachers and administrators;
- proofs of commitment to student success; and
- other corporate and user success factors.

Coming from a competitive bidding environment, I know these will be sought after must-bid/must-win contracts. I dreamt of these kinds of opportunities most of my career. Bidders must remain cost-conscious, but awards are based on overall *"Best Value"* determinations. And in this case, that is the **Best Value to the student's education**.

Bidders will be able to stretch their wings a bit and think outside of the usual restraints. Providers will be able to think about innovation and invention. **THAT is cool!**

— ♦ —

FUNDING ADVANTAGES OF THE FREE-MARKET SYSTEM

We're beginning to see now that **once we are unshackled from the government yoke and the bureaucracies** that infect today's public schools, the possibilities are endless.

> *Stepping away from a governmental system frees us up to explore our great American innovative spirit.*

Imagine being able to **innovate, explore, expand, and revolutionize** one of the most important industries that exists – the education of our children. So much more is possible under FMS that would not be possible under a government-based system of education.

Consider the following features, benefits, and advantages of funding an FMS system.

EFFICIENCY AND OVERSIGHT

Government programs are arguably inefficient, even when operating at scale. In fact, as government programs grow larger, they fail to take advantage of that scale and become **burdened with even more fraud, waste, and abuse**. Although any large system may struggle with these aspects, commercial free-market systems tend to operate more efficiently and with more internal controls to protect their bottom line – *the lifeblood of their corporate existence.*

In fact, one of the most powerful tools of the free-market world is the **ability and willingness to right-size when necessary** and level-set the business to ensure its survival. No government agency has ever done that (*with the exceptions of the forced downsizing of government agencies done in* 2025-2026).

> *Considering the fraud, waste, and abuse inherent in any government program, is there any doubt that a free-market school system could operate at <u>significantly reduced cost</u>?*

As we saw in **Chapter 10** and **Chapter 11**, the FMS system is built from the ground-up with checks and balances in place to protect all aspects of the system. The **contract and bidding processes**, **reporting mechanisms**, and **structured monitoring and oversight** by state and national FMS Associations ensure that any irregularities are quickly identified and corrected.

INNOVATION, IDEOLOGIES, AND IMPLEMENTATION

The importance of innovation and the **ability to implement new concepts and best practices broadly and quickly** is the driving force behind FMS education. This capability is necessary to keep up with the speed of today's world. The current monolithic school system is moribund in a structure that disincentivizes new ways of doing things and pushes back against change.

The FMS system allows for advances and changes based on our evolving understanding of education. Individual FMSEPs will be encouraged to **explore new ideas and innovate to better serve the needs of the students**. If this involves cost, the FMSEPs may absorb that as a cost of doing business, a value-added service by their organization, or they may seek grants from the state or national Associations to explore new concepts.

If these concepts prove superior, the Associations may propagate these concepts throughout the various school systems through contract modifications. Once proven, these educational concepts can be integrated and implemented quickly by those FMSEPs who choose to take advantage of them.

FUNDING FOR SUCCESS

Because FMS will be more competitive, efficient, functional, and able to minimize fraud, waste, and abuse, the system (managed through the various Association levels) will be able to **fund additional services without additional burden on the taxpayer**. The budgets submitted for each county, district, or state will include fungible resources for **innovation incentives**, **continuous improvement initiatives**, **performance and quality enticements**, and other commercial-type programs that were never possible before.

SOCIOECONOMIC BALANCING

We have a unique opportunity with FMS funding to help ensure that **ALL** **children** receive the best education possible. There are areas in our country where education has (*to put it kindly*) **fallen behind the rest of the U.S.** FMS can address this with additional support for low-income, inner city, rural and other school environments where children are faced with a substandard education that that does not prepare them for success.

This is NOT to be construed as *"equity"* but is focused on ensuring that all children have **access** to **quality educational opportunities** – especially those children in at-risk populations.

FMS support includes these important features.

- **Cost Averaging** as discussed previously will be a major element of socioeconomic balancing. Larger providers will be incentivized to bid higher levels of service than would normally be available in targeted areas and absorb those additional costs into their broader contract. Refer to the three cost averaging examples provided previously.

- **FMS Association incentives and grants**. The state and national Associations will provide grants and other incentives to place higher qualified teachers, improve educational programs, fund student activities, and provide additional services in at-risk areas.

- **Community involvement** through both *student-to-community* and *community-to-student* activities will be a primary focus of FMSEPS and the Associations. This may be funded in part through the FMSEPs broader contract. We will also explore additional funding from the community (see alternative revenue models discussion later in this chapter).

QUALITY AND PERFORMANCE INCENTIVES

A modern free-market educational system should operate efficiently and at lower cost. However, it is critical that contracts **never be awarded on the lowest price**. Such a practice almost always leads to a downward spiral that seeks the bottom levels of service. As noted above, FMS will award "**Best Value**" contracts that do consider price, but are focused on quality of service, user satisfaction (the students), parent ratings, performance ratings, and other measurable metrics. A Best Value procurement approach should still result in savings to the taxpayers.

Specifics will be determined later, but the FMS Associations will incentivize **quality and performance of teachers, administrators, and service providers** through monetary awards, incentives, and bonuses. This will motivate all elements of the system towards innovation, improvement, and higher performance goals.

FACILITIES, INFRASTRUCTURE, AND RESOURCES

You may have asked in your journey here, "*What about all the existing schools and infrastructure?*" FMS will use the existing schools, facilities, infrastructure, buses, and other resources. These will be funded in a similar fashion to what is done now with taxes, bonds, etc. However, operating as a business, **these capital and other expenses will be carefully evaluated, negotiated, and competitively bid (Best Value) by FMS to best serve the students**. All expenditures will be analyzed from a student-success perspective to ask, "*Is **this** expenditure a net positive need for **this** student population?*"

ALTERNATIVE INCOME STREAMS – GOING BEYOND TAXATION

And finally, one of the most exciting aspects of FMS is the possibility of **weaning the schools off of pure government taxation and developing other lucrative revenue streams to supplement the cost of operating the schools and provide enhanced services**. Although other options will be explored, capital expenditures like building schools will likely remain attached to property taxes, bond referendums, and the like.

However, it is entirely possible that **operating expenses and general overhead could be removed from the taxation cycle** and funded through alternative income streams. Initial goals would be to:

1. Eliminate Federal funding and involvement completely.

2. Minimize State tax collection and funding as much as feasible. The State FMS Association would act as the aggregator for distributed funds.

3. Minimize local taxation and ensure that local and state governments cannot interfere with the operation or functions of the schools.

4. Develop multiple alternative revenue streams and grow those to supplement and potentially replace most government funding.

The success and scope of alternative funding streams would depend on many factors, but **ANY reduction of reliance on government funding** through taxation would be a good thing.

> IMPORTANT NOTE → *ANY alternative funding stream must be carefully examined to <u>ensure that it will not have an adverse or negative impact</u> on the students and will be a net positive for them, the schools, and the FMS system.*

Important!

Revenue streams could be developed and/or managed by the **FMS Associations, FMS Providers, Teachers/Administrators, Parents, Students, people/organizations within the community,** or any number of **external entities**. This activity could also be tied into some of the community activities that we discussed earlier. A function such as this will obviously take work, but the possibilities are endless.

Below I offer just a few thoughts on alternative funding to create long-term revenue streams. All should be considered with caution and managed with care.

1. **STATE LOTTERIES**:

   Most states maintain a lottery system that generates some revenue for the K-12 schools. According to organizations such as NASPL[178], lotteries generate over $25 Billion per year in revenue to schools (about 1% of total education funding). However, lottery revenue that goes to the public schools varies within states from 0% to 30%. In some states, the lottery revenue is used to replace or offset other sources of school funding… resulting in little or no net increase in funding to the school.

   The FMS Associations will lobby to increase the percentage that goes to the schools in every state and to ensure that all revenue is supplemental to education budgets and not used to replace or offset other sources.

2. **DONATIONS AND ENDOWMENTS**:

   There is no reason that K-12 schools (particularly high schools) can't be treated similarly to higher education when it comes to school spirit and affiliation. Local fundraising can focus on donations from alumni, parents, or community members who want to support the local schools.
   Endowments for K-12 are rare, but there is one high school near me that received a huge endowment from an individual and has not sought government funding in 50 years. It is a very beautiful school and is respected for the quality of education received there. Correlation? Maybe.

3. **GRANTS**:

   Grants may be sought from nonprofits, foundations, corporations, or other organizations that may have an interest in improving public education in general, or that would like to address specific challenges or needs. In particular, these may be **sought to provide supplemental support to schools with high at-risk populations**. The FMS Associations may work as matchmakers to connect schools with these organizations.

4. **FEES FOR SERVICES OR PROGRAMS**:
[*Caution area, let us not forget that this is still a school and our children's education is the primary mission.*] Some schools could generate income from fees for services, programs, or rental of school facilities, equipment, or resources the school offers to the public. This could include adult education, after-school care, summer camps, use of sports facilities, and much more (when classes are NOT in session). This might also be an opportunity for Teachers and Administrators to earn additional income. Also, refer back to our previous discussions about partnering with home schools, private schools, and other alternative schools. Benefits could be gained through fees for use of the facilities (particularly sports facilities) or partnering with the alternative schools to assist in providing services or programs.

5. **PARTNERSHIPS AND LICENSING**:
[*Caution area, we don't want to experiment on our children.*] We discussed earlier the potential for external organizations such as EdTech or curriculum companies to partner with the schools in various configurations. This might include beta testing new EdTech software, or proof of concept application of educational tools, research, or other possibilities such as expanding their national footprint. Potential positive aspects for the schools could include direct revenue, free software/tools, or potential partnerships in development of software or hardware resulting in long-term licensing fees.

6. **SPONSORSHIPS, MERCHANDISING, ADVERTISING**:
[*Caution area, once again, this is still a school, and these are our children.*] Having said that, let me get a bit

entrepreneurial for a moment. You may remember our previous discussions about higher levels of involvement in the community. This is the perfect tie-in area. Most schools sell local business signage on the ball field fence or sell t-shirts and hats. Maybe it's time to take that up a notch and talk about building a real business within the school that caters to the local community and beyond.

Give the DECA[179], business, media, and computer students some real-world experience in building a business model to generate revenue for the school. This could be through more traditional advertising, marketing, or merchandising apparel, accessories, books, etc. They could seek out sponsorships from local businesses. Or, we could let them think beyond the limitations of classwork and tap into the student skill base and partner with media sites, social media, e-commerce, branding, blogging, etc.

As an actual example of things that could be done in an open free-market system, one teacher wanted to provide practice tests for his students to prepare for placement tests. The district wouldn't pay for it. He couldn't afford it. The answer? He sold advertising space on the tests. He had numerous requests from businesses, but approximately 67% of the ads were inspirational messages from the parents.[180]

The possibilities – and educational experiences – are boundless if we let them explore their interests. They might even generate significant revenue for the school.

7. **VOLUNTEER AND SERVICE PROGRAMS:**
Offer volunteer and service programs that engage students, parents, and community members to perform tasks and needed services within the community as fundraisers.

8. **NAMING RIGHTS OR LEGACY GIFTS:**
Within reason... seek out individuals or entities who would make large donations or endowments for naming rights associated with the school, or part of it such as programs, rooms, buildings, ball fields, etc.

By tapping into the resources, skills, and networks of the FMS system, the students, parents, staff, alumni, and community partners, we can diversify funding sources and reduce dependence on the government and taxation of citizens. **This also plays double duty in expanding exposure and integration of the school population into the community** to promote participation, engagement, and job prospects for the students within the community. The opportunities are endless.

————————— ♦ —————————

CLOSING THE BOOKS ON FUNDING

The critical factor to note in funding is that the structures for initial funding are already in place and the taxpayers are already paying taxes for the schools. **In a big, broad stroke**, the primary difference related to funding will be the payee (the FMS system) who will in general aggregate the taxes allocated and then manage and pay for all aspects of the public school system. This approach has no outward impact on the taxpayers. They will pay taxes as they always have and their children will get an education.

What will change for them is the result – **a new forward-looking generation of education and opportunity for their children** that is focused on *their* success, not the school's or the teacher's.

The efficiencies of the FMS system will allow for greater flexibility in ensuring that **the money goes to where the students need it most**. This will mean some centralization, some decentralization, the ability for the money to follow the student, and a flexibility to shift that was not possible before.

Note however that **this *flexibility* is NOT to be construed as taking away from wealthy communities to give to poorer communities**. The restructuring, efficiencies, and new funding approaches will allow the system to provide a net positive effect in all communities.

> *The critical takeaway is that the people managing the money are focused entirely on the SUCCESS OF THE STUDENTS… no matter where they might live.*

The focus is NOT the teachers, the administrators, the schools, what the teachers' unions want, or any kind of internal or external agenda. **Student Lifetime Success is always the #1 focus** of the entire system. As it should be.

───────── ♦ ─────────

Make no mistake, the current system is extremely complicated, unwieldy, and difficult to decrypt. This transition won't be easy. In addition to all the other pushbacks, there will be some conflict between how local and state dollars are allocated towards the various school districts.

In many states and localities **there is no end to the laws, regulations, and policies managing state and local revenues** and how they are applied to school funding. These include concepts such as tax swaps, state recapture policies, equalization methods, bond levies, foundation formulas, portability, and much more.

Unraveling all of this will be challenging as we work towards a free-market system that **liberates the money from bureaucratic overhead and allows the competitive system to naturalize towards the most efficient approaches to return the system to student success**. Approaches could even come in forms that I can't imagine as I write this book.

THAT is what's exciting about this entire approach → I may NOT be the smartest person in the room, but I do have a vision of this magnificent universe of education for all children. I understand the massive failure of our modern educational system and understand the risks of allowing bad influences back in.

No single person can accomplish this. It will take a large contingent of very smart, very dedicated people to execute this level of foundational change and maintain it.

Speaking of execution...

———————— ◆ ————————

I am sure you have many questions remaining, but to keep this exploration under 2,000+ pages, it is time to close the book on funding and open the door to the future. In the next chapter, we will **explore how to begin the journey** and map out our pathways to success.

CHAPTER

14

SO, HOW DO WE START?

Things to consider:

➢ Where do we even begin to begin?

➢ Is this kind of change too hard?

➢ Isn't the educational system too big to change?

"Take the first step in faith. You don't have to see the whole staircase, just take the first step."
—Martin Luther King Jr.[181]

"Never doubt that a small group of thoughtful, committed, citizens can change the world. Indeed, it is the only thing that ever has."
—Margaret Mead[182]

"Change will not come if we wait for some other person or some other time. We are the ones we've been waiting for. We are the change that we seek."
—Barack Hussein Obama[183]

A JOURNEY BEGINS WITH A SINGLE STEP

I know it is cliché to say it, but I must... No matter how big, important, or life altering a destination is, the journey begins with a **single, determined step**.

The time has passed us by for timid, uncommitted attempts to stick our toes in the water and it is now time to be daring enough to believe we can take on this challenge.

So how in the world do we **unravel this monolith that is our public school system** and convert it to a Free Market School (FMS) system? Is it too big to change? **By necessity, it must NOT be**; otherwise the future of education will likely never change. We must force it.

> ***We must be bold enough to say, "Our time has come!"***   BE BOLD!

But belief is only the beginning. We must also be smart, innovative, and strong-willed. Big change does not come easy.

You do not take a massive 1,300-foot, 230,000-ton freight container ship, yank the wheel hard to starboard, and spin the behemoth of steel and cargo in a different direction. IF you could even do that, it would lead to a disaster of epic proportions. **The chaotic ballet of inertia, resistence, and mass vs. momentum would quickly expose the folly of impromptu maneuvers** that would shred the weak points of the ship long before they could be identified and mitigated.

Which is a great segue into the two most obvious approaches to accomplish a transition to Free-Market Schools. In actual real-world implementation, the transition will likely be quite different than the **two simplistic models**, shown below.

Can you guess which one we'll explore in depth?

MODEL #1: The *"Rip the band-aid off, let the patient die, and go for national implementation all at once"* model. (1 year)

- In an amazing world of magic and unicorns, we would convince all local, state, and Federal governments (and a majority of voters) to joyfully participate in this foundational reformation.

- We would accomplish a national transition between graduation in the spring and back-to-school in the fall.

- Yikes!

MODEL #2: The *"Take it step-by-step and provide proof-of-concept at a small scale so we can launch from a position of strength"* model. (5-10+ years)

- Back in the real world, the Founders would identify a "friendly" state/county/district that is ready for change and court them to implement an FMS reformation. They would work with all stakeholders to carve out an **FMS Educational Zone** (county, district, or school) and lobby to adjust laws accordingly to allow operation as close to the FMS model and Guiding Documents as possible.

- Once the FMS Educational Zone proves successful as a model, use that one as **proof-of-concept to expand and develop other Zones within the state**. This will open the national discussion and we will use this State Zone as proof-of-concept to push for FMS in other states.

Obviously, **Model 2** has the higher probability of success. But **I'm still working on that unicorn**.

In the end, a better way may be found, but for now we're going to dive into **Model 2** as our likely approach. Considering today's highly politicized environment and highly monetized educational ecosystem, **starting small and growing through the what some might recognized as a Crawl, Walk, Run methodology** (adapted for this use case) seems like the best free-market approach to succeeding.

- **CRAWL**: Proof-of-Concept (*Does it work?*)

- **WALK**: Proof-of-Viability (*Can it be sustained?*)

- **RUN**: Proof-of-Success (*Is it viable large scale?*)

The biggest challenge of course will be to ensure that federal, state, and local governments do not contradict or undermine the FMS Educational Constitution (FMSEC) or FMS Guiding Documents. This is why the target for the first FMS Educational Zone must be chosen carefully and be properly nourished to embrace the entire FMS ideology.

It is clear that we would never get off the ground by trying to convert schools within areas that would be unfriendly to reforming their public school system. As with any other free market enterprise, we would need to study our market, develop the perfect target profiles, draft a strong business plan, nurture the right relationships, lobby for a platform to start, then succeed at a small scale before expanding to embrace the entire market.

———————— ♦ ————————

STEP-BY-STEP TO MODEL 2

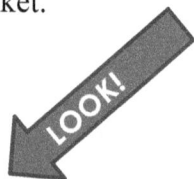

One of the most important concepts to remember is that FMS is **NOT an "alternative"** to public schools, **it is a "replacement"** of public schools.

Success will not be found in taking baby steps or being tentative about what we are trying to accomplish. We will not get everything we want in the first Education Zone, but we must make our case to get as close to the FMSEC requirements as possible. Proofs from *that* Zone will make our position stronger with each additional Zone we seek to add.

This is why **our first Zone must be in a concept-friendly environment** that is not only *willing* to work with us, but is excited and engaged with the entire reformation effort.

We must identify and court reform-minded states that are positioned for change in their educational system. The state must possess **bold and courageous state leadership and power centers who are willing to challenge the status quo** and implement meaningful educational reform. This boldness will flow down to the counties and districts that will be targeted for reformation.

By starting with a single school district, all of the resources of the FMS Associations and other stakeholders could be launched at this Zone to push a campaign of success that **engages the community and all elements of the education ecosystem** in that district.

The approach to transitioning a school or district from government-run to FMS-run must be handled with extreme care and forethought. Those who are firmly entrenched in our current system, even with all of its ills, will not willingly accept a reformation like this. **Even in our chosen "friendly" Zone, there will be many who will fight this every step of the way.** There will be even more **external forces** who will push back on every point (*teachers' unions, education associations, politicians, and other entrenched entities*).

> ***Even so, we will succeed because we must.***

So, how will we get from the **as-is government system** that is in place to the **to-be free-market system**?

What I provide below is a high-level framework that identifies many of the required steps. It makes **assumptions** that the Founders have already finalized the **FMS Education Constitution (FMSEC)**, the **FMS Student Bill of Rights (FMSSBR)**, formed the **Free Market School Association (FMSA)**, and developed all the other required **Guiding** and **Governance Documents** necessary to begin operations.

[It's okay if you find the process plan below boring and just want to skim. Personally, I love it, but I have been known to be weird.]

––––––––––– ♦ –––––––––––

Process to Identify and Transition the First FMS Educational Zone to Free Market Schools.

1. **PLANNING AND STAKEHOLDER ENGAGEMENT**:
   The first step is formation of an **Educational Zone 1 Task Force.** This will be comprised of education experts, policymakers, legal experts, parents, and representatives from potential education providers and related education organizations and services. They will identify the risks, issues, critical needs, and state and local processes required to implement an FMS Educational Zone (state, county, district). From this information, they will develop an **Implementation Plan and Timeline** to identify the Zone 1 target and complete a transition to FMS.

2. **IDENTIFY THE PRIME ZONE 1 CANDIDATE AREA**:
The Task Force will develop a profile of what the best Zone 1 candidate looks like and perform a nationwide analysis to identify the top targets for a transition to FMS. They will evaluate the social and educational environments, political climate, existing public schools, infrastructure, student demographics, assess community needs and desires, and analyze numerous other factors to home in on the "friendliest" reformation environment(s) possible. Along the way, it would be nice if a state or district stepped forward with a direct interest in converting.

3. **LEGAL AND REGULATORY ANALYSIS**:
Once a prime Zone 1 candidate area has been identified, the Task Force will collaborate with legal experts to perform legal reviews of existing educational laws and regulations and examine impacts from State Constitutional issues, funding requirements, tax laws, etc. The Legal Task Force will develop a **Legal Plan of Action** to transition Zone 1 to FMS.

4. **LOBBYING AND PUBLIC AWARENESS**:
Going public with the FMS Zone 1 location is where it gets fun and the opposition begins to ramp up. The FMSA, the Task Force, and others (internal and external) tasked for this will begin an awareness and influence blitz campaign to ramp up public awareness and begin lobbying for reformation in the selected Zone 1 area. They will reach out to politicians, school boards, county supervisors, and other stakeholders to provide information and convince them reformation is necessary. The goal will be to get them all on board for a transition to FMS. The team will also reach out to parents, students, school administrators, community leaders, potential community partners (see **Chapter 15**), and any others who could influence the county and state to take on this project.

5. **NEGOTIATION, AGREEMENT, AND LAW:**

Once all stakeholders have agreed in theory to transition, then negotiations will be required to resolve the final makeup, applicable laws, regulations, and other requirements to move forward. This may take the most time and could entail the Governor and State Legislature writing new law and working with the State Education Department and various State and County agencies to adjust regulations and other requirements to allow and support the FMS in the conversion of the schools in FMS Zone 1. Success here will require the Governor, numerous State Representatives and Senators, and others to be enthusiastic advocates for FMS in order to accomplish the mission. Activities here will drive the **Transition Timeline** based on potential implementation dates and start dates.

6. **FMS EDUCATION PROVIDERS AND OTHER SERVICES:**

At the same time, FMSA will also be working with potential FMS Education Providers (FMSEPs) to help them understand the system, the requirements of the Guiding Documents, and the processes for bidding for and executing on the program. During this period, the FMSA will also be learning from potential FMSEPs about the latest educational tools, methodologies, and processes that might be implemented in the new FMS system. Based on the developed Transition Timeline the FMSA may also be working with all of the various school service providers (transportation, food, maintenance, janitorial, trash, etc.) to prepare them for the requirements of the new FMS system.

7. **PHASED TRANSITION:**

If transitioning an entire school District, County, or a state, FMS may transition through a "Phased Transition" if it is deemed the safest approach for the students. This could entail transitioning a single school first, or only specific grades (elementary, middle, or high), or by other breakdowns until the entire targeted system is transitioned. A phased transition would allow more resources to be focused on fewer elements to improve the success profile. The need for a phased transition will be determined when the Transition Timeline is established.

8. **TRANSITION TIMELINE**:

Numerous activities will take place during the transition period according to the Project Plan and Timeline. Once the implementation and start dates are determined, the following activities will be performed per detailed plans.

- Notify and educate teachers, staff, administrators and other personnel of the upcoming transition to FMS. Educate them about their options for employment.

- Notify parents, students, and the community at large of the upcoming changes. Perform Town Halls, Workshops, and Public Meetings to provide information, instructions, and to address concerns, gather feedback, and build community support. Also notify parents of the opportunities available to them within the FMS Associations.

- FMS Education Provider (FMSEP) selection will be made from competitive bids through Requests for Proposals (RFPs) from potential providers. They will be onboarded as selected.

- Teacher and Staff Transition. Once awarded a contract, the FMSEPs will begin job fairs and other hiring events to select the teachers and others they will employ on their contracts. They will educate them on the requirements of the new system.

- Manage asset transfers of infrastructure and facilities including buildings, equipment, and resources.

- Negotiate new contracts with all external providers of services such as transportation, food, maintenance, janitorial, trash, groundskeeping, and other services.

9. IMPLEMENTATION AND EXECUTION:

With Day 1 of FMS schools approaching, it is time to bring it all together to ensure a successful implementation for all students. **Failure cannot be allowed.** These activities include, but are not limited to, the following.

- FMSEPs market their courses, curriculum, and approach to attract parents and students to use their services.

- Open enrollment for parent/student orientation and sign-up period to choose FMSEPs and classes.

- Evaluation and assessment of FMSEP readiness. This may include Dress Rehearsals and system validations with teachers, administrators, and support personnel.

- Open Houses for parents and students to meet the teachers they signed up with and learn more about the educational approach and possibilities with FMS.

- Perform final security assessments and validations.

- Open the doors for Day 1 of classes.

10. QUALITY ASSURANCE, EVALUATIONS, AND ASSESSMENTS:

Opening the doors to students is just the first step of proof of concept and successful implementation. The entire system will be continuously evaluated for performance, effectiveness, and adherence to the FMS Guiding Documents. Critical quality assurance and assessment activities will include at a minimum:

- **Ongoing Assessments**: Continuously evaluate effectiveness, efficiency, and compliance to the Guiding documents of the system and adjust policies and practices as needed.

- **Continuous Improvement**: Ensure that we are always exploring and identifying new ways to improve the system for the students.

- **Performance Metrics**: Define and track clear performance indicators such as student outcomes, student success, Master Achievement Grades (see **Chapter 12**), teacher qualifications, teacher retention, quality scores, and much more.

- **Oversight and Observation**: Establish independent oversight bodies (usually through FMSA and FMS Associations) to monitor and evaluate all elements of each school's performance, not just in the classroom, but throughout all elements of each facility (food, transportation, etc.).

- **Transparency**: Visibility throughout the entire system is critical to ensuring that all systems operate as designed and that there is no mission creep. Transparency (as much as is safe) to parents, students, external oversight, the FMSAs, and the public will keep the system operating efficiently and will maintain public trust.

———————— ♦ ————————

SUCCESS IS CRITICAL TO SUCCESS

Transparency, collaboration, and adaptability are crucial throughout the entire reformation process to ensure that each and every element performs as planned. **The ONLY way to ever get FMS into nationwide usage is to succeed masterfully**.

Success in one school, one district, or one county will drive our ability to grow into two schools, two districts, or two counties. Then three, four, and on and on. Only through success will we accomplish a move to the state level. Then two states and more. Eventually, **no state will be able to credibly deny the superiority of the FMS model** over the government model and will hopefully adapt in order to compete or due to parental pressures.

————— ♦ —————

Side Note:

One of the issues we are likely to face is that certain states will recognize the superiority of FMS but will **refuse to relinquish any controls**. In this case, a state may attempt to replicate FMS themselves, but retain the influence and oversight of government and external entities such as teachers' unions and the existing education associations.

Unfortunately, without guardrails like the FMSEC and other ironclad FMS Guiding Documents, the change consists only of band-aids and duct tape that will at some point erode under the external influences that are allowed access to the system.

This likely cannot be avoided and the only hope is that parents and others in those states recognize why a true FMS system works and can eventually force political change for their children. Note that FMS will eventually have a State FMS Association even in those states to advocate for change. We will leave no state or child behind.

————— ♦ —————

Even so, we will need to focus on a migration and assimilation approach as described above rather than a blitz-type wipe and reset of the entire nationwide system. It would be nice to help all students immediately and **get it all done in one swipe of a magic wand**. But that is not reality.

What IS real is that our children need a different approach. The government model is not working for them and, in fact... as we have seen throughout this book, **it is working against them**. Generations are failing and they don't need to be.

With a good **Project Plan** and **Transition Management Team**, a school or possibly even a district could be converted to an FMS over the summer break between one school year and the next. That one reformation won't help all of the nation's children, but it will be a start.

And once FMS proves itself in doing all that I believe it can, then parents throughout the country would begin demanding their school, their district, their county and state adopt FMS. **Once there is definitive, unquestionable data and results-based proof** that FMS provides a better education, that is when real change will happen.

———————— ◆ ————————

Again, **what I offer here in this short book is simplistic**, but it has to be. The actual plans for an endeavor such as this would take multiple books, manuals, and business plans that are **beyond the scope of this exploration into the possibilities**.

<u>Consider this a roadmap to what needs to be done.</u>

The good news is that we don't have to do it alone. **Chapter 15** provides a look into how we can reach out to our communities for help in making Free Market Schools even more amazing for our children. Imagine what would be possible if we engaged in public/private partnerships to expand the possibilities.

15

PUBLIC, PRIVATE, AND COMMUNITY PARTNERSHIPS

Things to consider:

➢ Do we need help?

➢ Who would benefit from partnering?

➢ Is the result larger than the sum of two parts?

"Alone we can do so little; together we can do so much."

—Helen Keller[184]

"I can do things you cannot, you can do things I cannot; together we can do great things."

—Mother Teresa[185]

CAN WE DO IT ALONE?

At its core, FMS is a public/private partnership in that the free-market educational system is primarily funded by tax dollars collected by the government. **This is the most efficient method of funding the schools** – at least in the beginning.

The government acts as the tax collector and distributes the necessary funds to the FMS system who manages it from there. **The <u>tax collector</u> does not partner in the management or operation** of the FMS educational system – that only happens in Government Schools and the Mafia.

What makes FMS fun though is that there are incredible opportunities to explore where **it would be beneficial to partner with other public, community, and private entities** to ensure the success of Free Market Schools and enhance the educational experience for students.

———————— ◆ ————————

The success of the FMS depends on much more than the people and elements *within* the system. To achieve the greatest education possible for students, we will push for the **active involvement and support of the broader community** as well as the businesses and organizations that inhabit that community. They have always had a stake in the quality of education the children of that community receive, but until now **there has been minimal opportunity for two-way interaction and direct involvement** to engage with the schools.

With an FMS educational system, the broader community should have a role in supporting the school system and helping to shape it in a way that they believe will benefit the community most. Communities will be encouraged to engage in various aspects of the schools that will benefit the students – *as well as the community at large*.

After all, **a large percentage of the students will be living within those communities** as productive citizens once they graduate.

Working closely together, the **stakeholders on both sides can create certain synergies and develop networks between** them to provide resources, expertise, and opportunities for the students and for the businesses within the community depending on their needs, skills, and capacities.

A school system that offers more choice, diversity, and flexibility to meet the needs and interests of each student can foster a more **engaged, motivated, and creative generation of learners and leaders** who will exit the school system ready to build and participate in a more cohesive and harmonious society – starting within their own community.

How does this happen?

You may remember our previous discussions about working with the community at large to participate in the schools, provide opportunities for students, and for the schools and students to support local businesses. We talked about numerous opportunities for interaction in **Chapter 13** related to **funding the schools** and in **Chapter 14** for **transitioning to FMS**. In this chapter, we'll start to explore what we can do with **partnering on an ongoing basis for the greater good**.

What do these partnerships look like?

These partnerships may take many forms, but are essentially voluntary and mutually beneficial arrangements between the FMS Elements and businesses, organizations, or individuals that aim to provide opportunities such as the following.

- Help provide funding for the schools.

- Expand the school's ability to educate or train in specific jobs and trades.

- Sponsor or host special activities and events.

- Internships, mentoring, and employment opportunities for students.

- Provide expanded support for low-income or at-risk students.

- Provide speeches, seminars, or training events of interest to the students.

- Help fundraise or sponsor fundraising events.

- Participate in sponsored business program challenges as discussed in **Chapter 13**.

- Support teachers to help them with classroom resources, tools, supplies, books, etc.

- Businesses and organizations could share facilities to enhance the capabilities or capacities of the school.

I'm sure readers can think of many other possibilities to drive specific positive outcomes and objectives of FMS. Mainly we seek to engage the collaborative and cooperative nature in working with stakeholders internal and external to create synergies and networks that can enhance the FMS education, reach stretch-goals, and address common challenges of schools such as absenteeism.

WHO WOULD PARTICIPATE?

As free-market entities, the Elements within the **FMS Educational system are truly partners with the local community and the ecosystems they operate in**. The FMS Associations and FMS Educational Providers (FMSEPs) will work closely with local entities to develop partnerships and support groups to enhance available educational services and opportunities.

Remember, the more successful each FMSEP is, the more contracts they may win in their efforts to expand their businesses.

Creating Educational Opportunity Zones will benefit the students and provide FMSEPs with proof points and discriminators to use in their proposals to extend their existing contracts and to win new contracts to expand. Continuous improvement and student success factors are critical to every FMSEP in keeping their contract.

With that vested interest in mind, and the support of the FMS Associations, the FMSEPs will want to explore every opportunity to get the community involved and keep them engaged.

Some examples of potential community and business partnerships include:

- Local businesses of course (*NOT just advertising, but brand exposure, promoting specific skills and trades, career exploration, offering jobs, internships, scholarships, and more to the most accomplished and/or motivated students*);

- Associations and non-profit organizations (*same opportunities as businesses, plus promoting social work, civic education, and volunteerism*);

- Alternative schools (*as discussed earlier*);

- Government agencies and public services (*city hall, police, fire, parks and recreation, and more to enhance civic education, safety, recreation, public service, and more*);

- Higher education institutions (*to provide academic enrichment, dual enrollment opportunities, college readiness programs, scholarships, etc.*);

- Gyms and sports facilities (*possibly something like golf driving ranges for use and golf training classes*);

- Transportation companies (*think small after school or event transportation, or possibly supplementing or replacing the school bussing system*);

- Private training organizations (*think public speaking, Karate, tutoring, test preparation, college counseling, career guidance, etc.*);

- Leadership and discipline organizations such as Civil Air Patrol (CAP) and other youth or paramilitary organizations;

- Arts and cultural institutions (*museums, theaters, libraries, galleries, etc. to expand their audiences and enrich students' learning experiences with diverse and creative activities and resources*);

- Health and wellness providers (*doctors, dentists, therapists, nutritionists, fitness trainers and more benefit from exposing students to different careers and promoting healthy habits and lifestyles among the students*);

- Alumni and families (*former students, parents, grandparents, and others to share their experiences, skills, connections, and resources*).

The possibilities are endless for the entrepreneurial free-market mind. The challenging aspect will be to identify the benefit for both the partnering entity AND the school or students. The intention is to **develop a long-term relationship** that will benefit the school financially, the teachers in their educational endeavors, and the students in their success in education as well as transitioning to the broader world.

————— ♦ —————

A Real-World Case Study.

Husco International[186] is private, family-owned business that manufactures hydraulic and electro-mechanical components for U.S. and overseas sales. About as far away from an "educational" environment as you can get... yet they have made some amazing investments in local education.

Gus Raimerez (one of the founders of Husco) has made **education and student success the focus of his community efforts due to his belief that education is the foundation of economic prosperity for students and the community**. The Raimerez family and the Husco company invested heavily in Milwaukee, Wisconsin's Southside to forward those beliefs.

- In 2010, they donated $1 million to help renovate and expand the St. Anthony Catholic school. The school serves mostly low-income, minority, and at-risk students.

- Husco also worked in collaboration with the Waukesha STEM Academy[187], a charter school. They built a state-of-the-art facility adjacent to the school and donated equipment, materials, and expertise to create a hands-on learning environment for students interested in science, technology, engineering, and math (STEM).

  This partnership also provides opportunities for students to visit the company's headquarters, participate in internships and apprenticeships, and interact closely with Husco engineers.

- In their biggest venture investing in education for the community, the Ramierez family and Husco invested in a new school in Milwaukee's Southside to improve the educational experience of students. Augustine Prep opened in 2017. Since they opened for classes, they have become one of the top-rated K4-12 schools in Wisconsin. They are now preparing to build another school, Augustine North.[188]

  Most of their students come from minority backgrounds and poorer socioeconomic backgrounds who qualify for state and city assistance programs. Of particular note, the State of Wisconsin ranked student academic growth at Augustine in the top 2% statewide. In 2024 the senior class earned over $10.5 million in scholarships, of which 70% are first-generation college students. 100% of the 2023 class were accepted into either 2- or 4-year colleges, or the military.[189]

They have done much more to partner within the community and around the world in education, but you get the point. Their donations helped fund scholarships, technology upgrades, teacher training, and more. **This is an amazing example of community investing in students**, their education, and their futures.

So what do the Raimerez family and Husco get out of it? I assume in big part, **the pleasure of helping in a community they are passionate about**. But they also gain the recognition and goodwill of the community, the parents, and the students. At times, they also receive some nice tax breaks. Not to mention a pipeline of future talent with a well-known quality education, access to a current and ongoing pool of talented and diverse potential employees, and fostering a culture of innovation and collaboration among current and future Husco employees.

The students benefit from a high-quality education, exposure to STEM careers, opportunities for mentorship and internships, and of course preferential access to jobs after high school, college, or the military.

These partnerships with Raimerez and Husco have been praised as a model of corporate social responsibility and educational innovation.

---------------- ◆ ----------------

This is the kind of partnership that we want to emulate in FMS and encourage among our potential partners.

FMS is not only a system that transforms the way education is delivered, but is also **a system that invites and involves the whole community to participate and benefit from the process and product of education**. By creating a more choice-driven, market-oriented, and community-supported school system, FMS can foster a more efficient, effective, and unbiased educational environment for every single student.

One last note on partnerships. We have focused here on the local community, but let's not forget there is a big, wide world out there that should have an interest in engaging with the schools. These might include EdTech developers, curriculum developers, hardware/software developers, large technology companies, and others.

It is a big world to explore, and it is well worth taking a step out of our comfort zone to imagine what might be possible in the future.

CHAPTER

16

WHAT DO FMS SCHOOLS LOOK LIKE?

Things to consider:

➢ What can the future look like if we imagine it?

➢ Are FMS schools better?

➢ What are the risk factors of success?

"We who live in free market societies believe that growth and prosperity, and ultimately human fulfillment, are created from the bottom up, not the government down."

—Ronald Reagan[190]

"The great advances of civilization, whether in architecture or painting, in science or literature, in industry or agriculture, have never come from centralized government."

—Milton Friedman[191]

WE LIVE IN A DIFFERENT WORLD

Let us make one more assumption as we near the end of this grand proposal. Let's **assume that we have decided to do this**, we have gathered our amazing **Founders**, initiated our first **Educational Zone**, and are moving towards an exciting new future for our children with Free Market Schools.

What would that look like?

It would look and feel pretty amazing to have that first Educational Zone. The excitement in the air would be palpable in anticipation of a new future brimming with unparalleled opportunities for our children that we never could have believed possible before. Imagine that feeling for just a moment.

But first… let me take you on a little side journey.

Some of you may be familiar with Milton Freidman's story of the **Manufacturing of a Pencil**. He uses this example to help us understand the complexity and interconnectivity of our incredible free market system.

In his exploration of how a pencil is made, he demonstrates that **no single person could make this everyday utensil happen** in bulk without the efforts of countless people from around the globe. Yes, you *could* make something like a pencil for yourself, and maybe your family and friends, but it would be difficult and time-consuming. It would be much easier to just run down to the store and buy a pack of 12 for about $5.00.

In order for you to be able to do that though, it takes a system that accounts for components coming from different places around the world and requires the use of specialized tools, equipment, skills, and labor. Everything comes together through an **intricate ballet of the balanced forces** within the free market.

What does it take to produce something as simple as a wooden pencil?

- **Wood**: Most pencil wood in America comes from cedar trees in the northwest. The trees are carefully managed and harvested in a sustainable manner to ensure continuous and reliable supplies. Hundreds of trades are required to get from tree form to pencil form.

- **Graphite**: The graphite is often sourced from mines in China, Sri Lanka, and other distant locations. The mineral must be extracted from the earth and processed to achieve the appropriate consistency for pencils. Specialized knowledge and equipment are needed to ensure the final graphite is pure and finely ground to specification.

- **Metal**: The ferrule (*the metal band that holds the eraser in place*) is typically brass (copper and zinc potentially sourced from places such as Chile or Kazakhstan) or aluminum (which might be mined in Australia). The refinement, shaping, and shipping involve numerous people and organizations.

- **Eraser**: Rubber for the eraser may derive from natural rubber (harvested from rubber trees in places like Indonesia or Thailand) or could be synthetically produced in industrial plants around the world. Again, specialized labor, tools, and technology are required to help us erase our mistakes.

None of this even gets into the other required elements such as paint, embossing, package design, packaging, marketing, shipping, and point-of-sale that puts these pencils on a shelf where you can buy them. Yet… somehow… **it all comes together**

through an amazing international choreograph of disparate parts that ends with you standing in the store, trying to decide between multiple different brands of pencils. Amazing!

The long and complex path of becoming a pencil exemplifies the **interconnectedness of our national and global economy** and the efficiency of a free market system. The beauty of voluntary cooperation and compounding efficiency is driven by each participant's own interests and their desires to contribute – and profit – on products and services that people want.

———————— ◆ ————————

So **WHY have I used precious space** in this book to belabor the manufacturing of a pencil? It is simply this…

Over the last 50 years or so, WE the people have overcome and surpassed the capabilities of governmental systems.

In the past, we always turned to the government when we wanted to do something big. We knew it was an inefficient bureaucracy, but **government was the only entity with the resources to do BIG things** like NASA and space exploration.

Today, we have a free-market private enterprise company (SpaceX[192]) building manned rocket ships, flying more direct missions than NASA, rescuing astronauts in space, and they are even planning a manned Mars mission. This has become so feasible that **there are now numerous private spaceflight companies**[193] such as **SpaceX** (*owned by Elon Musk*), **Orbital ATK**[194] (now owned by) **Northrop Grumman**[195], **Sierra Space**[196], **Blue Origin**[197] (*founded by Jeff Bezos*), **Boeing**[198], and many others around the world operating in various arenas of space travel, space tourism, supply, satellites, and operations.

These are massively complex endeavors that **we could not have imagined anyone but a government doing** just a few years ago. Yet today, it is common.

And it's not just space. There are additional sectors of our society now where **the common entrepreneur has exceeded and excelled beyond government-only capabilities**. Free market private enterprise has succeeded with many large-scale ventures:

- **Mail and Package Delivery**: The U.S. Postal Service (USPS)[199] was established by the U.S. government nearly 250 years ago. Today it ensures we receive our *Sears Christmas Catalog* on time every time. However, our government-based mail delivery system became overwhelmed early on and prices continue to go up and up as service became more and more troubled and erratic, especially with packages.

  Enter our incredible entrepreneurs to save the day and private enterprise companies like **Federal Express (FedEx)[200]** and **United Parcel Service (UPS)[201]** were born. They did their job so well that they are actually in competition with the Federal Government. In fact, FedEx was the primary air cargo supplier for the USPS until UPS took over that role in late 2024. Many wish that FedEx would just take over the entire government mail contract for the USPS and improve the entire service.

- **Shopping and Shipping**: No talk of massive enterprise would be complete without a discussion of the juggernaut that is **Amazon[202]**. There is no government equivalent to Amazon, but I include it here due to the sheer size of it and **the massive logistics involved in this operation**. What started as a small book-buying website, quickly ballooned into $575 BILLION dollars in annual revenue. They currently deliver over 8 BILLION packages per year worldwide. Imagine the U.S. Government trying to efficiently manage a logistics operation like this.

- **Privatization**: There has been a growing trend for several decades now for government to privatize (*or allow private enterprise to engage in*) sectors that have traditionally been exclusively government-owned and managed. These include **prisons**, **utilities** (*water, electricity, gas*), **transportation** (*railways, airlines, and public transportation systems within cities*), and **hospitals**. There have been some mixed results, but in general, the private sector operates more efficiently, effectively, and engages in innovation to succeed. Failures are often attributed to continued government interference and regulation of the privatized element.

So What?

Why in the world did I take you down that rabbit hole of what might seem irrelevancy? It was all to make one simple statement that is critical for you to accept as we wrap all of this up.

CRITICAL! | CRITICAL!

> *If <u>private enterprise</u> can accomplish all of the amazing, wonderful, complex, and massive ventures we discussed above...*
> *WHY can we not also manage our public educational system?*

If you still doubt that free market private enterprise is capable of operating and managing our educational system, then I refer you back to the previous few pages.

I challenge you to come up with viable arguments that a government bureaucracy can do a better job of educating our children than the incredible entrepreneurs of our nation can.

Before you do that, let me toss out a scrap of food for thought. Let's go back to our pencil story for a little "**what if**" moment based entirely on my opinion and beliefs – *and maybe a bit of tongue in cheek political rant just for fun*.

What If...

Let's assume for a moment that our government controls the production and distribution systems of America and, being the kind and benevolent leaders they are, have decided to let you have something new called a pencil (*which did not already exist for some weird reason in our "what if"*).

*Once it was decided by a **Blue Ribbon Panel** that pencils were an acceptable item for the people to own, they would pass the mandate to a committee whose job it would be to manage the "pencil" project.*

*Their focus in providing pencils to the masses would NOT be efficiency, competition, or the realities of the market. **Their focus would be to determine how this project could benefit their reelection,** who is owed favors, who they can curry favor with, what industries to enrich, and which industries to destroy. As a result, a political committee with no experience would decide what your pencil would look like, how it would function, and the materials it would be made of. No consideration would be given to cost or competition.*

In the end, ONE manufacturer would receive a contract to make them, and the resulting pencil would likely cost you around $20, assuming you could even get one. With limited availability and waiting lists to have the privilege of owning one, you would need connections to get your hands on a government pencil. They will of course create a set-aside quota for favored constituencies to curry favor and votes.

Absurd? *Maybe.* Maybe I'm just **poking the bear** a bit. But if we look at how government works, we see that the focus, intention, and execution of any government activity is far different from the free market. Part of that difference is that the **government does not "create" anything**. Nor do they have their own money. They use other people's money (OPM)... i.e., our tax dollars to fund what *they* think is important at that moment. Then they figure out how to spend your money... without consideration of running out. After all, they can just print more.

They also won't worry about *why* you need a pencil or *how* you are actually going to use it, or even the best aspects of a pencil to make it most useful. Instead, every decision from a government system will be determined by **how it gives them more power, gets those involved reelected, and how it supports the political and social agendas of the day**.

Nowhere in that equation do you see anything related to what is best for the end user. Nowhere do we see a calculation of how competition might do it better... because there is none. Nowhere in that math is there a consideration of the cost to the end user.

And if the final cost is too high (it will be), then government will just create another program to spend tax dollars to provide "assistance" to low-income people or schools so that they can own government pencils. They are always happy to help overcome a problem that they created.

– End of political rant and back to topic. – 😊

Fortunately, the government won't be building our new educational system... we the people will. This book provides the baseline of what is needed to build an FMS public school system. We know what it will take and, as complicated as it is, **our educational venture would be far *less* complicated (*but far more critical*) for our children** than building a new space enterprise from scratch or an international sales company that ships 8 billion packages per year.

On a side note, I would argue that government is necessary for the military. But the national defense is a **Constitutionally provided function** of our federal government. **Public schools are not.** And just for the record, I do NOT advocate privatizing our military.

So, even though the Military is a Government function, I would point out that the **military as a government entity relies on the free-market system and free-market contractors** to provide nearly all aircraft, ships, weapons systems, communications, transportation, tools, and so much more.

As I stated before, the government does NOT create anything, it only buys, with our money, what it needs from the private sector. There is no way to discern an actual number, but my best estimate from my years in government contracting is that more than **60% of all federal military spending** is on products and services derived from free-market sources.

WHAT WOULD AN FMS WORLD ACTUALLY LOOK LIKE?

So, we are finally there. We have broken through all the firewalls and the first Free Market Schools (FMS) fall session is operational in our first Educational Zone. What does it look like?

Initially, the schools would look very similar to what we have now. **We would keep the best of what exists and replace the elements that don't work.** Classes would be held in the existing buildings. Students would scurry from class to class when the bells ring. Teachers would teach students. The lunch bell would call them to the cafeteria on **Taco Tuesdays** and **Pizza Fridays**. And kids would still complain about dodge ball.

Most of the initial changes would be pretty much invisible to the students. **It would feel comfortable to them. Familiar.** The teachers would be trained to ease the students into broader changes while they are transitioned into the full power of the FMS environment.

As the methodologies prove themselves, more and more of the **amazing educational adventures** we have discussed here will be implemented and incorporated into the student's daily lives.

Within six months from Day One of FMS, all approved elements of FMS will be fully operational and the students will begin to experience the power of a true and bountiful education designed specifically for them.

———— ♦ ————

The big differences the students will notice at the beginning and as the first year progresses are:

- **A more diverse curriculum** with a primary focus on Core Academics, while allowing for a broader range of subjects designed to promote a well-rounded education **focused on *their* success** once they leave school. The balance will change throughout the student's career from grade 1 to grade 12.

- **Personalized learning paths** based on a customized learning plan tailored to their strengths, interests, and career aspirations allow them to thrive at their own pace.

- **A Culture of "Learning"** will be promoted rather than a culture of "Knowing". Students will learn how to understand, master, and apply subjects rather than just memorize enough facts to pass tests. This will promote a **Culture of Success** rather than just a culture of just *"passing the class."*

- **Master Achievement Grading (MAG)** that goes beyond a simple pass/fail system and takes into account personal progress, subject matter mastery, real-world application of learning, and more. As discussed in **Chapter 12**, MAG will create a more holistic evaluation of each student's performance and provide an accurate reflection of their ability to apply that knowledge outside of the classroom.

- **Innovative Teaching Methods** will be integrated into the learning paths that promote project-based learning, experiential education, creativity integration, critical thinking, and problem-solving skills.

- **Community Partnerships** will be expanded to create stronger ties with local businesses and organizations. Students will gain real-world experience through availability of internships, mentorship programs, and collaborative projects.

- **Enhanced Technology Integration** will be seamlessly woven into the fabric of daily education to provide students with dynamic and engaging learning experiences.

- **Positive and hopeful attitudes** will be promoted in all elements of the school by the FMS teachers and administrators to instill forward-looking positive beliefs as the natural state of being. This will be especially important for the high-risk schools and at-risk students.

- **Flexible Scheduling** will be adaptable to accommodate different learning methods and styles, and to support extracurricular activities, cross-FMSEP programs, community engagement, and more.

The changes will become more pronounced over time as the system evolves and the FMS Education Providers (FEMSEPs) **innovate new ways to ensure student success.** Many changes are highlighted in this book, but the real change will come from those who are involved in this when it becomes reality.

We have focused on the students here, but **teachers** will also notice changes.

- **Meritocracy**: For the first time, teachers will be employed within a true Free-Market Meritocracy rather than a stifled Bureaucracy. They will eventually realize that their successes, excellence, innovation, and self-growth will be rewarded with opportunities, promotions, higher pay, and recognition. They will be incentivized to succeed.

- **Focus on Student Success**: Sadly, many of our schools are focused in essence on pumping children through and graduating them to move them out of the school system. All stakeholders within FMS environments (no matter the socio-economic makeup of the school) will be encouraged, incentivized, and provided with the tools necessary to promote a **Culture of Success**.

- **Professional Development**: FMSEPs are competitive organizations, always seeking to be better than the other guys. Experience dictates that FMSEPs will support and incentivize teachers to enhance their existing skills, develop new skills, and embrace new technologies and methodologies to make the FMSEP more competitive when bidding on more locations.

- **Innovation and Creativity**: Teachers will have the freedom to explore and implement innovative teaching methods and creative solutions in their classrooms to encourage a dynamic and engaging learning environment (within the broad bounds of the individual FMSEPs and the FMS Guiding Documents). This freedom is not possible in the bureaucratic morass of our current schools.

- **Supportive Community**: Strong community partnerships will be established, providing teachers with resources and support from local businesses, organizations, and collaborative projects, enriching the educational experience.

The paradigm shift for teachers may be hard for some, but will be welcomed by many. To move to the next generation of education, **we need to be bold, embrace innovation**, be willing to fully commit, and be ready to face change.

---------- ◆ ----------

As long as we are imagining the future here, there are some other imaginings that are beyond the scope of this book that should be considered for discussion later. **I am not particularly advocating any of this**, but if we are going to reimagine the future of public education, why not examine everything?

Primarily, **the big question to imagine is if the K-12 public school structure is still valid?** Is having 12 grades really the best pathway to guide the children of today and the future into being productive and successful members of society. Society is not structured in a straight-line progression for everyone. The pathway is different for each individual. K-12 is an artificial construct that was developed out of necessity in the early days.

With all the advances in educational methods and technology that are available to us today, **wouldn't a more fluid structure that adapted to each individual provide a more powerful growth path for the students?** This fluidity would allow students to grow at their own pace and in a direction that best suits their strengths. There are many possibilities, but maybe something like the **color belts** in martial arts or **certifications of mastery** for each course of study.

Or imagine simply an **educational career curriculum managed by an AI system** that walks a student through their career from beginning to end. The AI system would learn through years of discussion and experience with the student and their parents as to where their education is leading them and help **guide them in the proper direction as they evolve** into who they are going to be. The AI (under parental guidance) would chart the best courses, the best speed, and adjust as the student learns. *Hmmmm... I sense another book there... or possibly a business... No, **forget that**... I said nothing... You heard nothing... Moving on...*

One last thought for our imagination exercise. **Will our traditional public-school buildings still be necessary in the future**, or will they become a relic of how we did things in the past? The <u>convenience</u> of the yellow school buses going to a single building, the singular kitchen and cafeteria with bad food, and the gymnasium with smelly locker rooms, etc. cannot be denied. But is there a better way? Do we still need to do that? Again, the communal public-school house is not what life is like in the real world.

It absolutely makes sense to <u>use the existing buildings now</u>. But **might it make more sense over time to move into smaller more specialized spaces**, commercial spaces, old malls, etc.? Or going the other direction, **might it make sense to build more campus-like settings that better serve our reimagined fluid educational system** (*sans grades* K-12) where all resources can be consolidated into an immersive and expansive educational environment?

———— ◆ ————

Just some thoughts to consider as we barrel towards our future. **Maybe it's time we evolved a bit**.

Can We Evolve?

17

NEXT STEPS TO AN AMAZING EDUCATIONAL FUTURE

Things to consider:

➢ What steps can WE take now?

➢ What steps can YOU take now?

➢ Are you ready for change?

"If you want to change the world, pick up your pen and write."

—Martin Luther[203]

EXODUS OR REVIVAL?

So here we are finally!

> ➤ We visited the **past**.

> ➤ We examined **today**.

> ➤ We explored a **tomorrow** that could be.

Why did I spend so much time doing this? Long ago, Martin Luther (and others throughout time) challenged us to pick up our pen if we want to change the world.

I am not famous. I am not an authority on public education. I don't have a big platform or following. I have no specific qualifications to change the world.

But I DO have a pen!

This book was a massive journey in the evolution of my thinking and a personal three-year exploration of this topic. But I took this on because of three things.

1. I am a father and recognize the failing state of public education for all of our children.

2. I understand that silence is acceptance of what is.

3. I have spent my professional career tearing apart large complex subjects and constructing simple pathways to understanding for those who may be unfamiliar with a topic, system, or methodology. I felt that I needed to apply that skill to something meaningful.

I hope ***my* journey now becomes *your* journey** and that I have laid out a clear understanding of the dangers of our current public educational system and the damage it is doing to generations of our children. I also hope that I have convinced you that **correction can only be found through the complete death and rebirth of our public educational system.**

There are no half-steps to this. We cannot "fix" the existing system, the systemic problems are too deep a wound to heal. There is no "repair" that will save ALL of our children.

Most importantly, I hope that readers understand that the **mass exodus from the public school system** will leave millions upon millions of children behind in a broken system that will only get worse. **Those left in today's system will suffer from an increasingly weak education that will focus on programming and indoctrination** on a scale that we never could have imagined before. If we leave vulnerable children behind, that failure is on all of us.

> *The Mass Exodus from Public Schools will leave millions of children behind to falter within a broken system.*

As I write this book, the **movement towards EXITING the public school system grows stronger and options expand to reach more children**. I absolutely understand this and do NOT condemn anyone who chooses or promotes that path. Parents are moving their children to private schools, parochial schools, specialized schools, and other alternates including home schooling **for a reason**.

I have made it clear throughout this book that **I am a big fan of homeschooling**. If it were feasible for all children to be homeschooled, I would advocate for that. A recent study claims that **1 in 3 children will be homeschooled by 2030** as millions flee the public school system.[204] Although I find that statistic to be a bit enthusiastic, I am excited to see continued growth in homeschooling.

But homeschooling is not a realistic option for everyone. **Mass public schooling is the reality of today** for most people.

*So… I MUST keep returning to
the premise that we are bound by
our nature to do something for
those left behind.*

According to the study noted above, the issue becomes more dire when we compound traditional students exiting the public schools while we also have **massive numbers of new enrollments from the immigrants that have been pouring into our country**.

If this trend to exit schools continues, **we risk progressing the United States into a systemic culturally tiered nation where we could potentially devolve into a true Caste system**[205] due to the disparity of quality and focus between alternate schooling and public schooling. Traditionally, once someone is born into an institutionalized Caste, it becomes nearly impossible to change one's hereditary class. **This would institutionalize discrimination (along many different lines), limit social mobility, and undermine the principles of equality and individual rights** that are the foundation and hallmark of American society.

Wouldn't a better path be to create an educational system that is so desired that most parents and children would *want* to be a part of that? There will always be those who prefer alternative schooling, that is great, but **our collective focus should be on developing competitive public schools** since they will be the primary education source for most children in America for the foreseeable future.

———— ♦ ————

So why am I beating all of this to death? We covered a lot of ground in this proposal, but I want to make sure that **readers walk away with the main point** of this entire book clearly in their minds.

So, pardon me for a moment while I whack readers one more time with the ***Obvious Stick***…

> **LOOK!** →
>
> All efforts to "*fix*" the broken public education system will result in **generations of children being left behind** in a broken system that they cannot escape as the sacred fire continues to burn out.
>
> We cannot allow that. We must **tear the government system down** and **replace it with an educational system that works for ALL students**. THAT is the only way we can be honest about the attempt to **secure success for future generations**.

Now that we're all on the same page, it is time to begin.

NEXT STEPS

I imagine your next question is, "*Where do we start?*"

We start by building a **coalition of incredible people** who understand the government system is irrevocably broken and that **"fixes" and band-aid solutions will not work.** We must understand in unity that the only way to truly reinvent public education is to burn down our current system (*metaphorically of course*) and build on that framework to take the best of the best and create a new entrepreneurial vision that is focused on the education and success of our children.

What are the next steps?

(*CAUTION* → *Shameless pandering below.* 😊)

1. **Buy** this book.
2. **Persuade** everyone you know to buy this book.
3. **Share** this book with anyone with a voice or platform.
4. *Are you sensing a common theme here?* 😛
5. **Join** the FMS Mailing List (*see next section*).
6. **Share** the FMS website with everyone you know and on social media (*see next section*).

7. **Imagine** what <u>YOU can do</u> to help FMS become a reality.
   a.   Who do YOU know?
   b.   Who do YOU know who knows other people who have influence?
   c.   Pick up YOUR pen and write to your blog, your list, your mother, your father, your friends, coworkers, associates, and anyone you can think of.
   d.   Write reviews of this book on Amazon and any other platform you belong to.

The point is that it will require many smart and connected people to step forward. We can only reach them if we can break through all the noise out there. We need that excitement and engagement before we can even begin developing this into a broad conversation beyond the confines of this book.

Primarily, it is necessary to **get this proposal into the hands of those who can truly lead and execute change** in a big way.

The steps beyond those noted above will evolve as more people get engaged and begin interaction, exploration, and discussions of *"what if"*.

You should be a part of that.

TAKE ACTION

We are a **nation in crisis** as we teeter upon a **fundamental tipping point of who we will be in the future**. You and I can take direct action NOW to influence laws, promote regulations, and vote as we push to fix our broader issues such as crime, inflation, immigration, international affairs, and more, but **OUR children and grandchildren will be the nation's leaders in the coming years** (*assuming any of our lifetime career politicians step out of the way*).

The **foundational education of our future leaders** is critical to ensure Truth, Justice, and the American Way remains the foundation for future generations.

We are the only nation in the world that **teaches our children to hate their own country**, their Founding Fathers, and the very U.S. Constitution that has held us together as the Great American Experiment for 250 years. The future of this amazing country will be **shaped by the students of today** as they become the leaders **of tomorrow**.

CRITICAL! ➤ *WHO do we want them to be?*

We have lost too many generations of our children already to **hatred, hopelessness**, and **hostility**. Just imagine an amazing world where ALL children are educated toward the potential to be **critical thinkers, independent minded, motivated to succeed**, and **aspirational in everything they do**.

HERE is what you can do now to make that happen![206]

ACTION	WHAT TO DO
Go to the **Sacred Fire** site where you can learn more about FMS and get the latest news and updates.	Go to **www.Gabberz.com** and follow links for more information or to **join the mailing list**.
Follow me to keep up to date on new information, updates, events, and more. Also, read more on Substack.	• https://X.com/davidnemzoff • https://davidnemzoff.substack.com/ • https://www.facebook.com/david.nemzoff
Buy the book for yourself, your friends, family, and others. Buy in BULK for board meetings, fairs, events, and other places.	Available on Amazon at: https://www.amazon.com/dp/0988273837 and through most online book sellers. Reviews and comments on Amazon are welcome.
Reach out with your thoughts, ideas, suggestions, recommendations, or to provide information.	Go to **www.Gabberz.com** and join the mailing list for more information or leave a comment. **WRITE A REVIEW HERE**: https://www.amazon.com/review/create-review?&asin=0988273837
Take action if you believe your schools are in a prime target area for FMS implementation. Begin taking back your schools for your children and to position your schools and	• Run for your Board of Supervisors • Run for your local School Board • Run for State Office • Get involved in your schools • Make your voice heard at Board Meetings.

ACTION	WHAT TO DO
communities for potential FMS engagement. If you don't believe your district is a prime target, then work towards reshaping your schools to be ready when the future comes to your schools.	• Write Op-Eds, commentaries, blogs, reviews, and post any other place your voice can be heard. • Spread the word wherever you can that there is another way and let people know about this book

YOUR voice is important, and you should be heard. **YOU are no less qualified to be heard than I am**… I just happened to have a pen handy to write this book.

I hope that it provides a framework
for others to build upon.

───────── ♦ ─────────

THE LAST WORD

It has taken us a while, but we have now reached the end of this proposal and the beginning of our arduous journey. The **Sacred Fire of Education** has been all but snuffed out in today's public education system. **This is not just a disservice to our children's education** but is a complete and utter **betrayal of their future potential**. And the potential of those who come after them.

I have dissected the flaws and pitfalls that plague our schools, and we have seen how systemically deep the wounds are throughout the system. Unfortunately, we must allow the fire to burn out, taking the schools with them before we can fan the flames into their glorious brilliance again.

To that end, **I have outlined here a transformative pathway to reignite the Sacred Fire of Education** in our public schools.

It will not be easy. Monumental change has always been driven by **unwavering courage and collective action** of those who believe we can do better.

Our mission is no different, but there will be tremendous forces arrayed against this at every step. To succeed, we must **harness the power of our collective voices** and advocate relentlessly for a new system that nurtures and honors the innate brilliance of every child.

The time for complacency is over.
The time to act is now.

The pathway to saving future generations does not lie in superficial or transitory remedies, but in a **bold reimagining** of what public education for our children can become. Together...

- We can reignite the Sacred Fire.

  - We can ensure that no child is left behind

    - We can throw light upon the shadows and darkness of a broken system.

      - We can rise to this challenge with unwavering resolve and boundless hope.

The future is OURS to shape for our children and for those who follow them.

Step Forward and Be Heard!

─────── ♦ ───────

David Nemzoff

Father, Husband, Author, Believer in America, and Lover of Imagination, Innovation, and a Glorious Future for Our Children

APPENDIX A –
ENDNOTES

A Parting Thought...

Please enjoy the references I have provided throughout this book to help you do your own research and come to your own conclusions. **These references are by NO means the only sources for information I used or that you can find**. For most of the topics, there are numerous sources for you to explore. I recommend you **look at sources from all sides of the political spectrum** to get the full picture.

> *They are _quite_ contradictory...*
> *but fun nonetheless.*

Finally, as I have noted throughout, I did my best to properly interpret the information I examined and provide a fair and accurate description of my understandings and beliefs of the information. If I have incorrectly portrayed anyone, any organization, or any information, **I welcome qualified corrections. There was _NO_ intention of falsely or incorrectly portraying any person, organization, or event**. If you identify an error, please let me know and I will do my best to correct the information going forward.

Enjoy!

1   **Seriously?** You are reading the endnotes and references? **Good for you, you hearty soul**. I appreciate your interest in these ideas and encourage you to jump down the rabbit hole to learn more. Enjoy!

2   **Thomas Jefferson** wrote this in a letter to Judge John Tyler on June 28, 1804. https://libquotes.com/thomas-jefferson/quote/lbi6k1k.

3   **George Washington** wrote this in his letter to Catherine Sawbridge Macaulay on January 9, 1790 expressing a few observations. https://founders.archives.gov/documents/Washington/05-04-02-0363#:~:text=The%20establishment%20of%20our%20new,as%20a%20govern ment%20of%20Laws.

4   There are many sources for the "*Great Experiment*" designation including George Washington and Thomas Jefferson. Alexander Hamilton did write in *Federalist #9* about the errors of our past and new principles in government that were integrated into the founding of our nation. Likewise, Abraham Lincoln talked in "**The Gettysburg Address**" about our "*new nation*" and "*testing whether that nation… so conceived…. can long endure.*" A quick search of the amazing and wonderful Internet will turn up numerous examples of the term. One I particularly enjoyed was David Rubenstein's book, "*The American Experiment: Dialogues on a Dream.*" https://en.wikipedia.org/wiki/David_Rubenstein

5   The first public school, the **Boston Latin School** was founded in 1635 and is the oldest existing school in the Unites States. Website: https://www.bls.org/apps/pages/index.jsp?uREC_ID=206116&type=d.

6   "*The Good, the Bad and the Ugly*", 1966 film starring Clint Eastwood. https://en.wikipedia.org/wiki/The_Good,_the_Bad_and_the_Ugly.

7   The zettabyte era. https://en.wikipedia.org/wiki/Zettabyte_Era.

8   There are numerous sources in the zettabyte's of data available to us. A couple of interesting ones include: https://www.statista.com/statistics/871513/worldwide-data-created/ and https://www.forbes.com/sites/bernardmarr/2015/09/30/big-data-20-mind-boggling-facts-everyone-must-read/?sh=4d2ad5317b1e,

9   As with many innovations, the **Band-Aid®** was invented out of need and the right person with the right knowledge recognizing that. We have Earle Dickson to thank for the magic Band-Aids we know and love so much. However, throughout this book, I use this as a generic term for patching things together and is not intended to imply anything about the company or the product. https://lemelson.mit.edu/resources/earle-dickson.

10   **U.S. Public Education Spending Statistics**, the Education Data Initiative, updated August 2, 2021. https://educationdata.org/public-education-spending-statistics.

11   The average cost of Private schools varies significantly based on location, demand, type of school, and other factors. Numerous sources for data can be located on the Internet, providing similar numbers. https://educationdata.org/average-cost-of-private-school and https://www.privateschoolreview.com/tuition-stats/private-school-cost-by-state.

[12] The numbers vary tremendously from different sources and different timeframes. The 10 times is an easy round number. But here are a few sources to feed your curiosity. https://nces.ed.gov/fastfacts/display.asp?id=372, https://www.edweek.org/leadership/education-statistics-facts-about-american-schools/2019/01.

[13] Mel Gibson classic movie. https://en.wiktionary.org/wiki/Thunderdome, https://en.wikipedia.org/wiki/Mad_Max_Beyond_Thunderdome.

[14] If you dig through Zappa's works, you'll find many wonderful thoughts. Zappa did say this. https://www.goodreads.com/quotes/33052-a-mind-is-like-a-parachute-it-doesn-t-work-if. However, the quote can be attributed to several others including Charlie Chan, Lord Dewar, and others. https://english.stackexchange.com/questions/517939/a-mind-is-like-a-parachute-who-coined-this-expression-and-when. I chose to attribute Frank Zappa because, well… it was more interesting that way.

[15] Peter Kreeft, Professor of Philosophy. https://en.wikipedia.org/wiki/Peter_Kreeft.

[16] Francis Bacon. https://www.britannica.com/biography/Francis-Bacon-Viscount-Saint-Alban.

[17] Variations of this quote are attributed to many. I make no claim to originality. https://quoteinvestigator.com/2016/01/05/done/.

[18] W.E.B. Du Bois, *The Freedom to Learn* (1949) In P.S. Foner (Ed.), *W.E.B. Du Bois Speaks* (pp. 230-231). New York: *Pathfinder*, 1970.

[19] I can't believe you clicked on a link for a reference that discusses **spear control** for ancient man! **Just kidding**. You have no idea how hard it is to make history fun.

[20] Many historical accounts are available through easy searches demonstrating the power of the Xettabyte Era discussed earlier. A good starting point of you want to know more is an excellent account on Wikipedia. https://en.wikipedia.org/wiki/History_of_education.

[21] Eighteenth-century schools had a common theme that play was counter to learning and becoming an adult, and education must be work and strictly, even brutally controlled. This was reflected in John Wesley's Rules for Wesleyan Schools. *Sohag University International Journal of Educational Research*, Vol. (1): pg. 7.

[22] Numerous sources bear out the prevailing thinking about education during that time, e.g., https://www.psychologytoday.com/us/blog/freedom-learn/200808/brief-history-education.

[23] As with most topics these days, there are numerous sources of information floating around in the zettabytes of data available to us. If you want to learn more, the Boston Latin School (BLS) website is the best to start. https://www.bls.org/apps/pages/index.jsp?uREC_ID=206116&type=d.

[24] Some of the awards and rankings are listed in Wikipedia at https://en.wikipedia.org/wiki/Boston_Latin_School.

[25] Attendance around 1840 according to the 1840 census per https://en.wikipedia.org/wiki/History_of_education_in_the_United_States.

[26] Sorry, I thought I made up the word "***deprovements***" but see now there is some debate about it. I use it to indicate the degradation of a system rather than improving it. https://www.urbandictionary.com/define.php?term=deprovement.

[27] Horace Mann and the Mann Reforms change education in America. https://en.wikipedia.org/wiki/Horace_Mann.

[28] National Education Association (NEA), https://www.nea.org/. https://en.wikipedia.org/wiki/National_Education_Association.

[29] The U.S. Department of Education website provides an excellent history of the Department and how it grew broader in scope over the following decades. https://www2.ed.gov/about/overview/fed/role.html.

[30] Jim Crow laws. https://en.wikipedia.org/wiki/Jim_Crow_laws.

[31] Lists multiple sources for this information. https://en.wikipedia.org/wiki/History_of_education_in_the_United_States.

[32] A basic primer on the history of education can be found at: https://en.wikipedia.org/wiki/History_of_education_in_the_United_States.

[33] This page just focuses on education during the Great Depression. https://en.wikipedia.org/wiki/History_of_education_in_the_United_States.

[34] NSBA. https://www.nsba.org/.

[35] One of many stories related to the NSBA letter to the Biden administration. https://www.nationalreview.com/news/national-school-board-association-at-risk-of-losing-millions-over-state-chapter-withdrawals/.

[36] "The Lanham Act" *History of Education Journal*, Vol. 3, No. 1, 1951. https://www.jstor.org/stable/3659219.

[37] Impact Aid Program. https://oese.ed.gov/offices/office-of-formula-grants/impact-aid-program/ and https://education.stateuniversity.com/pages/2079/Impact-Aid-Public-Laws-815-874.html.

[38] https://en.wikipedia.org/wiki/Brown_v._Board_of_Education.

[39] https://en.wikipedia.org/wiki/Civil_Rights_Act_of_1964.

[40] ESEA of 1965 passed by President Lyndon B. Johnson. https://en.wikipedia.org/wiki/Elementary_and_Secondary_Education_Act.

[41] The Coleman Report by Professor James Coleman. https://en.wikipedia.org/wiki/James_Samuel_Coleman and https://www.educationnext.org/what-matters-for-student-achievement/.

[42] "Report: "A Nation at Risk: The Imperative for Educational Reform"". https://en.wikipedia.org/wiki/A_Nation_at_Risk.

[43] https://en.wikipedia.org/wiki/No_Child_Left_Behind_Act.

[44] One source of information on the "Every Student Succeeds Act". https://www.everystudentsucceedsact.org/.

[45] Project H.O.O.D. https://www.projecthood.org/.

[46] "Rooftop Revelations: Pastor Brooks 100-Day Rooftop Vigil. https://www.foxnews.com/opinion/rooftop-revelations-pastor-brooks-shares-the-lesson-he-learned-from-thomas-sowell-on-school-choice.

[47] Thomas Sowell. https://en.wikipedia.org/wiki/Thomas_Sowell.

[48] Dunbar High School, Washington, D.C. https://www.dunbarhsdc.org/.

[49] I explore Dunbar's "Unintended Consequences" a bit more in my Substack. A Tale of Glory and Woe - by David Nemzoff (substack.com)

50 Quote from Thomas Sowell's appraisal of Dunbar High School.
https://en.wikipedia.org/wiki/Dunbar_High_School_(Washington,_D.C.).

51 Melinda Harmon, U.S. District Judge in a ruling in 1996.
https://en.wikipedia.org/wiki/Melinda_Harmon.

52 Britannica offers a historical background on CRT as well as broad strokes on racism: https://www.britannica.com/topic/critical-race-theory. Wikipedia provides another look at CRT, though I believe one that is softened a bit: https://en.wikipedia.org/wiki/Critical_race_theory.

53 There are numerous stories related to this gubernatorial race, this is but one. https://www.npr.org/2021/11/02/1049026183/virginia-governor-election-mcauliffe-youngkin.

54 Again, there are numerous stories related to this important (for many reasons) race. Here are two links. https://thehill.com/opinion/campaign/578885-education-blunder-igniting-suburban-parents-driving-mcauliffe-panic-in, and https://www.newsweek.com/mcauliffe-saying-parents-shouldnt-tell-schools-what-teach-big-factor-election-poll-1649488.

55 Home School Legal Defense Association's (HSLDA) analysis of the U.S. Census Bureau's Household Pulse Survey (HPS). The numbers indicated will likely decline some after all the schools reopen and the COVID hysteria dies down. https://hslda.org/post/homeschooling-continues-to-grow-in-2021.

56 McKinsey & Company did several studies related to education during COVID. https://www.mckinsey.com/industries/education/our-insights/covid-19-and-education-the-lingering-effects-of-unfinished-learning#:~:text=In%20fall%202020%2C%20we%20projected,end%20of%20the%20school%20year.

57 Well of course, I couldn't write a book about education without crediting Einstein. https://en.wikipedia.org/wiki/Albert_Einstein.

58 The actual numbers vary tremendously depending on year and the study done, but the differences generally remain within a similar range. These are from the Bureau of Labor Statistics 2021. https://www.bls.gov/news.release/hsgec.nr0.htm#:~:text=The%20labor%20force%20participation%20rate%20(the%20proportion%20of%20the%20population,percent%20and%2037.9%20percent%2C%20respec tively.

59 Horace Mann, considered the father of the common school offered many discussions regarding the power and importance of a public or common school. https://files.eric.ed.gov/fulltext/EJ842412.pdf.

60 The annual PDK Polls of the Public's Attitudes toward the public schools provides extensive insight into the public school system. https://pdkpoll.org/wp-content/uploads/2020/05/pdkpoll48_2016.pdf.

61 The **45 Communist Goals** are based on an excerpt from "*The Naked Communist*", by Cleon Skousen. There is more background over how these came to be, and how they came to light, but that is a story you can read in Skousen's book. https://www.beliefnet.com/columnists/watchwomanonthewall/2011/04/the-45-communist-goals-as-read-into-the-congressional-record-1963.html.

62 No matter what your feelings are towards Malcolm X, the truth of this quote from him cannot be denied. https://en.wikipedia.org/wiki/Malcolm_X.

[63] **Momentum of Stasis** is a phrase I *think* I coined that captures the phenomenon of individuals and families staying in place, even in the face of incredible degradation of their environment. It's what they know, who they know, where they've always been. They cannot conceive of leaving except through extraordinary fortune.

[64] A simplistic way of saying that signs of disorder lead to more and more disorder. https://www.psychologytoday.com/us/basics/broken-windows-theory. Also in https://en.wikipedia.org/wiki/Broken_windows_theory.

[65] A pithy paraphrase of Thomas Jefferson's, "*A government big enough to give you everything you want, is a government big enough to take away everything that you have.*" https://www.monticello.org/site/research-and-collections/government-big-enough-give-you-everything-you-wantspurious-quotation.

[66] The full text of the U.S. Constitution and The Bill of Rights can be found here: https://www.archives.gov/founding-docs/constitution.

[67] K-12 Public Schools. https://en.wikipedia.org/wiki/K%E2%80%9312.

[68] There are many versions of the old fable, but Wikipedia provides some interesting background. https://en.wikipedia.org/wiki/The_Scorpion_and_the_Frog.

[69] The USDA-FN announcement is a perfect example of government mandating social issues by controlling the purse strings. https://www.fns.usda.gov/building-back-better-school-meals. https://www.usatoday.com/story/news/politics/2022/06/02/noem-lawsuit-trans-inclusive-school-lunch/7490200001/. https://www.foxnews.com/politics/biden-admin-holding-school-lunch-money-hostage-force-transgender-policies.

[70] Executive Order used as a basis for Federal Agencies holding school funds hostage for compliance with social agenda rules. https://www.whitehouse.gov/briefing-room/presidential-actions/2021/01/20/executive-order-preventing-and-combating-discrimination-on-basis-of-gender-identity-or-sexual-orientation/.

[71] "Play-for-Pay" is a play on words for the common phrase, "Pay-for-Play". Play-for-Pay means exactly that… play along if you want to get paid. This works best when you have hooked someone on the money.

[72] Rubber Rooms. https://www.newyorker.com/magazine/2009/08/31/the-rubber-room. https://en.wikipedia.org/wiki/The_Rubber_Room. https://en.wikipedia.org/wiki/Reassignment_centers.

[73] One of Thomas Sowell's highly relevant quotes. I highly recommend that you take a look at some of his writings. https://www.ocregister.com/2010/03/11/thomas-sowell-creating-artificial-stupidity/. https://www.amazon.com/Dismantling-America-other-controversial-essays/dp/0465022510/ref=sr_1_1?s=books&ie=UTF8&qid=1280529320&sr=1-1.

[74] As always, Thomas Sowell is right on point. https://www.amazon.com/Dismantling-America-other-controversial-essays/dp/0465022510/ref=sr_1_1?s=books&ie=UTF8&qid=1280529320&sr=1-1.

[75] The **45 Communist Goals** are based on an excerpt from *"The Naked Communist"*, by Cleon Skousen. Based on the writings from *"The Communist Manifesto"*, by Karl Marx in 1848.
https://www.beliefnet.com/columnists/watchwomanonthewall/2011/04/the-45-communist-goals-as-read-into-the-congressional-record-1963.html.
https://en.wikipedia.org/wiki/The_Communist_Manifesto.

[76] His quotes can be found in numerous places. Here is one.
https://www.goodreads.com/quotes/search?utf8=%E2%9C%93&q=children%2C+Marx&commit=Search.

[77] Developed from multiple sources including *Intellectuals: From Marx and Tolstoy to Sartre and Chomsky* (New York: Harper Perennial edition, 2007).
https://www.academia.edu/12009844/Intellectuals_From_Marx_and_Tolstoy_to_Sartre_and_Chomsky_by_Paul_Johnson.
https://www.goodreads.com/quotes/search?utf8=%E2%9C%93&q=children%2C+Marx&commit=Search.

[78] **Cultural Marxism** is a highly charged term looked at and described very differently from the left and right as demonstrated by the various links below. Ludwig von Mises said, *"Social institutions, [people] assert, must be just. It is base to judge them merely according to their fitness to attain definite ends, however desirable these ends may be from any other point of view. What matters first is justice. The extreme formulation of this idea is to be found in the famous phrase: fiat justitia, pereat mundus.* **Let justice be done, even if it destroys the world.***"* in his book **"Theory and History: an Interpretation of Social and Economic Evolution"**.
https://www.amazon.com/b?node=19419898011&ref=ac_ilm_april_storefront_1&pd_rd_w=besyQ&content-id=amzn1.sym.0570d964-fc4d-4cee-83b3-fd2bfaca2247&pf_rd_p=0570d964-fc4d-4cee-83b3-fd2bfaca2247&pf_rd_r=T2A4CVVW0M54EFC95VM9&pd_rd_wg=McXWQ&pd_rd_r=c4538f61-e44c-4bea-822a-13953189ac2f. The Mises Institution dives deeper into this here: https://mises.org/wire/what-cultural-marxism. The Urban Dictionary provides an interesting take on Cultural Marxism at: https://www.urbandictionary.com/define.php?term=Cultural%20Marxism.
Finally, Wikipedia presents Cultural Marxism **entirely as a "conspiracy theory"**: https://en.wikipedia.org/wiki/Cultural_Marxism_conspiracy_theory. I recommend you do a little light reading and decide if the term is appropriate.

[79] Although *"Indoctrinational"* already existed as a word, it is a term I coined here to *capture the essence of* **a system that is designed to indoctrinate**. The very structure of a system like this is built to open numerous avenues for indoctrination into whatever socio-political philosophy is prevalent at the moment.

[80] There are many discussions of **Action Civics** available. This short article is a good primer. https://www.dailysignal.com/2020/11/02/action-civics-is-teaching-our-kids-to-protest/. The Wikipedia entry is more robust, but I believe it misses the flavor of what is really happening regards using Action Civics and does not address how this leads to the indoctrination of children. https://en.wikipedia.org/wiki/Action_civics.

[81] As always, **Thomas Sowell** is right on point in his book, *"Dismantling America: and other controversial essays."* https://www.amazon.com/Dismantling-America-other-controversial-essays/dp/0465022510/ref=sr_1_1?s=books&ie=UTF8&qid=1280529320&sr=1-1.

82 Stories related to the Grade School Barrack Hussein Obama songs: https://www.huffpost.com/entry/school-children-singing-t_b_300126. https://www.cbsnews.com/news/elementary-school-students-taught-pro-obama-songs/.

83 Simulated Black Power Rally in elementary school was reported in multiple sources. https://dailycaller.com/2021/02/11/william-d-kelley-school-philadelphia-christopher-rufo-black-power-rally-angela-davis-communist/. https://christopherrufo.com/bad-education/.

84 Numerous articles include: https://policetribune.com/school-paper-tells-pre-teen-students-how-to-protest-sets-different-rules-for-white-kids/. https://minnesotarightnow.com/2022/02/25/justice-page-middle-schoolers-get-blm-protest-advice/. https://www.foxnews.com/politics/minnesota-middle-school-students-blm-protests-white-students.

85 Some links regarding the **Black Lives Matter at School Week of Action**: https://www.blacklivesmatteratschool.com. https://www.blacklivesmatteratschool.com/guideforblmas.html. https://www.nea.org/resource-library/black-lives-matter-school. https://www.nationalreview.com/news/blm-week-of-action-teaching-students-nationwide-to-affirm-transgenderism-disrupt-nuclear-family/. https://www.foxnews.com/us/parents-outrage-black-lives-matter-week-of-action. https://www.foxnews.com/opinion/americas-kids-lgbt-failing. https://defendinged.org/investigations/2024-black-lives-matter-at-school-week-of-action/. https://www.blacklivesmatteratschool.com/starter-kit.html. https://www.blacklivesmatteratschool.com/13-guiding-principles.html.

86 Although the report was focused on American Universities, I believe the study translates well into today's K-12 environment. In fact, I would venture to believe that the percentages for K-12 would be higher if a similar analysis were to be done. https://www.nas.org/reports/making-citizens-how-american-universities-teach-civics/full-report#Recommendations.

87 The NEA reportedly supports using **Political Activism** in the schools to further agendas such as CRT. https://www.msn.com/en-us/news/us/national-educator-s-association-approves-of-critical-race-theory/ar-AALLton. https://christopherrufo.com/national-teachers-union-commits-to-critical-race-theory/. Note that I was unable to find **2021 New Business Item 39** on the NEA website. Reports are that they removed any reference to this. I queried NEA, but received no response from them. https://www.nea.org/.

88 **Civics Secures Democracy Act**. https://www.congress.gov/bill/117th-congress/senate-bill/879. https://www.nationalreview.com/corner/the-greatest-education-battle-of-our-lifetimes/. https://www.nas.org/blogs/article/the-second-act-of-civics-secures-democracy. https://www.realcleareducation.com/articles/2022/06/23/congresss_controversial_1_billion_civics_bill_110740.html. https://eagleforum.org/publications/focus/a-stealth-plan-to-radicalize-students-common-core-civics.html. https://www.coons.senate.gov/news/press-releases/sens-coons-cornyn-and-reps-delauro-cole-blumenauer-introduce-bipartisan-bicameral-bill-to-expand-access-to-and-strengthen-civics-education. https://www.nationalreview.com/corner/the-greatest-education-battle-of-our-lifetimes/.

[89] Randi Weingarten, President of the **American Federation of Teachers**. https://www.nbcnews.com/politics/politics-news/schools-become-political-battlefield-culture-wars-trump-cultivated-n1278257. https://www.azquotes.com/author/24819-Randi_Weingarten. https://federalobserver.com/2022/05/18/the-way-in-which-wars-start/.

[90] **National Education Association** (NEA). https://www.nea.org/.

[91] **American Federation of Teachers** (AFT). https://www.aft.org/.

[92] The NEA and AFT almost exclusively support Democrats at all levels of government. https://en.wikipedia.org/wiki/National_Education_Association. https://en.wikipedia.org/wiki/American_Federation_of_Teachers.

[93] Documentary "*Whose Children Are They*?". https://whosechildrenarethey.com/.

[94] American Petroleum Institute. https://www.api.org/.

[95] George Orwell's most wonderful book, "*Animal Farm*". https://www.amazon.com/Animal-Farm-George-Orwell/dp/0451526341.

[96] Salaries for School Board members span a broad range of annual income. https://www.salary.com/research/salary/posting/board-member-salary.

[97] Total campaign costs for the California LA Unified school district in 2017 was around $15 million total. https://www.latimes.com/local/la-me-edu-school-election-money-20170521-htmlstory.html. https://laschoolreport.com/heres-whats-really-fueling-the-nations-most-expensive-school-board-race-ever/.

[98] George Orwell's most wonderful book, "*Animal Farm*". https://www.amazon.com/Animal-Farm-George-Orwell/dp/0451526341.

[99] This is the President of the United States of American saying that your children do not belong to you when they are in the classroom. https://news.yahoo.com/biden-claims-school-children-don-234147454.html. https://www.nationalreview.com/news/biden-claims-school-children-dont-belong-to-parents-when-theyre-in-the-classroom/.

[100] In an ad campaign for "**Lean Forward**," on MSNBC Melissa Harris-Perry claimed that "*...kids belong to the whole communities.*" Interestingly, as I tried to find a reference link, all instances of the video have been purged from MSNBC, YouTube, and other places. You can read about it at these sites. https://www.msnbc.com/melissa-harris-perry/why-caring-children-not-just-parent-msna56151. https://www.washingtonpost.com/blogs/erik-wemple/wp/2013/04/08/msnbc-hits-home-run-with-harris-perry-ad/. https://www.cnsnews.com/news/article/msnbc-we-have-break-through-idea-kids-belong-their-parents.

[101] The Carnegie Council on Children background, activities, and publications. https://www.lib.uchicago.edu/e/scrc/findingaids/view.php?eadid=ICU.SPCL.CCCR&q=clinton. https://snaccooperative.org/view/9465191. https://www.washingtontimes.com/news/2016/sep/15/hillary-clinton-believes-state-can-raise-children-/.

[102] Massive amounts of data are available on fatherlessness. Much of it is different and some conflicting, but they all tell the same story. https://www.fatherhood.org/father-absence-statistic. https://fathers.com/statistics-and-research/the-extent-of-fatherlessness/. https://www.foxnews.com/opinion/america-crisis-fathers.

[103] Parents must "earn" the right to information about their children. https://www.wisconsinrightnow.com/2022/03/01/eau-claire-school-board/. https://thefederalist.com/2022/03/08/wisconsin-school-district-parents-are-not-entitled-to-know-if-their-kids-are-trans/.

[104] Once again, Thomas Sowell is right on point about the quality of our public schools. Can be sourced in many places, but here is one. https://www.azquotes.com/quote/566452.

[105] The Learning Counsel researched the future of K12 education, and it looks grim. https://thelearningcounsel.com/articles/the-future-of-k12-education-so-you-can-prepare-for-it-public-education-is-set-to-lose-16-million-enrollments-by-2030/. https://www.campussafetymagazine.com/news/public-school-enrollment-decline-why-students-are-leaving/122644/.

[106] U.S. Department of Education home page. https://www.ed.gov/.

[107] Henry Louis Mencken was an influential journalist, essayist, satirist, and scholar. https://menckenhouse.org/. https://en.wikipedia.org/wiki/H._L._Mencken.

[108] Kevin Cooper (aka Cole Summers) was an amazing individual who never said "it can't be done." https://www.amazon.com/dp/B0B1HN84HL?&linkCode=sl1&tag=knowledgehous-20&linkId=17014c6d81a338d99314f3d2202bcd25&language=en_US&ref_=as_li_ss_tl. https://www.deseret.com/2022/8/22/23309244/cole-summers-died-newcastle-utah-warren-buffett-charlie-munger-bari-weiss-unschooled?utm_source=substack&utm_medium=email. http://homeschoolingteen.com/article/rip-kevin-cooper-aka-cole-summers-an-ambitious-homeschooler/. https://www.willowliana.com/writing/remembering-cole-summers.

[109] Kevin Cooper's (aka Cole Summers') autobiography. https://www.amazon.com/dp/B0B1HN84HL?&linkCode=sl1&tag=knowledgehous-20&linkId=17014c6d81a338d99314f3d2202bcd25&language=en_US&ref_=as_li_ss_tl.

[110] Florence Thomas, President of South Dakota Parents Involved in Education (SDPIE). https://www.foxnews.com/media/south-dakota-flame-school-board-meeting-over-pornographic-books-marxist-revolution.

[111] Comprehensive Sexuality Education (CSE). https://en.wikipedia.org/wiki/Comprehensive_sex_education.

[112] American Principles Project (APP) poll of voters in May of 2022. https://americanprinciplesproject.org/media/new-app-poll-swing-state-voters-strongly-oppose-transgender-agenda/.

[113] Drag Queen Story Hour NYC (Now "Drag Story Hour"). https://www.dshnyc.org/about. https://nypost.com/2021/05/22/doe-treats-nyc-students-to-virtual-drag-queen-story-hour/.

[114] The librarian and the kid sex workers. https://redstate.com/nick-arama/2022/05/29/shocking-new-loudoun-county-story-about-school-librarian-and-child-sex-workers-n571722. https://thepostmillennial.com/virginia-school-librarian-describes-students-as-sex-workers. https://washingtonstand.com/news/loudoun-co-school-library-book-promotes-prostitution-authorities-investigate-1.

115 "Queer Book Library" in classroom.
https://sjhexpress.com/feature/2020/11/21/lgbtq-book-care-packages-from-the-queer-book-library/. https://pjmedia.com/culture/robert-spencer/2022/09/08/california-public-high-school-teacher-boasts-about-her-classrooms-queer-library-n1627983.
https://www.washingtonexaminer.com/news/california-teacher-boasts-queer-library.

116 181 K-12 Educators Arrested in first half of 2022.
http://www.iheartmyteacher.org/index.php?threads/at-least-181-k-12-educators-charged-with-child-sex-crimes-in-first-half-of-2022.254386/.
https://headlinehealth.com/181-teachers-charged-with-child-sex-crimes/.
https://www.foxnews.com/us/181-k-12-educators-charged-child-sex-crimes-2022.

117 AFT Promotes Pronoun Changes and Hiding from Parents.
https://www.foxnews.com/media/aft-promotes-method-teachers-help-kids-change-pronouns-without-parents-knowing.
https://sharemylesson.com/teaching-resource/why-pronouns-are-important-school-student-introduction-card-400128. https://sharemylesson.com/iact.

118 Radical gender lessons. https://christopherrufo.com/radical-gender-lessons-for-young-children/.

119 New Jersey's Sexuality-based school curriculum.
https://www.northjersey.com/story/news/education/2022/09/22/nj-sex-education-curriculum-how-schools-will-teach-avoid-discipline/69510211007/.
https://amaze.org/. https://nypost.com/2022/04/08/nj-kids-to-learn-about-gender-identity-under-sex-ed-curriculum/.
https://www.foxnews.com/politics/nj-sample-lesson-plans-push-videos-5th-graders.

120 California promotes transitions to kindergartners.
https://www.foxnews.com/media/california-department-of-education-advocates-books-promoting-gender-transitions-kindergartners.
https://www3.cde.ca.gov/reclitlist/displaytitle.aspx?pid=42101.
https://www3.cde.ca.gov/reclitlist/displaytitle.aspx?pid=42153.
https://www.teachingbooks.net/annotations.cgi?id=67914#t_cid_1.

121 L. Frank Baum, author of *"The Wizard of Oz"* and many children's books.
https://www.amazon.com/s?k=L.+Frank+Baum&i=stripbooks&crid=36J7N SSL76025&sprefix=l.+frank+baum%2Cstripbooks%2C55&ref=nb_sb_noss_1
. https://www.goodreads.com/quotes/405508-stunt-dwarf-or-destroy-the-imagination-of-a-child-and.

122 There are numerous versions in the Bible based on version and translation. They all mean the same thing. https://biblehub.com/proverbs/22-6.htm.

123 Frank Warren, author. https://www.amazon.com/Frank-Warren/e/B001H6N9M2%3Fref=dbs_a_mng_rwt_scns_share.
https://en.wikipedia.org/wiki/PostSecret.
https://www.goodreads.com/author/quotes/8655.Frank_Warren.

124 George Orwell's most amazing book, *"Animal Farm"*.
https://www.amazon.com/Animal-Farm-George-Orwell/dp/0451526341.

125 National Center for Education Statistics (NCES). https://nces.ed.gov/. Also see their Wikepedia page for additional information.
https://en.wikipedia.org/wiki/National_Center_for_Education_Statistics.

126 The Nation's Report Card (gov.). https://www.nationsreportcard.gov/.

127 National Assessment of Educational Progress (NAEP). https://nces.ed.gov/nationsreportcard/about/.

128 United States Census Bureau Statistics in School. https://www.census.gov/schools/.

129 Research.com various statistical studies related to education. https://research.com/education/american-school-statistics.

130 Millennials tied for last in the world. https://www.edweek.org/policy-politics/opinion-why-other-countries-keep-outperforming-us-in-education-and-how-to-catch-up/2021/05. https://www.oecd.org/unitedstates/.

131 General school statistics. https://www.edweek.org/leadership/education-statistics-facts-about-american-schools/2019/01.

132 Wall Street Journal report on college seniors. https://www.wsj.com/articles/exclusive-test-data-many-colleges-fail-to-improve-critical-thinking-skills-1496686662?mod=trending_now_1.

133 NEA poll shows more than half of teachers want to leave profession early. https://www.nea.org/about-nea/media-center/press-releases/nea-survey-massive-staff-shortages-schools-leading-educator. https://www.npr.org/2022/02/01/1076943883/teachers-quitting-burnout.

134 Charter Schools. https://en.wikipedia.org/wiki/Charter_school.

135 National Association of Independent Schools. https://www.nais.org/.

136 Homeschooling. https://joinmodulo.substack.com/p/21-statistics-and-trends-that-show?. https://hslda.org/post/homeschooling-continues-to-grow-in-2021. https://joinmodulo.substack.com/p/pros-and-cons-to-homeschooling. https://en.wikipedia.org/wiki/Homeschooling.

137 Jess Lair, author. https://www.goodreads.com/author/quotes/359196.Jess_Lair.

138 Maria Montessori. https://en.wikipedia.org/wiki/Maria_Montessori.

139 Home School Legal Defense Association (HSLDA). https://hslda.org/.

140 Listing of state homeschool organizations that fight to keep homeschooling free and legal. https://hslda.org/post/state-homeschool-organizations.

141 Downward enrollment trends in K-12. https://www.edweek.org/leadership/opinion-public-school-enrollment-is-down-by-more-than-a-million-why/2022/11. https://nces.ed.gov/programs/coe/indicator/cga/public-school-enrollment. https://michaelbhorn.substack.com/p/downward-enrollment-trend-in-school.

142 National Commission on Excellence in Education. https://en.wikipedia.org/wiki/National_Commission_on_Excellence_in_Education.

143 A Nation at Risk: The Imperative for Educational Reform. https://en.wikipedia.org/wiki/A_Nation_at_Risk. https://edreform.com/naep/. https://nationalparentsunion.org/wp-content/uploads/2023/05/Nation-At-Risk-5-12.pdf.

144 Quote from A Nation at Risk, pg. 10, 1983. https://edreform.com/wp-content/uploads/2013/02/A_Nation_At_Risk_1983.pdf.

145 National Center for Education Statistics (NCES). https://nces.ed.gov/. https://en.wikipedia.org/wiki/National_Center_for_Education_Statistics. Note that NCES is now a part of the U.S. Department of Education.

[146] James Samuel Coleman and the *Coleman Report*.
https://en.wikipedia.org/wiki/James_Samuel_Coleman.

[147] The *Equality of Educational Opportunities* report (*Coleman Report*).
https://files.eric.ed.gov/fulltext/ED012275.pdf.

[148] Department of Government Efficiency (DOGE).   https://doge.gov/.

[149] Oregon's Preschool Promise Program.
https://oregon.public.law/statutes/ors_329.172.
https://www.foxnews.com/media/oregon-department-of-education-doles-out-millions-in-under-enrolled-preschool-program.

[150] Oregon Office of the Auditor reports.
https://sos.oregon.gov/audits/Pages/default.aspx.

[151] "Public ed is not to teach kids what parents want."
https://www.facebook.com/photo.php?fbid=557931896356215&set=a.23215
8348933573&type=3.   https://www.foxnews.com/media/parents-dream-school-district-become-woke-nightmare-jokes.

[152] Pastor Brooks and Rooftop Revelations.
https://www.foxnews.com/opinion/rooftop-revelations-pastor-brooks-shares-the-lesson-he-learned-from-thomas-sowell-on-school-choice.

[153] Bebasish Mridha on the true nature of education.
https://www.goodreads.com/quotes/tag/true-education.
https://www.linkedin.com/in/dabasishmridha/.

[154] Nelson Mandela, President of South Africa.
https://en.wikipedia.org/wiki/Nelson_Mandela.

[155] Milton Friedman on the Free Market System.
https://en.wikipedia.org/wiki/Milton_Friedman.

[156] Investopedia description of a "Free Market".
https://www.investopedia.com/terms/f/freemarket.asp.

[157] A slight often-used misquote from the movie, "Field of Dreams". "If you build it, he will come." https://en.wikipedia.org/wiki/Field_of_Dreams.

[158] President John Tyler (1790-1862). https://en.wikipedia.org/wiki/John_Tyler.

[159] Judge Janice Rogers Brown.
https://en.wikipedia.org/wiki/Janice_Rogers_Brown.

[160] Readers might be interested in exploring my Substack, "The Art of Unintended Consequences" where I explore unexpected results from our actions.   https://davidnemzoff.substack.com/.

[161] James Madison, Founding Father and author of the Federalist Papers: No. 10.
https://avalon.law.yale.edu/18th_century/fed10.asp.

[162] Book discussing pornography in a public-school library. https://www.city-journal.org/article/have-you-looked-inside-any-of-these-books.
https://washingtonstand.com/news/as-book-battles-break-out-across-the-country-idaho-turns-to-legislation.   https://www.foxnews.com/media/alaska-board-members-brawl-silencing-dad-exposing-book-kinks-porn-im-going-interrupt-you.   https://www.christianpost.com/news/school-district-offers-books-promoting-porn-gay-sex-apps.html.   https://www.amazon.com/Lets-Talk-About-Talking-Children/dp/1736788493.

[163] Quote from John Holt's book, "How Children Fail".
https://www.amazon.com/Children-Fail-Classics-Child-Development/dp/0201484021.

164 Bill Bennett, Ronald Reagan's Education Secretary.
https://en.wikipedia.org/wiki/William_Bennett.

165 Bill Bennett on today's schools in 2024 interview.
https://www.foxnews.com/media/reagans-education-secretary-urges-schools-become-temple-learning-not-social-experimentation.

166 Alex Newman quote in an article from Freedom Project Media, June 3, 2019.
https://www.freedomproject.com/2019/06/03/study-common-core-had-significant-negative-effect-on-students/.

167 There are many sources, and all differ slightly, but here two that have some interesting statistics. https://www.edweek.org/leadership/education-statistics-facts-about-american-schools/2019/01.
https://educationdata.org/public-education-spending-statistics#public-education-spending-statistics.

168 The term was first coined by Alexandr Wang of Scale AI, Inc. as as his hiring principle and an apparent swipe at DEI.
https://fortune.com/2024/06/24/mei-elon-musk-alexandr-wang-anti-dei-hiring-merit-excellence-intelligence/. https://scale.com/blog/meritocracy-at-scale. https://www.foxbusiness.com/fox-news-tech/scale-ai-ceo-explains-why-his-company-hire-mei-not-dei-merit-excellence-intelligence.

169 Here are just a few links to discussions regarding small/micro schools.
https://reason.org/innovators/national-microschooling-center-founders-illustrate-how-microschools-are-changing-k-12-education/.
https://smallschoolscoalition.org/a-primer-on-the-power-and-tradition-of-small-schools/. https://www.usnews.com/education/k12/articles/what-is-a-microschool.

170 Frances FitzGerald, "The Evangelicals: The Struggle to Shape America". A phrase repeated by many to warn of the risk of taking government money.
https://www.amazon.com/Evangelicals-Struggle-Shape-America/dp/1439131333.

171 Transcript of the U.S. Constitution for reference.
https://www.archives.gov/founding-docs/constitution-transcript.

172 Various resources for additional research include (in no particular order:
https://nces.ed.gov/. https://pdkpoll.org/wp-content/uploads/2020/05/pdkpoll51-2019.pdf.
https://www.usnews.com/education/k12. https://eddataexpress.ed.gov/.
https://www.ed-data.org/.

173 SpaceX information. https://www.spacex.com/.
https://en.wikipedia.org/wiki/SpaceX.

174 Blue Origin information. https://www.blueorigin.com/.
https://en.wikipedia.org/wiki/Blue_Origin.

175 Virgin Galactic information. https://www.virgingalactic.com/.
https://en.wikipedia.org/wiki/Virgin_Galactic.

176 Rocket Lab was founded in New Zealand and established their headquarters in the U.S. in 2013.. https://www.rocketlabusa.com/.
https://en.wikipedia.org/wiki/Rocket_Lab.

177 Relativity Space information. https://www.relativityspace.com/.
https://en.wikipedia.org/wiki/Relativity_Space.

178 North American Association of State and Provincial Lotteries research and data. https://www.naspl.org/where-the-money-goes.

[179] DECA: Distributive Education Clubs of America are active in many high schools to prepare students for careers in business, marketing, finance, and management. https://www.deca.org/.

[180] A teacher sells ad space on test papers to pay for the tests. https://mises.org/mises-daily/free-market-education.

[181] Martin Luther King Jr. Quote on first steps. https://en.wikipedia.org/wiki/Martin_Luther_King_Jr. https://www.xavier.edu/jesuitresource/online-resources/quote-archive1/martin-luther-king-quotes#:~:text=%22Change%20does%20not%20roll%20in,%2D%20Martin%20Luther%20King%20Jr..

[182] Cultural anthropologist Margaret Mead on change. https://en.wikipedia.org/wiki/Margaret_Mead.

[183] Barack Hussein Obama on change. https://en.wikipedia.org/wiki/Barack_Obama.

[184] Helen Keller, author of 14 books and the first deafblind person in the U.S. to earn a Bachelor of Arts degree. https://en.wikipedia.org/wiki/Helen_Keller.

[185] Mary Teresa Bojaxhiu, better known as Mother Teresa. https://en.wikipedia.org/wiki/Mother_Teresa.

[186] Husco Int. investments in community education. I've done my best to summarize their activities. I welcome anyone at Husco to correct me if needed. https://husco.com/.

[187] Waukesha STEM Academy. https://sdw.waukesha.k12.wi.us/o/stemes/page/about-us.

[188] Augustine Preparatory K-12 North Campus. https://husco.com/husco-news/aug-prep-announces-bold-new-plans-for-k-12-north-campus/.

[189] Augustine Preparatory Academy (Aug Prep). https://sdw.waukesha.k12.wi.us/o/stemes/page/about-us.

[190] Ronald Reagan, 40th President of the United States. https://simple.wikipedia.org/wiki/Ronald_Reagan.

[191] Milton Friedman, economist, statistician, and Nobel Memorial Prize winner. https://en.wikipedia.org/wiki/Milton_Friedman.

[192] SpaceX. https://www.spacex.com/.

[193] Private spaceflight companies. https://en.wikipedia.org/wiki/List_of_private_spaceflight_companies.

[194] Orbital Sciences Corporation merged with Alliant Techsystems, then was purchased by Northrop Grumman. https://en.wikipedia.org/wiki/Orbital_Sciences_Corporation.

[195] Northrup Grumman. https://www.northropgrumman.com/.

[196] Sierra Space. https://www.sierraspace.com/.

[197] Blue Origan. https://www.blueorigin.com/.

[198] Boeing. https://www.boeing.com/.

[199] U.S. Postal Service (USPS) started in 1775. https://www.usps.com/.

[200] Federal Express, now FedEx. https://www.fedex.com/en-us/home.html.

[201] United Parcel Service, now UPS. https://www.ups.com/us/en/Home.page.

[202] Amazon. https://www.amazon.com/.

---

[203] Martin Luther on changing the world.
https://en.wikipedia.org/wiki/Martin_Luther_King_Jr.
https://www.azquotes.com/author/9142-Martin_Luther/tag/writing.

[204] Study shows that 1 in 3 children will be homeschooled by 2030. Also contains some other statistics worth looking at. https://libertysentinel.org/1-in-3-homeschooled-by-2030-as-16-million-flee-public-school-forecast-finds/?utm_source=substack&utm_medium=email. See the study here -> https://thelearningcounsel.com/articles/the-future-of-k12-education-so-you-can-prepare-for-it-public-education-is-set-to-lose-16-million-enrollments-by-2030/.

[205] The Caste system in India as described on Wikipedia.
https://en.wikipedia.org/wiki/Caste_system_in_India.

[206] **HERE ARE SOME IMPORTANT LINKS RELATED TO THE BOOK**

LINKS

BOOK PAGE	Sacred Fire of Public Education | Gabberz
AMAZON	https://www.amazon.com/dp/0988273837
LEAVE A REVIEW	https://www.amazon.com/review/create-review?&asin=0988273837
Substack	https://davidnemzoff.substack.com/
X (Twitter)	https://X.com/davidnemzoff
Facebook	https://www.facebook.com/david.nemzoff
BookBub	https://www.bookbub.com/authors/david-nemzoff

I hope you enjoyed the book. Please join the **Mailing List**, follow me on the sites listed above, and definitely leave a **REVIEW ON AMAZON** and/or your favorite sites.

Thanks!

David Nemzoff